About the author

Garth Andrew Myers is director of the Kansas
African Studies Center and professor in the
departments of geography and African/
African-American studies at the University
of Kansas. He is the author of *Verandahs
of Power: Colonialism and Space in Urban
Africa* (Syracuse, 2003) and *Disposable
Cities: Garbage, Governance and Sustainable Development in Urban Africa* (Ashgate,
2005), and the co-editor (with Martin Murray)
of *Cities in Contemporary Africa* (Palgrave
Macmillan, 2006). He has published or co-
authored more than forty articles and book
chapters, with the vast majority on African
urban development topics. His research emphasizes eastern and southern African cities,
primarily.

AFRICAN CITIES

alternative visions of urban theory and practice

Garth Myers

Zed Books

LONDON · NEW YORK

African Cities: Alternative visions of urban theory and practice was first published in 2011 by Zed Books Ltd, 7 Cynthia Street, London N1 9JF, UK, and Room 400, 175 Fifth Avenue, New York, NY 10010, USA

www.zedbooks.co.uk

Set in Monotype Sabon and Gill Sans Heavy by Ewan Smith, London
Index: ed.emery@thefreeuniversity.net
Cover designed by Rogue Four Design

A catalogue record for this book is available from the British Library
Library of Congress Cataloging in Publication Data available

ISBN 978 1 84813 508 6 hb
ISBN 978 1 84813 509 3 pb

Contents

Figures and tables

Abbreviations

AAPS	Association of African Planning Schools
ANC	African National Congress (South Africa)
BNG	Breaking New Ground (Cape Town)
CBD	central business district
CBO	community-based organization
CCM	Chama cha Mapinduzi (Revolutionary Party, Tanzania)
CUF	Civic United Front (Zanzibar)
DRC	Democratic Republic of Congo
JSP	Joe Slovo Park (Cape Town)
MONGO	My Own NGO
RDP	Reconstruction and Development Programme (Cape Town)
SCP	Sustainable Cities Program
SMOLE	Sustainable Management of Lands and Environment (Zanzibar)
SUD	sustainable urban development
UMMM	*Umoja wa Mradi wa Maji na Maendeleo* (Unity in the Project for Water and Development, Zanzibar)
UNDP	United Nations Development Programme
WNLA	Witwatersrand Native Labour Association
ZIFF	Zanzibar International Film Festival
ZILEM	Zanzibar Integrated Lands and Environmental Management
ZSP	Zanzibar Sustainable Program

Acknowledgments

The inspirations for writing this book are numerous and diverse. I am grateful for the opportunity to conduct research on a project funded by the National Science Foundation Geography Program (2006–08, award no. 0549319), but felt it was important to broaden my book geographically and conceptually from the grant's focus on land reform in Zanzibar, based on what I'd already seen in research elsewhere. I also benefited from participation in the International School at Rhodes University in Grahamstown, South Africa, in June/July 2009, and the Cities Alliance Workshop on the State of African Cities Reporting Project held at the African Center for Cities of the University of Cape Town, in April 2009. I am particularly thankful to Sue Parnell, Edgar Pieterse, Jenny Robinson, and Vanessa Watson for the latter opportunity. Besides the NSF funding, I also used funding from the US Department of Education Title VI National Resource Center grant of the Kansas African Studies Center to travel to various cities in Africa during 2008–10. Chapter 1 emerged from the final study tour of Lusaka on the Kansas African Studies Center's US Department of State affiliation grant with the University of Zambia in 2004. The Hall Center for the Humanities at the University of Kansas offered me the sanctuary of a Resident Fellowship in fall 2009 to write Chapters 2 and 3. Chapters 4 and 6 owe their existence to a spring 2010 sabbatical leave from the University of Kansas. Chapter 5 has its origins in the 2006 fall faculty seminar at the Hall Center on Representations of the Middle East that I was invited to co-chair, with Robin Rowland, following the untimely death of our colleague, Misty Gerner, whose idea the seminar was. The Hall Center and the Office of International Programs also supported research that led to the production of one section of Chapter 6. The Nordic Africa Institute assisted me by granting me the opportunity to write a concept paper for their research cluster on Urban Dynamics in Africa in spring 2010, the key ideas of which are found throughout this book. Small segments from articles of mine that have appeared in *Urban Geography*, *African Affairs*, and *Geography Compass* are paraphrased here, and I gratefully acknowledge the permission of each of the publishers for doing so.

I have presented portions of the book or the research behind it in a number of lecture series, conferences, or workshops, including talks at the Nordic Africa Institute (2007 and 2010), Texas A&M University, University of Sciences and Arts of Oklahoma, UCLA, University College London, the Ohio State University, University of Chicago, University of Florida, Colgate University, Binghamton University, Kansas State University, the European Conference on African Studies (Leipzig, 2009), and annual meetings of the African Studies Association in San Francisco (2006) and New York (2008), the Association of American Geographers in Denver (2005), Chicago (2006), San Francisco (2007), Boston (2008), Las Vegas (2009), and Washington (2010), the Institute of British Geographers in London (2007 and 2008), and the Mid-America Alliance for African Studies in St Louis (2006 and 2008) and Lawrence (2007 and 2010). My sincere thanks to all who have commented and critiqued these presentations over the past five years, including Charisma Acey, Onyanta Adama, Bill Bissell, Christian Brannstrom, Deborah Bryceson, Andrew Byerley, Jenny Cadstedt, Jennifer Cole, Steve Commins, Julio Davila, Filip de Boeck, Brian Dill, David Donkor, Rosalind Fredericks, Matthew Gandy, Jacob Gordon, Amanda Hammar, Karen Hansen, Goren Hyden, Peter Hugill, Rachel Jean-Baptiste, Wendy Jepson, Anthonia Kalu, Kalechi Kalu, Stephen Kandeh, Ed Keller, Tom Klak, Miles Larmer, Todd Leedy, Loretta Lees, Charlotte Lemansky, Agnes Leslie, Ilda Lindell, Abdulaziz Lodhi, Tina Mangieri, Gordon McGranahan, Fiona McLaughlin, Claire Mercer, Martin Murray, Heidi Nast, Wilma Nchito, Jeremia Njeru, Simon Nkemba, Rob O'Donaghue, Francis Owusu, Ben Page, Sue Parnell, Edgar Pieterse, Debby Potts, Carole Rakodi, Jenny Robinson, Rick Schroeder, David Simon, Maliq Simone, Jonathan Smith, Ed Soja, Bill Stites, Beverly Taylor, Evalyn Tennant, Leo Villalon, Vanessa Watson, Ian Yeboah, and probably many more people than that. My debt to Ed Soja is obvious from the first chapter, but I thank all of my mentors, stretching from David Vail, Sarah McMahon, and especially Randy Stakeman at Bowdoin through to Ed, John Friedmann, Susannah Hecht, Judy Carney, Ned Alpers, Nick Entrikin, Michael Curry, Jim Coleman, Steve Commins, and most of all Gerry Hale at UCLA, for making me work more than my brain wants to on its own to make my work better, if still never what it could be. Jenny Robinson has read these chapters thoroughly, talked me through the ideas, and offered constant encouragement, challenging me to think harder about the material, sharing so much of her world, thinking through life's puzzles together. None of these people above, I hasten to add, can be blamed for any shortcomings this book has – its faults are entirely my own.

My graduate students at the University of Kansas have been a constant source of ideas for the book over the years: Ken Aikins, Almokhtar Attwairi, Emmanuel Birdling, Mohamed Dosi, Victoria Downey, Levi Gahman, Ryan Gibb, Aaron Gilbreath, Ryan Good, Ang Gray, Abdi Gutale, Andy Hilburn, Megan Holroyd, Hilary Hungerford, Ryan Lash, Josh Long, Anton Menning, Cort Miller, Makame Muhajir, John Oakes, Amy Potter, Heather Putnam, Peter Sam, Peter Self, Jamie Shinn, Shimantini Shome, Sarah Smiley, Luke Struckman, and Karen Wetugi. Muhajir has been a cheerful and thoughtful analyst of this project from the beginning. I thank him, and his entire family, for their help and hospitality in Zanzibar on many occasions. Abdi is a great part of any understanding I've gained, however incomplete it may be, of Mogadishu. I thank Anton for my appreciation, however incomplete it also may be, of the US Army in that same city. Peter and Ken helped me immensely in gaining a sense of Accra, as Mokhtar has done with Tripoli, Emmanuel with Maiduguri, and Hilary with Niamey.

Anyone who reads this book will see my debts to Ali Zungu (Ali Hasan Ali) in numerous places, and to Zuhura Abdulrahim Mohamed, and their wonderful children, for their warm friendship and ideas, to say nothing of their hospitality to Sarah, Jamie, Megan, Heather, and others. My other Zanzibari family, Jussy Singh, Parmukh Singh, and Kul Kaur, and all of my neighbors in Kikwajuni, Mwera, and Mazizini, are as ever an inspiration.

I've been blessed with the priceless opportunity to share ideas that have gone into this book with colleagues at the University of Kansas, and their feedback has contributed to its improvement. Byron Caminero-Santangelo, in particular, has read and commented on several chapters and helped keep me sane in the traumas of basketball season. In addition, the comments and suggestions of Glenn Adams, Folabo Ajayi-Soyinka, Shawn Alexander, Elif Andac, Victor Bailey, Jonathan Boyarin, Hannah Britton, Chris Brown, Brian Daldorph, Khalid El-Hassan, Johan Feddema, Tanya Golash-Boza, Majid Hannoum, Susan Harris, Thomas Heilke, Bob Hemenway, Peter Herlihy, Paul Hotvedt, Jane Irungu, Jay Johnson, John Kennedy, Liz MacGonagle, Yoonmi Nam, Ebenezer Obadare, Peter

Ojiambo, Shannon O'Lear, Robin Rowland, Gitti Salami, Pete Short-
ridge, and probably more colleagues than that have been helpful. As
ever, my family, Atlee and Phebe Myers and Melanie Hepburn, have
helped me through the long process of producing this book through
their encouragement, companionship, and love.

I finally declared myself an urban geographer in 2000. I was sitting
in a geography department meeting at the University of Kansas,
where the faculty was considering a list of courses that had not been
taught in five years for possible elimination from our course list.
A class entitled 'Advanced Urban Geography' was on the chopping
block because, the chair was saying, we had no faculty members
who did advanced urban geography. I sheepishly suggested that,
actually, I could teach this course. In the days that followed my
rescue of Advanced Urban Geography from erasure, it dawned on
me that nearly every publication I had ever had was a piece of urban
geography. I started to trace out why I would not have been thought
of – or have thought of myself – as an urban geographer. In graduate
school, I had taken more graduate course work in urban planning
than I had in geography, but somehow, somewhere in the subliminal
messages of my trip through the 'LA School' of urban studies during
a particularly heady time, my urban geography credentials earned
an asterisk, as an exception, even in my own head, because I studied
cities in Africa. This is a book about removing the asterisk on cities in
Africa.

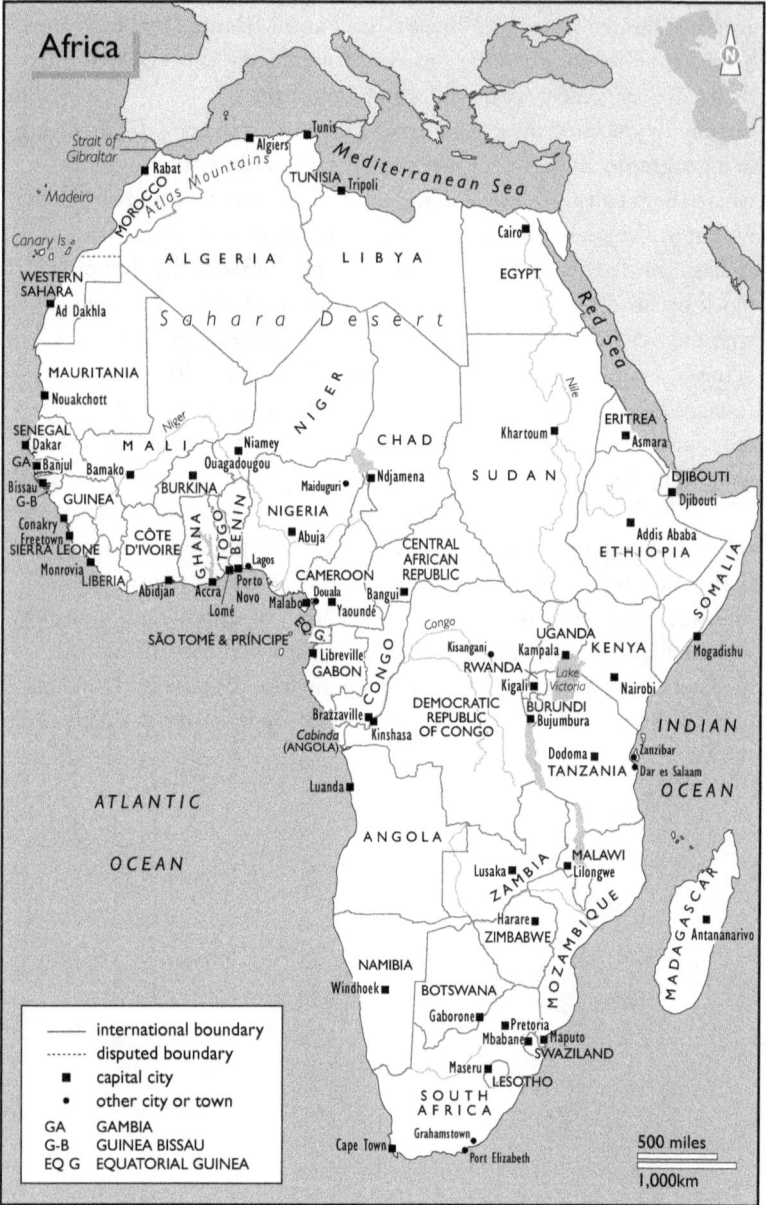

Africa

Strait of Gibraltar

Madeira

Canary Is.

WESTERN SAHARA

Ad Dakhla

MOROCCO

Rabat ■

Algiers ■

Tunis ■

TUNISIA

Tripoli ■

Atlas Mountains

Mediterranean Sea

Cairo ■

ALGERIA

LIBYA

EGYPT

Sahara Desert

Red Sea

MAURITANIA

Nouakchott ■

SENEGAL

Dakar ■

GA ■ Banjul

Bissau ■

G-B

GUINEA

Conakry ■

Freetown ■

SIERRA LEONE

Monrovia ■

LIBERIA

Bamako ■

MALI

Niger

Niamey ■

Ouagadougou ●

BURKINA

Maiduguri ●

NIGER

CHAD

Ndjamena ■

SUDAN

Khartoum ■

Nile

ERITREA

Asmara ■

DJIBOUTI

Djibouti ■

Addis Ababa ■

ETHIOPIA

SOMALIA

GHANA TOGO BENIN

NIGERIA

Abuja ●

CENTRAL AFRICAN REPUBLIC

CÔTE D'IVOIRE

Abidjan ■

Accra ■

Lomé ■

Lagos ●

Porto Novo ■

CAMEROON

Douala ●

Malabo ■

Yaoundé ■

Bangui ■

EQ. G

SÃO TOMÉ & PRÍNCIPE

Libreville ■

GABON

Kisangani ●

Congo

UGANDA

Kampala ■

RWANDA

Kigali ■

KENYA

Nairobi ■

Mogadishu ■

Congo

DEMOCRATIC REPUBLIC OF CONGO

Brazzaville ■

Cabinda (ANGOLA)

Kinshasa ■

BURUNDI

Bujumbura ■

Lake Victoria

Dodoma ■

Zanzibar ●

TANZANIA

Dar es Salaam ●

INDIAN OCEAN

Luanda ■

ATLANTIC OCEAN

ANGOLA

Lusaka ■

ZAMBIA

MALAWI

Lilongwe ■

Harare ■

ZIMBABWE

MOZAMBIQUE

MADAGASCAR

Antananarivo ■

NAMIBIA

Windhoek ■

BOTSWANA

Gaborone ■

Pretoria ■

Mbabane ■ Maputo ■

SWAZILAND

Maseru ■

LESOTHO

SOUTH AFRICA

Cape Town ■

Grahamstown ●

Port Elizabeth ●

international boundary

- - - - - - disputed boundary

■ capital city

● other city or town

GA GAMBIA
G-B GUINEA BISSAU
EQ G EQUATORIAL GUINEA

500 miles

1,000km

Introduction

As African societies urbanize, it becomes evident that they do so in ways that challenge prevailing theories and models of urban geography, sociology, anthropology, and planning. But these are just as surely cities in 'a world of cities' (Robinson 2004). My aim in this book is to use African urban concepts and experiences to speak back to theoretical and practical concerns in urban studies and disciplines that study cities more generally, while at the same time contributing to African studies as a field. I am arguing for a revision – a seeing again, and a revising – of how cities in Africa are discussed and written about in both urban studies and African studies.

Most urban social studies are still built on theories utilizing US or European cities to stand as the universal models, or measuring cities in non-Western settings by the models and metrics of the West. As the geographer Jenny Robinson (2006: x) has shown, African cities are still typically studied through the lens of development, or in a manner that remains stuck, as her book's subtitle puts it, 'between modernity and development,' where 'these "other" cities have been thought to borrow their modernity from wealthier contexts.' Most of the time, to say that African cities come up short in measurements based on Western indicators in these studies is an understatement. We are more likely to see what the urbanist Edgar Pieterse (2008a: 2) describes as 'a relentless catalogue of the utterly devastating conditions that characterize the daily lives of the majority' living in African cities.

Of course, as Robinson's and Pieterse's books show, African urban studies is emerging, or re-emerging, in its own right (e.g. Beall et al. 2010; Bryceson and Potts 2006; Demissie 2007a; Freund 2007; Grant 2009; Mbembe and Nuttall 2008; Murray 2008a; Pieterse 2010; Simone 2004, 2010; Simone and Abouhani 2005; Weiss 2009). There is a significant literature of African urbanization which began more than fifty years ago, and it certainly continued to build throughout all of this half-century (e.g. Epstein 1958; Kuper et al. 1958; Cohen 1969; Mitchell 1969; Cooper 1983; O'Connor 1983; Stren 1985, 1994; Mabogunje 1990; or Simon 1992). In general, though, urban studies retreated to the background on the continent from the late 1960s to the early 1990s, even leading some to speak of a rural bias to African studies scholarship (Freund 2007). The last ten years have brought a resurgence of interest in urban Africa in the social sciences and humanities. In this decade, several important historical surveys of urbanization in Africa have appeared, along with intensive and often multidisciplinary studies of individual cities in Africa, and edited volumes examining an eclectic variety of the continent's cities (in addition to those cited above, see: Bekker and Leilde 2006; Coquery-Vidrovitch 2005a; Falola and Salm 2004, 2005; Goodwin 2006; or McDonald 2008). Within virtually every African country, there is also a growing research capacity on urban studies questions, resulting in impressive, empirically rich, and theoretically engaged analyses on many cities, but with more narrow global distribution; for Tanzanian examples, see the works of Fred Lerise (2005, 2000), Wilbard Kombe (2005), Lusugga Kironde (2000), or Tumsifu Nnkya (2007); Nigeria's urban research internally is a library of its own (Adama 2007; Ayeni 1998; Elleh 2002; Ikejiofor 2006); and South Africa, Ghana, Zambia, Cameroon, Senegal, Niger, Kenya, and many other countries have substantial urban research capacity. In this book, I seek to expand on the trend encouraging African studies and urban studies scholars to engage with the vibrancy and complexity of African cities with fresh eyes, and to learn from African scholarship.

African cities, African studies, and urban studies

What is going on in African cities that anyone interested in cities or anyone interested in Africa should care about? Answering this question should immediately appear to be an impossible undertaking. The breadth, diversity, and complexity of the continent and its urban areas seem to make it absurd and reductionist to speak of 'the African city,' or even of 'African cities,' as my title has, as if there is a type, or even several types that belong to a distinct set. Where it once seemed plausible to model *an* African city – even if, as in the case of geographer Anthony O'Connor (1983), one's attempt led to not one but six types – it now seems illogical to shoehorn cities into types just because they reside on the same continent.

And yet over and over again, media voices and scholars alike make exactly this sort of generalizing logic the prevailing mode of thinking about 'Africa' and its cities. What the anthropologist James Ferguson (2006: 2) calls 'this Africa talk' has, as he puts it, 'a certain intensity, full of anguished energy and (often vague) moral concern.' Ferguson (ibid.: 3) argues that in his discipline of anthropology many colleagues have taken the 'principled' but 'ineffective' tactic of 'refusing the very category of "Africa,"' instead writing about only the narrow corner of the continent that they have come to know. He sees this as an ineffective tactic because it leaves the discussion of 'Africa' to the 'journalistic and policy visions' that are 'misleading, factually incorrect, and often racist' (ibid.: 3).

Other scholarly disciplines, notably political science, continue quite confidently with their discussions of 'Africa,' typically as a place of grand and broad crisis. Political scientist Robert Bates tellingly entitled his 2008 book *When Things Fell Apart: State Failure in Late-Century Africa*, and he begins it with these two sentences: 'In late-century Africa, things fell apart. By way of illustration, consider Figure 1.1, which lists civil wars in African countries from 1970 to 1995, as judged by the World Bank' (Bates 2008: 1). The figure lists only nineteen countries, on a continent with more than fifty, and its bizarre calculations for what constitutes a civil war, with each year a full year of war across a whole country by the graph, when most were localized geographically and distinct temporally within that year, make it as 'misleading [and] factually incorrect' as the journalistic visions Ferguson critiques. For just one example, the occasional skirmishes of the Cassamance region of Senegal which cause that country to appear on Bates's chart from 1990 straight through to 1995 could not be remotely comparable militarily to the long all-out civil war of Mozambique, 1975–92 on the chart, a war that created millions of refugees and caused hundreds of thousands of deaths. One would be hard pressed to find a serious analyst of Senegal who would describe it as a country in the grips of 'state failure' in 'late-century Africa' alongside Somalia, just below it on this chart. It is as if the staggering differences between places and circumstances and history and geography just don't matter – in Bates's (ibid.: 16–29) aptly labeled 'fable' of African politics all of 'Africa' is in the throes of 'state failure' because of the 'specialists in violence' that seek the 'rewards of predation' that government leadership offers.

The Africa-wide fable-making is not much different when we come to the discussion of cities. In urban studies, it is often the case that theorists and scholars think and write across the whole of the continent, and often in a way that is 'obsessed with the less palatable particularities of African [urban] politics and society' (Chabal 2009: 18). Although there is some evidence here and there of changes, it is still generally the case that cities in Africa are ignored, banished to a different, other, lesser category of not-quite cities, or held up as examples of all that can go wrong with urbanism in much of both the mainstream and even critical urban literature. As more and more global urban studies scholarship does now seek to engage with the growing body of work of Africanist urbanists, it is nonetheless still not uncommon to find a token Africa article in edited volumes, written by one of a small handful of scholars, burdened with the tall order of speaking to cities in 'Africa.'

It is impossible and unhelpful to attempt to catalog every major urban studies scholar and her or his shortcomings in relation to Africa. A growing set of exceptions exist to the trends I am suggesting, and it is rather daunting to imagine demanding all urbanists take full account of African cities in developing their analyses. But I think it is vital to highlight some examples of the consequences that flow from the visions of Africa that still prevail in the urban disciplines, particularly urban geography. For instance, in mainstream textbooks of urban geography, African cities are typically discussed in a seg-regated chapter about 'urbanization in the less developed countries' (Knox and McCarthy 2005: 171) or 'cities in the less developed world' (Kaplan et al. 2004: 399) that is somewhere near the back of the book. In a best-case scenario (Pacione 2004: 429–576), 'urban geography in the Third World' might comprise about a third of the book; but it is still carved out as a distinct, lesser kind of urban geography, and African cases take a back seat to those of Latin America and Asia.

Of course, of necessity such books must simplify and generalize; likewise we can see that the market for most urban textbooks in Eng-lish is skewed toward the developed West, such that it is unsurprising to find that their coverage of cities in Africa is diminished. Yet the analysis of the 'Third World' in these texts is substantively distinct, too. For instance, the well-researched catalog of environmental prob-lems in Third World cities that comprises Chapter 28 in geographer Michael Pacione's enormous textbook *Urban Geography: A Global Perspective* presents no sense that anyone in these cities does anything about their problems. In fact, the proliferation of community, public sector, and global initiatives aimed at environmental governance in Asia, Africa, and Latin America is astounding. The Western city chapters are by contrast full of juxtaposition of problem with policy. The highly generalized discussion of rampant corruption in Third World urban governance in Chapter 29, similarly, appears without comparison to widespread forms of corruption of urban governance in more developed cities. And this is a skewing one finds in the best of the mainstream textbook approaches in urban geography.

One might conclude that perhaps the more economistic mainstream textbook approaches devalue African creativity or urban cultures, and that a humanistic approach in the field might lend itself to more sensitive theory. Yet humanistic geography is often no more progressive in dealing with Africa or African cities than mainstream urban textbooks; and the reality is that non-Africanists among humanistic cultural geographers don't really even venture into discussions of African cities at all, referencing the continent only as a repository of ancient, backward, rural traditions (Sack 1997: 15; Sack 2002).

The dominant voices of contemporary urban studies, those of critical, progressive, or materialist thinkers, still seem sometimes to be several steps off the mark in their thinking in relation to Africa. Although the urbanist David Harvey has inspired a number of important scholars who work on African cities, he himself has little to say about Africa in most of his works. Where he does make reference to the continent, for instance in his book *Justice, Nature, and the Geography of Difference*, the references are suggestive of the problem with starting from Harvey to try to understand African cities. He notes that as 'places in the city get red-lined for mortgage finance, the people who live in them get written off as worthless, in the same way that much of Africa gets written off as a basket-case' (Harvey 1996: 320). On one hand, this is suggestive of the keen understanding of Africa as a region struggling with misrepresentation as well as underdevelopment evident in several of Harvey's works, such as *A Brief History of Neoliberalism* (Harvey 2005). On the other hand, the *urban* portion of Harvey's image, 'the city,' clearly belongs to the West here, and, despite his appreciation for the internal heterogeneity of places in general, it is not implied that *parts* of African *cities* would be written off in the manner that parts of Western cities are written off, but that 'much of Africa' is written off that way. And Harvey thus falls into a similar write-off. Harvey belongs at the end of the spectrum identified by Pieterse (2008a: 2) where urban scholars and policy activists gather who 'insist that without addressing the framing conditions of the global economy it is not possible to solve urban poverty.' Henri Lefebvre, Doreen Massey, Saskia Sassen, Manuel Castells, and many other widely cited stars of urban studies, like Harvey, seldom make reference to Africa in their works, or put its cities in footnotes and margins, even as they may also belong at this progressive end of the spectrum. This end of the spectrum may be on target about 'the framing conditions of the global economy,' but it is continually missing opportunities for seeing African cities as important loci of global processes or generators of urban stories worth telling and worth learning from.

When critical urbanists who have not made a career out of the study of African cities do turn their attention to the continent, what we find in their scholarship may not be much of an improvement. Mike Davis, in *Planet of Slums*, devotes a considerable amount of attention to the continent's cities. Unfortunately, from the book's first sentence, which imagines a woman giving birth 'in the Lagos slum of Ajegunle' as part of a Dickensian vision of megacities in a Third World hell, it is an extreme portrait (Davis 2005: 1; Fredericks 2009). We read of 'Kinshasa, Luanda, Khartoum, Dar es Salaam' and other African cities as growing 'prodigiously despite ruined import-substitution industries, shrunken public sectors, and downwardly mobile middle classes,' and in his crisis-driven narrative he notes that 'the African situation, of course, is more extreme' (Davis 2005: 16, 18). He uses United Nations (UN) Habitat data for a chart that shows more than 75 percent of the urban population of Nigeria (79.2 percent), Tanzania (92.1 percent), Ethiopia (99.4 percent), and Sudan (85.7 percent) living in 'slums' where nearly all other developing countries listed have percentages below the 50 percent mark, without any critical discussion of where these data come from or what really constitutes a slum. Having spent two decades studying Tanzanian cities, I cannot fathom how one would conclude that more than nine out of ten urban Tanzanians live in 'slums,' if slums are equated with the ghoulish belching squalor Davis portrays (I discuss these data in Chapter 3 in more detail). Davis (ibid.: 19) is so fixated on exploding slums, with no hope for poverty alleviation, and urbanisms that seem to him comprised mostly of 'pollution, excrement, and decay,' that one often loses the valuable insights and broad reading behind the book, such as his dissection of the 'brutal tectonics of neoliberal globalization' (ibid.: 174). He is so driven toward the worst of the worst-case scenarios and 'pathologies' that we, the readers, can only abandon hope, and turn tail heading elsewhere (ibid.: 128).

Thus, with Ferguson's argument that African studies scholarship needs to challenge this sort of 'Africa talk' in mind, in this book I take on the task of seeing how 'African' cities are or can be represented and interpreted. My contribution to comparative urban studies lies in comparing African cities with one another. Other scholarly projects underway in various networks may contribute to building a more robust, globalized comparative urban studies crossing divides of North and South, First and Third World, regions of the South, and so on. There is also scope for a project directly engaging with Western urban theories and critiquing Anglo-American urban studies in relation to Africa – some of which I do here and in other chapters – without detailed empirical cases from Africa. My goal is more to suggest ways in which we might *see again*, to point to the multifaceted urbanity in African contexts as of great value to global understanding of urbanism, for scholars, researchers, and practitioners whose focus may not be on Africa. My starting place, appropriately enough, lies within the recent work of a multidisciplinary group of scholars working to explore, in different ways, alternative visions of both urban theory and urban practices *from* African urban contexts.

Alternative visions of theory and practice

Let us start the discussion of this literature with a cursory glance at some of those urban contexts. Looking at the demographic data on Table o.1, we can see that according to the UN-Habitat program the population growth rates for cities that I examine in this book vary from a high of 8.32 percent per year (Abuja) to a low of 1.17 percent (Cape Town). Recent studies suggest that certain truisms held as common for African cities seem to be falling by the wayside. For instance, geographer Deborah Potts's (2009, 2011) examination of census data from a variety of cities has suggested that the long-assumed high rates of urbanization for Africa have leveled off or, in some cases, reversed, as economic stagnation and decline lead people back to patterns of circular migration, or back to rural lives, in countries such as Zimbabwe. By contrast, recent works by geographers Ian Yeboah (2008a) and Richard Grant (2009) document the growing wealth of Accra, with its staggering number of ritzy gated communities where homes are valued in the hundreds of thousands of US dollars and residents shop in fancy new shopping malls. The great variability and variation in the reliability of data on African cities makes comparability highly problematic. The first step toward any alternative vision lies therefore in the recognition that African cities are quite different from one another in patterns, processes, forms, and functions. The second step comes in arguing that, rather than a search for a strict, measured comparison, the plausible option for beginning to theorize about 'African' cities involves engagement with themes that hold somewhat constant as they manifest themselves in different ways in this diversity of cities.

TABLE 0.1 Population estimates for selected cities

City	2010 population in 000s[1]	City growth rate[1]
Nairobi, Kenya	3,363	3.76
Cape Town, South Africa	3,346[2]	1.17
Dar es Salaam, Tanzania	3,319	4.29
Accra, Ghana	2,332	3.23
Tripoli, Libya	2,324	2.04
Douala, Cameroon	2,108	3.54
Abuja, Nigeria	1,994	8.32
Mogadishu, Somalia	1,500	2.60
Lusaka, Zambia	1,421	2.39
Nelson Mandela Bay (Port Elizabeth), South Africa	1,053	2.10
Niamey, Niger	1,027	4.40[4]
Maiduguri, Nigeria	969	4.52[5]
Lilongwe, Malawi	669[3]	4.30[3]
Zanzibar, Tanzania	391[3]	4.50[3]
Dodoma, Tanzania	324[3]	2.30[3]
Saint Louis, Senegal	155[3]	2.50[3]

Notes: 1. All figures from UN-Habitat, *The State of African Cities* (2008), except where indicated. 2. Calculated from the 2008 population given in UN-Habitat (2008), with the growth rate listed on the corresponding chart, since the Habitat report inexplicably left Cape Town off the chart from which these other figures come. 3. From the census offices of the United Republic of Tanzania, 2002 and 1988; Senegal, 2002 and 1988; and Malawi, 1998 and 2008. 4. Balzerek (2003). 5. Balzerek (2001).

I've spent quite some time struggling with just how to select or *see* these 'somewhat constant themes' through which to address both theory and practice. My book's subtitle is meant to draw attention to the importance of vision, but I am also interested in re-vision. I refer to vision both in the sense of observing closely and in the sense of cities and their residents having a vision. As the late geographer Denis Cosgrove (2008: 8) wrote, 'vision is more than the ability to see and the bodily sense of sight … Vision has a creative capacity that can transcend both space and time: it can denote foreseeing as well as seeing.' I am not claiming such a capacity for myself, but examining the 'foreseeing as well as seeing' one finds in African cities among scholars, politicians, planners, writers, artists, and ordinary residents, the themes that recur in their conceptualizations in writings, plans, or interviews, and in the practice of urban life.

African urban studies as an academic field is beginning to provide some of these visions, in a broad, diverse array of insertions into discussions of citiness, responses to Western urban theory, and the innovations that arise outside of such a response. Theorists working principally on African cities generally do not reject theories or analysts like Harvey or Davis emanating from the West, and I am not suggesting one needs to do so in approaching cities on the continent. But finding the right sort of engagement that deals with both externally derived ideas and African concepts can be a challenge, as can be seen in many Africanist works wrestling with urban theory.

Achille Mbembe and Sarah Nuttall (2008: 6) point to what they consider the last decade's 'four major attempts at reading African cities into contemporary [urban] theory,' in balancing African and Western conceptualizations, through the works of Jane Guyer, Rem Koolhaas, Filip de Boeck, and Abdoumaliq Simone. Guyer seems an odd choice for urban studies, given that for the balance of her important, prolific career she has turned an economic-historical anthropologist's lens on gender and rural labor relations, and even in the books they cite as attempts at 'reading African cities into contemporary theory' she only tangentially addresses the literatures related to urban theory (Guyer 2004; Guyer et al. 2002). But at least Guyer has made a major contribution to African studies for over thirty years. Koolhaas (2002, 2003; Koolhaas and the Harvard Design School Project on the City 2000) is a more troubling selection, given that his oeuvre on Africa is so thin – a DVD on Lagos and a few essays that form part of the work of the *Harvard Project on the City* that he has led, a project in which Lagos played the stock role in what Okwui Enwezor (2003: 108) calls the 'nightmare scenario' of modernity. Koolhaas and his project team perversely seem to celebrate Lagos as the 'terminal condition of urbanization' (Koolhaas and the Harvard Design School Project on the City 2000: 719; Myers and Murray 2006). Enwezor (2003: 113) icily wonders what Koolhaas intends in his 'investments' in Lagos 'beyond the expansion of Koolhaasian conglomeratisation of architecture and urbanism' where 'the architect rides on the poetics of decay.' Koolhaas, he writes, has 'been aperceptive' in 'his idealization of Lagos' desperation' where the 'aura of power' he possesses 'inoculates him against local resistance to his anthropo-urbanism' (ibid.: 114). To be fair, Koolhaas's architectural firm, OMA, has now worked with a number of Nigerian architects over the last decade in Lagos, and some observers claim that OMA's 'approach has moved on considerably' from its 'aperceptive' days (Egbo 2010: 5). One is still left to wonder what made Koolhaas one of Mbembe and Nuttall's four major theorists on African urbanism when dozens of dynamic African architects are breaking new ground in the conversation between Western and African urbanisms, literally and figuratively, across the continent (as in the Bukka Trust in Lagos itself; Njoroge 2009; Elleh 2002; or the entire ArchiAfrica network, discussed in Chapter 2 of this book).

Mbembe and Nuttall's other two choices, de Boeck and Simone, have made contributions that are considerable in the effort to read African urbanism and urban theory into the same intellectual landscape, and works by both appear frequently in this book. De Boeck's (De Boeck and Plissart 2004: 34) deeply personal excavation of Kinshasa, with the photographer Marie-Françoise Plissart, emphasizes how the people of its peripheral 'annexed areas' have moved the city away from the 'place' colonialism shaped for it, to instead 'infuse the city with their own praxis, values, moralities and temporal dynamics.' De Boeck plays off of Italo Calvino's fanciful *Invisible Cities*, with Kinshasa as the fantastical Venice, a set of 'micro cities' where each one 'reflects the others' as if in a hall of mirrors (ibid.: 18). Rich as the book is with passion, imagery, and well-researched stories, it is readably in conversation with, and challenging, Western urban theory (whether Harvey, Foucault, Lefebvre, de Certeau, or others), but also with representations of Kinshasa and of the Congo. De Boeck brings to life the novel notion of Kinshasa's relationship with its invisible other, its 'second world' in the 'shadows' (ibid.: 57–8).

However, de Boeck is writing about Kinshasa, making no claims to be speaking about or for 'African' cities, perhaps staying within the boundaries of the 'principled' argument of many Africanist anthropologists that Ferguson discusses, albeit in a manner that uses Kinshasa to speak back to Western urbanists in various ways. Simone's books and articles are more explicitly comparativist and engaged with addressing representations of 'African' cities. In his most well-known book, *For the City Yet to Come: Changing African Life in Four Cities*, he develops a vision of the myriad 'possibilities of becoming' one finds in African urbanism (Simone 2004: 3). He deploys several 'specific conceptual notions' – informality, invisibility, spectrality, and movement – as 'a means of focusing attention on a process of interconnection in the gaps between clearly designated and defined urban institutions, spaces, and actions' (ibid.: 22). He sees his notions as 'heuristic entry points ... to help make sense of what otherwise appear simply as disparate and irrational dimensions of urban life' in his chosen settings of Pikine, Senegal, Winterveld, South Africa, Douala, Cameroon, and the African Sufi Muslims in Jidda, Saudi Arabia (ibid.: 13). Actually, a wider set of contexts come into play in the book's other, more applied, empirical and policy-oriented chapters, with Nairobi, Dar es Salaam, Kinshasa, Lagos, Abidjan, the Copperbelt, and other urbanisms featuring in Simone's extended reviews of colonial urban history, municipal management, and land and shelter policies. Ultimately, Simone's (ibid.: 241) goal is to 'provide a theoretical basis for promoting a sense of the "multiplex" in African urban development ... the ability to negotiate among locally and externally generated urban development knowledge and to enhance the impact of African experiences and contributions to the consolidation of urban knowledge in general.' This image of a multiplex is where this ambitious book breaks new ground, and moves us farther along in the attempt to 'read' African cities into 'contemporary theory.'

Simone (2010) has continued with groundbreaking and ambitious work since publishing that book, notably in *City Life from Jakarta to Dakar: Movements at the Crossroads*. Although *City Life* is written intentionally as an advanced undergraduate textbook, it also works as a contribution to urban theory. Simone (ibid.: 14) broadens his geographical lens to connect cities from Southeast Asia to West Africa, intending to bring the 'periphery' back into 'our considerations of urban life.' He argues for opening up the discussion, connecting processes in African cities with those elsewhere – in this case, mostly Southeast Asia. With his trademark storytelling woven into larger theoretical claims, Simone (ibid.: 268) stretches an idea he calls 'black urbanism' around an effort to tie 'together the various situations and tactics that have been at work in the long history of African people moving out, into and around a larger urban world.' His use of the concept of blackness rests on his hope for the possibility of the term being freed from its racial baggage, which is a tall order to contemplate despite his deft argumentation in favour of doing so.

Simone on one hand refuses the 'Africa' box, and yet he seizes one of its key apparent tenets, 'blackness,' as a tool for renegotiating city

life. For Simone, the way to work is to start the discussion of citiness in the world from the movements, experiments, and 'peripheral'
experiences of 'black' cities. This is an exciting move, to in effect
embrace peripheral status and turn it on its head. He seeks to develop his discussion by highlighting five manifestations of peripheral
urbanism: the preponderance of strategies and tactics of mobility; the
sense of the 'colonial present' for these cities, where dominant core
countries continue to practice their schemes in the periphery first;
the apparent invisibility (and not non-existence) of working-class
and working-poor neighborhoods in academic literature and planning
dynamics; the idea of 'seeing what might happen' as a quintessential
tactic; and the actual urban practices and dynamics at the periphery,
specifically in peri-urban zones.

Among Simone's signal insights, there is much that is appealing
and much that I seek to expand upon in this book. Urban studies
can gain from his insistence that cities of the global North and South
'"move toward" each other ... in gestures and inclinations shaped by
the search for economic and political strategies that enhance their
"normalization" as viable cities according to standards still largely
shaped by occidental notions of modernity' (ibid.: 15). His work
contains a hopefulness about cities in the South taking the lead
in creating new 'synergies, cross-investments, commodity chains,
distribution networks, production complementarities and alliances'
(ibid.: 16). Seeing people as 'infrastructure' – where the people themselves are the 'stuff of the shifting circuitries of connections' – can
be a profound means of revalorizing the humanity of the citizenry
regardless of economic status in African cities (ibid.: 124–5). That
leads him to redefine the 'right to the city' in part as the 'right to be
messy and inconsistent, or to look disordered' (ibid.: 331).

Simone (ibid.: 175–86) also adds to the appreciation of the particularly geographical aspects of African urban development. His idea
of the 'trans-territorial city' is potentially useful to an understanding of globalization and cosmopolitanism at the same time that
he draws our attention to the relocalization occurring in African
cities. One key element of the relocalizing is found in the polycentric
metropolitanization reshaping the cityscape, as he points out, and
diversifying the peri-urban zones. Finally, in his rather indirect answer
to the key question he poses toward the book's end, 'what is Africa
in the larger urban scheme of things?', he suggests that it has to do
with how peripheralized citizens create and re-create 'a new urban

sociality even under dire conditions' through various experiments, 'trial balloons' and possibilities for popular culture (ibid.: 314–16).

While one is sympathetic to and inspired by Simone's approach, his ethereal prose can pose some unnecessary challenges for interpretation. Simone returns again and again to experimentation, possibility, uncertainty, flexibility, and provisionalism, to 'seeing urban life as a context for intersection', and a variety of similarly broad generalizations (ibid.: 115). Nowhere is this more of a problem than with his notion of 'blackness as a tool for materializing connections among all the disparate things black people across the world have experienced' (ibid.: 296–7). His black geographies seem too vague – where are 'black' cities, where are cities not 'black,' why do we hop around Africa and Southeast Asia but see so little of Central and South America or the Caribbean – let alone Europe? It is evident that, as Simone (ibid.: 28) puts it, 'the sheer enumeration of how bad slums are … does not tell us what specific cities are capable of.' He is successful in his effort to 'stretch the imagination' of urban studies, particularly to connect cities across Africa and Asia in the ways he envisions for us (ibid.: 267). But we need something more tangible, even if 'enumeration' is perhaps untenable as a solution.

If we widen the net for examining theoretical contributions along these lines that seek to validate urban practices of the African poor, we begin to see patterns in a much larger, though sometimes less poetic, scope. A great many theoretically minded scholars, whether those who explicitly root their work in post-structuralist ideas or those who choose to build on African thought and practice, frequently emerge with emphases on informality, invisibility, spectrality, or new geographies of connectivity, movement, fluidity, flexibility, and contingency as relevant in the creation of African urban areas. Urban majorities find themselves entangled within power dynamics that position them at the city's margins, literally and figuratively, working to make places they can live with in the face of injustice, inequality, violence, or underdevelopment – 'remarkable forces of dynamism and transformation' mix with 'remarkable blockages and resistance' (Simone 2004: 242; Konings and Foeken 2006). Let me briefly provide a few examples of this growing arena of scholarship.

Perhaps the most significant corollary work to Simone's belongs to Robinson, in particular in *Ordinary Cities*. Robinson (2006: 1) is, like Simone in *City Life*, articulating a vision for cities beyond those on the continent alone, across the 'Third World' or the Global

South, 'post-colonialising urban studies' by seeing a whole 'world of ordinary cities, which are all dynamic and diverse, if conflicted arenas for social and economic life.' South African cities, and several other cities on the continent (including Lusaka and the Copperbelt), are the main, though not at all exclusive, empirical homes for her argument that 'thinking about cities ought to be willing to travel widely ... in search of understandings of the many different ways of urban life' (ibid.: 169). Much of her subsequent work has applied these claims to practical urban development concerns in Johannesburg or Durban and policy circulations around the globe, playing off of dynamics and concepts in planning in the West and in South Africa, seeing the 'multiplexity' (Healey 2000: 526) in circulations of urban ideas (e.g. Robinson 2008).

De Boeck, Simone, and Robinson are hardly alone in this widening terrain. The sociologist Martin Murray (2008a: vii and ix) begins his recent book on Johannesburg, like de Boeck, with Calvino's *Invisible Cities*, for Johannesburg is also a 'prismatic, kaleidoscopic, and ever-changing metropolis that contains many cities in one,' and he takes methodological inspiration from Walter Benjamin to identify 'persistent themes or common threads that, when brought into relation with one another, constitute something akin to a unified totality.' Pieterse (2008a: 2–3) (who, astoundingly, also begins with a quotation from Calvino's *Invisible Cities*!) points to a 'seam of analysis' that struggles with how the '"everyday practices" of the urban majority' in informal, marginalized neighborhoods might be seen as creating 'a zone of possibility and autonomy in various interstices of the city, even if in circumscribed ways.' The geographer Andrew Byerley (2005), anthropologist Eileen Moyer (2004), literary theorist Joyce Nyairo (2006), or anthropologist Basile Ndjio (2006a), and a host of other scholars are all working to use African urban contexts to speak to concerns in urban theory across the world.

Scholarship articulating the sorts of conceptions of fluid African urbanism present in works like those by the authors above is growing exponentially. The challenges for African urban studies no longer lie simply or solely with paying more theoretical attention to the marginalized informal, invisible, spectral, necropolitan or ordinary settings across the cities of the continent – important as this may be. I argue that they lie equally in *practice*, in then attempting to articulate how such urbanization processes might contribute to efforts to improve the quality of life for the inhabitants of these places (Roy 2007). It is notable, for instance, how often the theoretical works I have been discussing above zero in on practical, applied issues like housing, land, crime, or service delivery. Even in Simone's rather conceptual *City Life* (2010: 331, 333), he ends by asking 'how platforms of engagement can be built' that address 'essential services, security and livelihood.' One of the most striking distinguishing features of this expanding new urban literature in Africa is its wide intersection between urban theory and urban planning practice, and things happen at that intersection of great potential value to both urban studies and African studies.

Specifically, I am interested in five moments of intersection between theory and practice in African cities. The considerable outpouring of urban studies scholarship from Africa has gone in so many different directions that it is difficult to encompass. Typologizing or categorizing this literature is a challenging task also because so many conventional categories or disciplinary boundaries are transgressed. There are eddies of discussion and debate, though, that are noticeable enough to provide us with at least these five themes, by which we may begin to see cities in Africa through questions and debates on *postcolonialism, informality, governance, violence,* and *cosmopolitanism* which serve as the organizing principles for my chapters. Though African cities are quite different from one another, these are the main struggles that most African cities share: overcoming colonial inheritances of poverty, underdevelopment and socio-spatial inequality; dealing with informal sectors and settlements; governing justly; forging non-violent environments; and coping with globalization. My comparative thematic approach enables us to address the different outcomes and processes across the continent in regard to those struggles. In each case, theoretical conceptualizations meet with practical empirical questions for city life. These are hardly the only themes of African urban studies, nor is it possible for my discussion of any one of them to be comprehensive. But taken as a whole, and seen for their interconnections with one another, these themes enable us to work toward a potential agenda for African urban studies.

That agenda, though, must come to terms with questions posed by the South African urban planner Philip Harrison (2003, 2006a) that tie into urban studies practice more broadly. Are African urbanisms genuinely new forms that manifest local knowledge which can then be deployed in alternative planning? Harrison (2006a: 325) helpfully wants us to eschew any notion that we are recovering 'hidden essentialism' in terms of some 'authentic African way of thinking and making' cities. Instead, he draws our attention to 'rationalities and practices that have emerged as the subalterns [in the sense of excluded or marginalized people] have found ways to live in circumstances of marginality and domination.' He argues for thinking across the borders between Western rational planning and these alternative rationalities and practices, seeing particular hopefulness in 'zones of exchange where different modes of thinking intersect within a common space' (ibid.: 326). What these new forms of thinking about urban practices actually *mean* for cities becomes a key theme for me, particularly in exploring hybrid and relational engagements within the five themes. In that exploration I seek to ground theoretical debates and discussions in the political and social practices of a wide range of actors.

Some of the theoretical writing in relation to African cities holds within its core a 'language that is unfortunately prone to a level of abstraction in which the issues of everyday life are translated into plans and policies that often bear little resemblance to the real concerns of people' (Harrison 2003: 23). This level of abstraction, indeed, seeps into some of the literature I've discussed above. The theoretical concerns are important, but the need to cut through abstraction may be equally so, given how pronounced the 'real concerns of people' are in most cities, where the poor comprise visible majorities. I believe that Pieterse (2008a: 89–106) brings us closer to those real concerns, in his model of how urban development practitioners (be they state, private sector, or civil society actors) work through five domains of political engagement toward a 'relational city.' By 'relational' cities, Pieterse means ones that have a fuller understanding of the 'plurality of action spaces,' where the broad and 'variegated' collection of actors in urban development engage with one another across divides between 'formal and informal, symbolic and concrete, collaborative and contestatory' (ibid.: 106). Pieterse (ibid.: 106) hopes to incite 'more comprehensive analytical accounts of political practices in the city' through his examination of representative politics, stakeholder forums, direct action, grassroots development, and symbolic politics (such as the political contestation of the city's image). One of the most valuable advances in Pieterse's (ibid.: 95) conceptualization is his recognition that many different overlapping agendas clash in the urban policy arena, operating at different scales and in different discursive fields; his multidimensional understanding of power relations in the city allows for 'relational interdependency between various domains of political practice.' This sort of interactionist or relational approach to studying urban practice is essential if one is to grasp the 'multiplex' Simone and others see in African cities. Thus in this book I seek to draw attention to these domains of political practice within my five themes.

The plan of the book

I use my own research and a close reading of works by other scholars, writers, and artists, African and non-African, based on the continent or based elsewhere, on a reasonably broad range of cities in Africa, to highlight the five themes. My choice of cities is governed by several factors. First, I prioritize cities in which I have lived, conducted research, and/or engaged with local scholars. The cities I know best get greater emphasis, owing simply to my greater familiarity. Since Zanzibar is the city in which I conducted my dissertation research twenty years ago and to which I have most often returned in other research, it shows up fairly often in this book, but in the company of Nairobi, Dar es Salaam, Lilongwe, Lusaka, Dodoma, Grahamstown, or Cape Town (as cities with which I am personally familiar); I work to pair or compare those more familiar research settings with the experiences of and processes in Dakar, Accra, Abuja, Mogadishu, Kinshasa, Douala, and other cities where I have not conducted research or stayed but from which significant works of African urban studies have emerged. My methods include the use of my research findings from interviews, surveys, archival research, and literary criticism, as well as my reading of these secondary sources. I open every chapter with a small story or anecdote, most often involving my own experiences, not to draw undue attention to myself but to engage readers as directly as I can, out of those experiences, as an interpretive, grounding device.

To some extent, the cities I emphasize are the hometowns of my graduate students, cities in which my graduate students have conducted research, and/or cities wherein the Kansas African Studies Center where I work has research relationships with African universities. I also seek to provide at least some measure of coverage for the whole continental region, with an inevitable emphasis on eastern and southern African cities given my experience. That experience also means an emphasis on anglophone scholarship, but not to the point of excluding areas of French, Portuguese, Belgian, Spanish, Italian, or German influences or scholarship. I seek to balance familiar cities that are frequently researched with less commonly studied ones. Finally,

I include analysis of some of the continent's larger, more economically significant cities with smaller secondary cities, to afford greater appreciation of the range of urban experiences on the continent. Ultimately, the cities I discuss provide us with a chance to see the great diversity that exists in the contemporary experiences of cities on the continent.

Chapter 1 lays out my five themes of African urban scholarship in relation to Lusaka. My structuring of the discussion in the chapter is also part of a long intellectual conversation with one of my professional mentors, the geographer Edward Soja, whose works – and particularly the books *Postmodern Geographies*, *Thirdspace*, *Postmetropolis*, and *Seeking Spatial Justice* – have been sources of major inspiration throughout my career. In the chapter, I explore the five themes in dialog with Soja's 'six discourses of the postmetropolis,' by asking 'What if the postmetropolis is Lusaka?' I then take up my five themes in turn in the ensuing chapters.

Like Simone's 'conceptual notions' in *For the City Yet to Come*, these themes are meant as terms that can open up onto the discussions and debates in the expanding African urban studies bookshelf and in planning offices or community organization headquarters. The first of these concerns the impacts and legacies of European colonialism for the continent's cities. Chapter 2 surveys what it means to be postcolonial for African cities, in theoretical and practical terms. A key empirical dynamic in this chapter entails discussion of the created capitals of the independence era – many of which can literally be described as postcolonial urbanisms. Specifically, I move from more theoretical discussions of postcolonial cities to an analysis of the cases of Lilongwe, Malawi, Abuja, Nigeria, and Dodoma, Tanzania. I seek to uncover the degree to which these new capitals move beyond the citiness and planning dynamics of the colonial era.

Chapter 3 concentrates on the everyday livelihood struggles and political-economic challenges for residents of the informal settlements common to African cities, focusing primarily on the struggles over land and housing that shape the cityscape from its cores to its peri-urban edges. I use material from Zanzibar, Dar es Salaam, Accra, and Cape Town in the chapter. My goal is to illuminate what is termed informality to city life in Africa and connect with wider discussions of the informal sector and especially of informal settlements, and clashes of rationality between these and what get labeled modern or formal zones or processes in cities within urban studies, working toward what political transgressions or alliances would need to transpire to produce the relational cities of Pieterse's model from the familiar and normal cities one encounters across the continent.

The governance challenges of African cities and the responses of city governments and ordinary residents to them are the basis of Chapter 4. I seek to look at African cities as they appear from their marginalized edges and discarded populations as well as their planning units, with a particular emphasis on governance and service delivery, raising questions about justice. I analyze neoliberal, materialist, post-structuralist and empiricist approaches to governance and service delivery, mixing research results from my work in Zanzibar and secondary sources on Nairobi, Douala, Kinshasa, Dakar, and urban South Africa. African urban governance problems often play a central role in the creation of outside authors' negative or nightmarish depictions, such as in Davis's *Planet of Slums* and its long segment on 'living in shit.' My intention in this chapter, without glossing over potential crisis areas, is to interrogate efforts to return agency to African urban residents in new modes of governance and to ask what cities are *possible*, as a means of re-envisioning our understanding of urban dynamics on the continent, seeking a path toward justice in what I refer to as 'hybrid governance' in a relational city.

Most Western students and most urban studies scholars will have a notion somewhere in their heads of African cities as wounded places, whether wounded by war, famine, disease, poverty or political turmoil. Violence, crime, and urbicide are indeed prominent arenas of contemporary research for African urban studies. Yet a recent major edited volume in urban studies called *Wounded Cities* (Schneider and Susser 2003) had no chapter on an African city, and most of the analysis found in books like *Planet of Slums* is alarmist and purely pessimistic. Mogadishu is my primary focus in Chapter 5, as it would rate highly on most lists of cities wounded by violence and yet can be an ideal setting for alternative ideas about cities. The chapter builds from postcolonial literary criticism. I examine the vivid representations of urban history and geography in the writings of Nuruddin Farah (2003, 2007a), particularly through his novels *Links* and *Knots*, that address the relationships of Somali exiles to the city. I use Farah's Mogadishu to suggest the importance of African cultures' urban visions, to guide us to a sense of African cities as both firmly linked in to the rest of the world and deserted by its dominant powers – or scholars – in other ways.

Chapter 6 seeks to place African cities in the broad sweep of globalization, in line with African urban studies' growing intellectual interest in diasporic and transnational relationships. I seek to show how the cosmopolitan human geographies of the city have stretched out and crossed oceans through transnational migration and technological innovations, circumscribed or produced by postcolonial nation-state politics and underdevelopment. To illustrate this, I discuss numerous cities and sites, particularly as their transnational cultures are made manifest in the creative arts, but with my main interest in Zanzibar and on Zanzibaris. The goal here is to show that, in deep contrast with what is commonly supposed in urban studies standard texts about global cities, globalization and cosmopolitanism have had major impacts for African cities, within them and beyond them, not all of which are nightmarish. My approach brings home the importance of connecting African cities with cities across the world, given the vital roles and experiences of Africans in cities outside of Africa every day. In the chapter, I again build from literature as well as the arts, in an effort to emphasize the imaginative character of cities in Africa. Recent scholarship in African urban studies has pointed us toward understandings of cities as centers of generative, imaginative, or creative energies, in part to consciously contest the wounded urbicides of so much of the popular imagination outside the continent. Various international arts festivals, novelists, artists, and photographers animate my discussion of alternative visions and re-visions of cities in Africa.

In the book's conclusion, I summarize my main arguments and suggest an agenda for research and action in relation to African cities. My key goal is to return us to Harrison's questions and Pieterse's notion of a relational city discussed above: what, among the 'practices that have emerged as the subalterns have found ways to live in circumstances of marginality and domination,' can be deployed to re-envision cities in Africa, for African studies and for urban studies? How can we work toward a relational city? In retracing my five themes, I suggest how a comparative approach to African cities might contribute to changing urban theory and practice on the continent, and urban studies more broadly.

ONE

What if the postmetropolis is Lusaka?

Introduction

In June 2004, I stood with several American friends waiting for a minibus in Roma, a hilly neighborhood in the eastern part of Lusaka, Zambia. The hoot of the minibus horn caused me to turn my head and look up the street, and to notice a fancy new sign planted by the bus stop. In bright letters at the top of a square board covered by an elaborate green awning, the sign read 'Please Keep Lusaka Clean.' It was the bottom of the sign which really caught my attention: 'Otherwise the Pirates Will Attack You.' A black shield identified something called the 'Ng'ombe Pirates' with a pirate flag and skull-and-crossbones insignia (Figure 1.1).

This sign appeared on a Lusaka street long before piracy on the high seas off the East African coast gained the world's attention, and Zambia is, after all, a landlocked country. Thus, after my friends and I boarded the minibus, we debated, with some good humor, about who the Ng'ombe Pirates might be. The Pirates of Zambia's football league are the team from Livingstone, not Lusaka, so it wasn't a football reference. Was Roma, an elite, formerly whites-only township until its forced incorporation into Lusaka in 1970, infested with pirates from the poor informal settlement, adjacent to it, Ng'ombe? Were there pirates among us – either us foreigners or our fellow passengers who had entered the minibus on the previous stops, all of which are located in Ng'ombe, in which Roma's maids and gardeners live? If so, what was their role: did they help keep the city clean by attacking its polluters, or did the city end up more vulnerable to evil pirate attack if its citizens did not clean up? Was there a new pirate movie playing at the cineplex of the shiny new South African-owned shopping mall, Arcades, to which the minibus was heading? Or were the pirates merely metaphorical phantoms deployed by the clever advertising department of the sponsoring company, Harvey Tile, to make people dispose of their garbage?

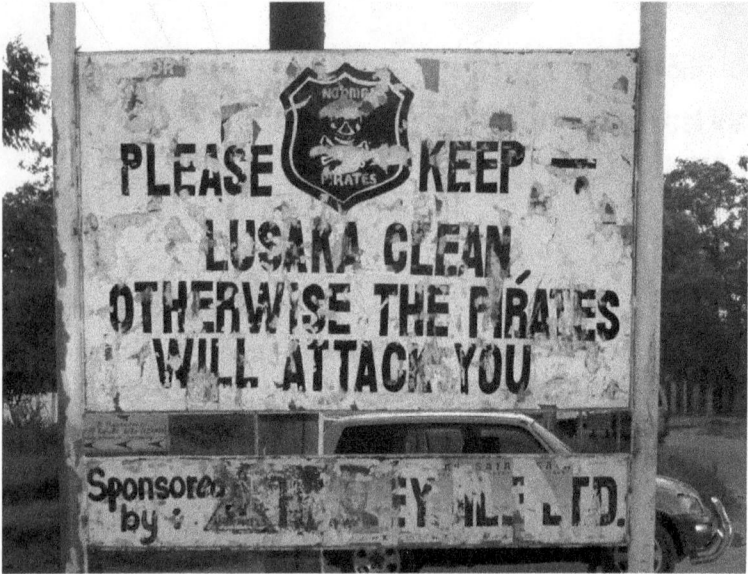

FIGURE I.I The pirates of Ng'ombe (*source*: Simon Nkemba)

I have never located the pirates of Ng'ombe, nor have I found the answer to the question of the sign's intent (five years later, it was covered with political campaign posters that a Zambian friend, Simon Nkemba, cleaned off to take this photograph). But I have found myself thinking of how the message, site, situation, and experience of the sign encapsulate my understanding of themes that predominate in many cities in Africa and writings about them. First, even forty or fifty years after the end of formal colonial rule, it is easy to see colonialism's scars, as in the gashes of space and injustice that separate the Romas and Ng'ombes of many cities on a continent where every country but Liberia spent at least some years being ruled by Europeans. Second, the bouncing, fluid chaos of the minibus ride, with the spontaneous relationships passengers made with one another, re-creates countless times a day in myriad ways in almost any major city the informal interactions that encapsulate much of everyday life and economy in many versions of urban Africa.

The sign itself was attempting to encourage cleanliness, to build on a decade of awareness-raising about the environment, made most manifest in Lusaka in governance programs for solid waste management. The garbage around the sign's base when we first saw it in 2004 and when Simon took the photo in 2009 made a mockery of these attempts. The rise of efforts to promote urban environmental planning and good governance is similarly hard to miss across Africa, and similarly struggling nearly everywhere. The everyday struggles of the ordinary residents of places like Ng'ombe, where residents told me in 2003 interviews that two or three armed robberies may happen each night, parallel those of informal settlement residents in many African cities. Most of Lusaka's residents live in substandard housing in such settlements, which are often illegal (or 'unauthorized' in local parlance), crime-ridden, struggling with HIV/AIDS, and home to many refugees from past wars in the Democratic Republic of Congo, Angola, or Mozambique. This too is a theme one finds resonating across many African cities, wounded and limping into the second decade of this new millennium.

Yet in Lusaka, the marks of globalization, a transformed modernity, and a distinctive cosmopolitanism, like the Arcades mall, are fast becoming visible, as they are in many African urban areas. Through this globalizing trend, perhaps, we return to the pirates. Much of what happens in African cities is invisible or unpredictable and might seem bizarre to the unfamiliar visitor, like those Ng'ombe Pirates. Sometimes, this invisibility is inexplicable, and sometimes it seems deliberate. The widely available road map to Lusaka one can buy in the bookstore in the Arcades mall has advertisements scattered all around its edges that cover up the vast majority of Lusaka's 'peri-urban areas,' where two-thirds of the city's population resides (Sivaramakrishnan 1997: 229; Waste Management Unit, Lusaka City Council 2006). Many of the names of these areas appear on the map, but none of the roads that cut across and through them does. One could never use the map to navigate them. This symbolizes an invisibility that haunts a great many areas in African cities. Yet in and around this invisibility, incredibly imaginary and imaginative facets of the city emerge, creative, propulsive, innovative, and strongly linked with a wider world. As Sivaramakrishnan (1997: 229, and in Davis 2005: 37) pointed out, in Lusaka, these areas are 'called "peri-urban" but in reality it is the city proper that is peripheral.' In cities like Lusaka, one needs to turn one's imagination inside out, to see the world in the city.

The paragraphs above lead me to a set of questions. What about Lusaka is actually the way many cities in Africa are, or even the way many cities in the world are becoming? What do those patterns say about the way people think about, write about, or understand cities in Africa or in the world today? As I have argued in the introduction, many major debates and theorists in urban studies bypass the continent, dismiss its cities from the cartography of urban areas that matter, banish them to minor footnotes of exception, or make of them exemplary dystopias and horror shows of future terror. What happens if we place them in the center of urban studies instead?

The postmetropolis according to Soja

In this chapter's title, I have made a deliberate reference to the third book of Ed Soja's trilogy of critical urban theory, *Postmetropolis* (2000). In this book and a related book chapter published the next year, Soja (2001: 38) uses the term postmetropolis to draw attention to 'profound material changes' in 'the modern metropolis.' He describes the restructuring, deconstruction, and reconstitution of space that he sees in cities in 'broad brush sketches' for a 'multi-sided picture ... of what has been happening to cities over the past thirty years' (ibid.: 39). Soja (2000: 145–348) suggests six broad themes, which are articulated in his provocative and inventive style (he names the themes his 'six discourses,' on the postfordist industrial metropolis, cosmopolis, exopolis, the fractal city, the carceral city/archipelago, and simcities).

It is seldom noted in analyses of his later works that Soja began his career as a scholar of the geography of urban development in East Africa (Soja 1968, 1979; Soja and Weaver 1976). Soja started to take a much more critical stance toward modernization and modernity, but left African studies by the early 1980s. In the trilogy, Soja uses Los Angeles as his primary, though not exclusive, empirical backdrop for an engagement with a wide range of social theorists, without revisiting Africa (though he does make meaningful reference to South Africa in the more recent *Seeking Spatial Justice*; Soja 2010: 39–40, 84).

The first book, *Postmodern Geographies*, had the phrase of its subtitle, 'the reassertion of space in critical social theory,' as its principal aim. Drawing on his interpretation of the writings of the urban theorist Henri Lefebvre, Soja's (1989: 80) central achievement lies in his articulation here of what he termed the 'socio-spatial dialectic,' whereby urban space is recast as a product of society that 'arises from purposeful social practice.' Soja sought to illustrate his claims along these lines in two successive chapters that close the book, entitled 'It All Comes Together in Los Angeles' and 'Taking Los Angeles Apart.' It is the latter chapter which gave inspiration to the style of this particular chapter in *my* book. Soja (ibid.: 223) was aiming to deploy 'fragmentary glimpses, a freed association of reflective and interpretive field notes' in order to 'appreciate the specificity and uniqueness of a particularly restless geographical landscape while simultaneously seeking to extract insights at higher levels of abstraction.' The vignettes I use below in discussing my book's themes in relation to Lusaka are similarly fragmentary glimpses meant to convey something specific about the city but also about the more abstract themes.

It is also this more creative end of the first book which gave rise to the approach in the second, *Thirdspace: Journeys to Los Angeles and Other Real-and-Imagined Places* (1996); but this second book is less significant for my interests here than the third book of the trilogy, *Postmetropolis: Critical Studies of Cities and Regions* (2000), which is structured in three parts that work to articulate each of the three dimensions of Lefebvre's spatial triad, 'the spatiality of human life as it is simultaneously perceived, conceived, and lived' (ibid.: 351). My concern here is with his Part II, the 'Six Discourses on the Postmetropolis.'

Again with Los Angeles as the empirical referent, Soja explores each of his discourses in distinct chapters. The first of these, the *postfordist industrial metropolis*, highlights emerging regionalism at the expense of industrial urbanism, with the formation of extended metropolitan regions built around flexible specialization production systems with the collapse of 'fordist' assembly-line industrialism. The second, on *cosmopolis*, emphasizes how globalization has changed the spatiality of power relations and society in global and world cities like Los Angeles. *Exopolis* gives rise to a discussion of 'the urbanization of suburbia and the growth of Outer Cities,' or the changed 'geographical outcomes of the new urbanization processes' of a 'city turned outside-in' (ibid.: 238, 234, 250). The fourth discourse, on *fractal city*, is meant to refer to the 'fluid, fragmented, decentered and rearranged' social mosaic of the city through rising socio-spatial polarity, inequality, and ethnic segmentation (ibid.: 265). Soja's final two discourses mark a bit of a departure. The *carceral archipelago* refers to the increasingly fortified character of urban space, via 'privatization, policing, surveillance, governance, and design of the built environment,' as in gated communities, homeowner associations, and the like (ibid.: 299). The final discourse focuses on 'the restructuring of the urban imaginary' in philosophy, urban studies, film, and computer games (ibid.: 324).

Reading through Soja's six themes of the postmetropolis is an entertaining experience. Is it a plausible suggestion for me to simply take his discourses and do a compare-and-contrast exercise? Soja (ibid.: 154, italics in original) in fact invites us to do exactly this: 'what will be represented here,' he writes in the introduction to Part II of *Postmetropolis* (on the six discourses), 'is an *invitation to comparative analysis*, to using what can be learned from Los Angeles to make practical and theoretical sense of what is happening wherever the reader may be living.' This is, I admit, part of what this chapter is about, given my chapter title: indeed, what if the postmetropolis is Lusaka – or Luanda, or Lubumbashi, for that matter – and not Los Angeles?

One problem with such an approach is that it might perpetuate the sense that we must learn about African cities by studying Western urban theory and then applying it on the continent. Los Angeles is not necessarily a completely false start for understanding African cities – the Nigerian-Angeleno novelist Chris Abani (2009), for example, has said that LA is 'the quintessential African city' because he recognizes so many aspects of its social geography as more than comparable to Lagos. As I've noted in the introduction, there is no reason why African studies must categorically reject Western urban theory, and many authors in the recent wave of African urban studies put Lefebvre, Harvey, de Certeau, or Massey to good use. But as with these other theorists, we find that references that stretch far beyond Euro-American cities are rare in and tangential to Soja's discussion of his six discourses. It would take some limbo dancing to finesse an African postindustrial fordist city under that discourse's bar, if you will – though Africa's Detroit, the Nelson Mandela Bay Municipality (Port Elizabeth-Despatch-Uitenhage) in South Africa, might perform the function if required (Port Elizabeth has a huge informal settlement called KwaFord, after all, next to Ford's manufacturing complex). Many African cities have always been cosmopolitan, exopolitan, fractal, or carceral, but in different ways than Soja means the terms (see Murray 2008b on Johannesburg, for example). Likewise, we can say that a 'restructuring of the urban imaginary' is ongoing across the continent, but not necessarily owing to or coterminous with computer gaming and postmodern cyber-architecture (see Diouf 2008 on Dakar).

Soja's latest book, *Seeking Spatial Justice*, picks up its narrative right where *Postmetropolis* ended, with the Bus Riders Union of

Los Angeles. While the first half of the book is a concise and helpful restatement of his arguments over the last twenty-five years, the
second half again concentrates on Los Angeles, albeit in new ways.
Here, Soja makes the connections between academia and activism
for social change explicit. He seeks to bridge theory and practice, to
take a 'critical spatial perspective' into the hard work of 'cross-cutting
coalition building' that he sees as crucial to forging more just and
relational communities, cities, and urban regions (Soja 2010: 199). As
with the earlier trilogy the challenge lies in dealing with the relationship between his example, Los Angeles, and cities in Africa. But the
twist here is that he develops the idea of 'spatial justice' out of his
consideration of the work of Gordon Pirie on apartheid South Africa.
It stands as a stark reminder of what urban studies can gain from
building from African urban studies, rather than having its directional
arrows ever flowing from the North and the West into the continent.

I take inspiration from Soja's six discourses in creating an organizing principle for the book, and in a sense a methodological approach
(rather than a set of theoretical or empirical concerns per se); but I
am still operating under the premise of African studies talking back
to urban studies, not the other way around. What happens, I ask,
if we start the discussion about 'what has been happening to cities
over the past thirty years' *from* Lusaka, or any other African city,
rather than LA? I choose Lusaka for many reasons, not least of which
is that its very ordinariness at first glance – no grand skyline, no
obvious spectacle, just a few million people living their lives in close
proximity – challenges the grandiosity that often inheres to urban
theory. That does not necessarily make my task of de-centering any
smoother. 'It is easy enough,' Robinson (2006: 167) writes, 'to raise
a critique of ethnocentrism in urban studies; it's so much harder to
instigate new kinds of practices for studying cities and managing
them.' I seek to follow her lead in 'decentering the reference points ...
in a spirit of attentiveness to the possibility that cities elsewhere [e.g.
cities in Africa] might perhaps be different and shed stronger light on
the processes being studied' (ibid.: 168–9). In so doing, I still share
Soja's (2000: xiv) under-appreciated 'commitment' throughout his
trilogy and *Seeking Spatial Justice* 'to producing knowledge not only
for its own sake but more so for its practical usefulness in changing
the world for the better.'

Instead of Soja's six themes, in this chapter and in the rest of
the book, I substitute five others – with Lusaka as my touchstone

city in this chapter – for an experimental vision of cities in Africa as seen through concerns with *postcolonialism, informality, governance, violence,* and *cosmopolitanism.* What has been happening to Lusaka over the past few decades? Lusaka has continued to deal with its colonial inheritance of poverty, underdevelopment, and deep inequality; the functions and forms to Lusaka's growth contain a high degree of informality; the methods, processes, and networks for governing Lusaka have seen dramatic changes in institutional terms via democratization and neoliberalism; the city is coping with rising domestic insecurity and a variety of seeping wounds to its social fabric; and Lusaka is globalizing at a variety of scales at once. My hunch is that this bundle of phenomena speaks much more strongly to the experiences of cities in Africa over the last thirty years or so than do Soja's six discourses. These themes are really an amalgamation and restatement of concepts developed and debated in African urban studies over the last few decades or more by many scholars in and out of Africa. They are sometimes themes that are hard to tease out from one another (particularly informality and governance), but ultimately I examine distinct phenomena under each. Since these themes provide the backbone for the next five chapters, I should note that I am merely sketching them here in this chapter in terms of how they might appear in 'broad brush strokes' in reference to Lusaka, to set the stage for the further excavation each chapter brings.

Postcolonial city

The cover image for my book *Disposable Cities* is based on an air photo of the boundary zone between Roma and Ng'ombe, the hilly former white township and the crowded informal settlement. I used the image in part to show that Lusaka, like many African cities, still bears the scars of colonialism nearly fifty years after Zambia earned independence from Britain. 'Catastrophic inequalities between juxtaposed neighborhoods all over the city, an absence of drinking water, overabundance of surface water, and toxic drainage, to say nothing of failing sewerage, sanitation, solid waste management, rates collection, or land control' – I called these 'the oldest stories of Lusaka' (Myers 2005; Cheatle 1986; Collins 1986).

Ng'ombe was a part of a white-owned farm estate from the 1930s, when Lusaka was formally constructed and designated as the capital of Northern Rhodesia, a colony of Britain that had been only recently transferred (in 1928) to the Crown from the British South

Africa Company (BSAC). The BSAC had founded the colony in the 1890s essentially as a mining concession. By the 1950s, most of what became Ng'ombe was leased to the Witwatersrand Native Labour Association (WNLA), which recruited mineworkers for South African mines. A neighborhood formed for a time around the WNLA camp, such that people began to call the area 'Winella,' a place-name that appears in maps and reports of the decade. About one hundred people lived in Winella's twenty houses as of 1957 (NAZ 1957–61: LUDC 1/4/24, f. 34).

By independence, though, the white landowner was back to using this area for occasional pasturage. He more than tolerated settlement on his land – like many white landowners around Lusaka, he engaged in what was derisively called 'kaffir farming,' where they were 'growing' huts for black squatters (for whom the derogatory term, kaffir, was used in Northern Rhodesia as in South Africa) who rented their rights to be on his land. The Director of African Affairs expressed some slight concern: 'This charging of rents ... for houses in unauthorized locations is an additional complication which requires early investigation because of the effect on perpetuating slums in which no services are provided.' Nevertheless, the director noted that the district commissioner was in fact doing much the same thing in similar places around the city, in allowing black squatters on government land (ibid.: LUDC 1/4/24, f. 142).

By 1966, the name Ng'ombe (cows) was affixed to the community emerging on this hillslope. The settlement began in the low-lying areas near to Roma and the creek. As it expanded (the 1990 census had 17,288 people, and the 2001 census counted more than 30,000 in Ng'ombe, while local household surveys at the same time counted more than 40,000 people) it moved up the hillside, encroaching on properties belonging to the Roman Catholic Church, for what was called the Roma Convent. The informal settlement's residents on church lands were then forcibly evicted by order of the Lusaka City Council in December 2002; some seven hundred homes were demolished. 'Some people in Ng'ombe threw off their crosses and rosaries after that, saying we won't be in this church,' one resident told me. Yet Ng'ombe was one of a dozen neighborhoods subject to demolitions that rainy season, and major demolitions had come every few years, across the scarred cityscape of peri-urbanism, in the late 1970s, the early 1990s, the late 1990s, and again after 2002's episode. The 'geographies of exclusion' that colonialism formed have hardly disappeared from the landscape of Lusaka (Sibley 1995; Tait 1997; Rakodi 1986). If anything, they have morphed into new forms.

Lusaka might be conceived of as postcolonial in the two ways that term is most often used. That means, first, that it is a city living in the 'temporal aftermath' of – i.e. the 'period of time after' – colonialism, and second, that it is a city amid the 'critical aftermath' – meaning the 'cultures, discourses and critiques that lie beyond, but remain closely influenced by, colonialism' (Blunt and McEwan 2002, in McEwan 2009: 17). The first sense, the conditions of the temporal aftermath, suggests how societies live with the legacies of colonialism. African societies certainly experienced a diversity of forms of colonialism, and it is unsurprising to see a divergent set of responses to what should be pluralized as postcolonial conditions. As Lusaka suggests, many aspects of colonial relationships have not ended; over and over again, for instance, demolition, removal, and upgrading processes in the postcolonial era replicate colonial tactics (Myers 2006; Davis 2005: 111). Postcolonial conditions are conditions that aren't really *post*colonial in very many senses, other than the temporal dimension alone. But that also does not mean that postcolonial conditions are not dramatically diverse – Lusaka is not any more or less typical than any other city in Africa in this. When postcolonial is used in that second sense, of a critical aftermath, where a 'set of theoretical perspectives' aim at 'hearing or recovering the experiences of the colonized,' it comes under fire for its abstractions (Sidaway 2000: 591, 594). The challenge lies, as geographer Cheryl McEwan (2009: 252) puts it, with connecting postcolonial thought's 'powerful discursive insights to material consequence,' as I seek to do in Chapter 2.

(I)n(f)ormal city

Most of Lusaka's people live in places like Ng'ombe, which are called compounds, or *komboni* in Chinyanja. The term has its origins in the colonial era. Legally, blacks only had the right to live in the city if they resided in the compound of their white employer. From the beginning, there were exceptions and violations of this rule. Lusaka had fewer than two thousand residents in 1928, but with the 1931 decision to make it the colonial capital its population began to climb. The planned 'Garden City' was meant for white settlers, but few whites ever came. Whites did control large farmsteads all around the town, but most of the poorly drained region was ill suited for farming. Some were able to mine limestone on their plots instead, but most white settlers made some money by renting land to blacks, and the rents they collected became their 'crop.' The compounds and the houses erected on them essentially had no legal status within the City of Lusaka, and each grew through the informal rules that governed the landholder's relations with his or her people. These long-forgotten settlers remain on Lusaka's map nearly everywhere one turns – John Laing, George, Misisi ('the Mrs'), John Howard, Jack, Marapodi (named for an Italian contractor, G. B. Marapodi), Villa Elizabetha (named for Marapodi's daughter), or Mandevu ('Beards,' the nickname of the landholder). Many developed adjacent to private whites-only developments built by these same settlers that were typically separate townships from the City of Lusaka, such as Roma. There are also many parts of informal Lusaka that Lusaka's African people have named, and still more where they have made the European names their own. By 1963, nearly 14 percent of Lusaka's population lived in unauthorized compounds and another 38 percent lived in 'employer' housing – an impossible percentage when compared with the real numbers of 'employees' for any supposed employers (Collins 1986: 125). By 1974, a clear majority of the city resided in what were by then being called 'informal areas' (ibid.: 131).

Some of the most interesting early urban studies research in Africa occurred in these peri-urban settlements in the 1950s, often through what was then the Rhodes-Livingstone Institute (RLI). These works document that the real life of the actual majority of Lusaka's population, from the very beginning, was found in the peri-urban edges. 'It has been interesting,' wrote an RLI researcher compiling a Gazetteer of African Housing Areas for Lusaka's district commissioner in 1957, 'to discover the extent to which the inhabitants of the unauthorized locations provide services for their fellows in the Municipal Locations as … vendors of herbs and dried caterpillars, indigent carpenters, shoemakers, wise women, and snuff grinders.' The RLI's 1958 report on unauthorized locations cautioned that the government would be 'mistaken to think of these people as criminals. The great majority of them are very decent people.' They had no alternative but to take up residence on the fringes – it was in fact economically logical: they had cheaper accommodation, and could replicate something more like the rural life they had left behind, while exercising nearly complete freedom of action and living nearer to work.

But then this 1958 report moved on to discuss what its authors called the 'five political effects of the squatter problem.' First: the 'unauthorized locations corrupt the average African coming to Lusaka from a rural area.' Second: the lack of stability leads to 'a lack of social conscience or sense of responsibility' in the peri-urban edges. Third, as independence and anti-colonial movements progressed, the authors feared that 'the physical disadvantages of life in these compounds [would] afford opportunities for the agitator.' Fourth, thinking of places much like Ng'ombe vis-à-vis Roma, the authors warned that 'the location of some of these locations adjacent to European residential areas does not make for harmonious race relations.' Finally, the report turned to the 'psychological effect' of informal settlements, because a 'man' there could be 'very apt to regard himself as opposed to the forces of law' (NAZ 1957–61: LUDC 1/4/24, f. 25).

This report lays bare common assumptions implicit in how one side of the gashed city has looked at the other from colonial times onward. To what extent throughout their history have these 'informal' or 'unauthorized' parts of Lusaka really been noticeable hotbeds of corrupted culture, irresponsibility, agitation, racial revenge, opposition to the rule of law? Hardly ever, it turns out, at least in ways one could ever distinguish from the rest of the city. They are just poorer, often astronomically so, and poorly treated by the power structure.

African urban studies scholars owe an incredible debt to Ann Schlyter and Karen Tranberg Hansen for their remarkable decades-long dedication to what are now anthropological time-series data sets on George and Mtendere compounds in Lusaka. As Schlyter (1999: 9, 21) wrote, 'all over Africa there are cities with collapsing urban services, environmental degradation and poor and overcrowded housing conditions. Lack of urban services, such as fresh water and energy provision' and other aspects of the problems hit especially hard in peri-urban neighborhoods like George which 'physically and socially manifested structures of power and patterns of everyday life.' Her work and Hansen's work demonstrate, in different ways, exactly this neighborhood-level manifestation of how municipal planning power works (or doesn't work) and how people actually live in informal settlements – even when these settlements began most formally, as Mtendere did. Once a model site-and-services scheme of the postcolonial regime, built in a neat, tight rectangular grid form with major international funding, Mtendere is now just another 'informal' 'peri-urban' 'compound' to most analysts and observers (Hansen 1997, 2008).

Informality, as Mtendere makes manifest, is as complicated a term as postcolonialism. For now, let me put it this way. We can say, with whatever confidence we have in a given set of statistics, that a high percentage of this city or that city lives in informal housing. But by that point, we may have in effect said that the city is so dominated by informality that it *is* an informal city. What formal sector activity does exist is so permeated by and interpenetrated with informality as to render a separation of them ridiculous in many cities. It may be time, in essence, to find a new language for this theme, to see it – as my brackets in the section subheading suggest – as (i)n(f)ormal, and familiar. Lusaka opens up the issues of terminology as well as any city in Africa, despite significant variations in what informality means across the continent.

City governance

Mzamose Mbewe was secretary of Samalila Ukhondo (SU) Waste Group in Kamanga, an unauthorized compound east of Ng'ombe. SU was started with International Labor Organization funds in 2000. Their name meant 'Taking Care of Cleanliness.' They started with eleven members and were down to five by the time the Zambian geographer Wilma Nchito and I interviewed Mzamose in December 2002. She told us of the grand ambitions with which they had begun their work, to collect the trash of the compound. 'In February 2000 we began the actual collection, door to door … We had targeted 1,333 households since that was the total number of households according to Irish Aid in all of Kamanga – Then! – in the time since it has grown. At one time we managed six hundred. Now we are down to perhaps two hundred.' They moved the collected waste out to 'midden boxes' and slabs, from which the Lusaka City Council was supposed to collect again (what is called secondary collection) to take it to a dumpsite. There were piles of waste along the road from 2000 to 2004 that the city council had not removed. 'Council told us they have no capacity,' Mzamose told us. 'Customers are saying that they will not pay. "We see where you are putting it and we can do that ourselves" … Our plans have been disturbed somehow … The thing we want the most is to have the waste removed. If we had it removed we would be talking of other stories.'

With Lusaka being one of the early adaptors of the UN's Sustainable Cities Program (SCP) framework, its experiences encapsulate the struggles of governance reform and sustainable urban development on the continent (Myers 2005). The Sustainable Lusaka Program (SLP) focused on a number of priority environment-and-development issues, but solid waste management was the first priority, as it was in nearly every one of Africa's twenty-nine participant cities. Less than 10 percent of the residential solid waste of the city at the beginning of the SLP was collected and deposited in a landfill.

Seven years of the SLP's operation did little to expand that collection rate, particularly in peri-urban areas. The seven years since it closed have been marked by straightforward privatization of waste services that meant modest improvements in the wealthiest areas and little or no headway in the compounds. The UN-Habitat's own published assessment of the SLP, for which principal authorship belongs to the hydrogeologist Daniel Nkhuwa (with Jonathan Mwanza and Kangwa Chama), is quite clear-eyed about the program's problematic outcomes. The main challenges came in the struggle to 'rally key stakeholders to work together for effective change in attitude and behavior' (UN-Habitat 2009: 1).

Some achievements are noted in the report, particularly in the main priority area of solid waste management. The authors cite some raised consciousness about the potential for private sector and community group involvement in waste management, and in some cases a cleaner environment with reduced epidemic diseases (ibid.: 19). On the other hand, most people in peri-urban communities proved too poor to pay for waste services. The Lusaka City Council never followed through on its end of the bargain, while 'political interference' and an 'unrealistic' schedule for waste collection in a 'learning-by-doing' environment debilitated the project (ibid.: 19–20). Nkhuwa and his team argued that 'the local authority has completely abrogated its responsibilities to the community' and also that a group they refer to as 'participatory elites' emerged to 'appoint themselves as representatives of the community … to dominate as many community projects as possible for personal gain; the less educated community members usually do not have the courage to confront them, hence they continue to dominate' (ibid.: 22). Multiparty democratic politics has come to Lusaka, in hotly contested local government elections as well as in the local races in national elections in 1991, 1996, 2001, and 2006, but Zambia's national governments have continually undermined and underfunded local authorities like the Lusaka City Council – and particularly when, as has been the case for the last decade, the council has an opposition majority. And any optimism that the opposition party that has been winning control of the council of late would somehow be more genuinely pro-poor in Lusaka, were it not undermined and underfunded, is immediately tempered by the recognition that this party's leader, Michael Sata, has twice been the cabinet minister responsible for widespread demolitions in peri-urban compounds in *previous* central governments!

UN-Habitat's other participant cities in the SCP and related urban environmental programs in Africa show Lusaka to be typical of patterns across the continent, and the SCP is just one of a great many efforts at the recasting, rescaling, and reinventing of urban governance to see mixed results in Africa. Chapter 4 takes on the task of assessing governance in a range of African cities, examining neoliberal governance, materialist and post-structuralist critiques of it, and more empirical assessments on the ground (like that of Nkhuwa and his colleagues) of both urban service delivery and socio-environmental justice.

Wounded city

James, his wife and four children, his sister, and her two kids live in two rented rooms in Garden, a peri-urban compound whose name is a joke: it was built in the low-lying outfall field from Lusaka's sewage treatment facility. Here, a 'Garden'-style apartment is a house with an extension in the back with two, three or even four two-room units rented to different households. James's place is crammed with many residents, lacking electricity and using only a standpipe for water. Garden, perhaps more than any compound, betrays the hydrological contradiction that is probably Lusaka's biggest wound: too much putrid surface water, not enough water for human consumption.

James walks from there to Kabulonga for work. Among compound dwellers in 1986, 48 percent were estimated to walk to work, sometimes, like James, walking 6 or 7 kilometers. Garden's roads are nearly all eroded away, full of garbage, mixed with water-filled potholes and charcoal-colored water. When I drove James home one day in my landlady's rental car, we had to drive around and around to get past crater-sized potholes to get as close as we did to his house. Then he insisted we had to have his sister watch the car while we walked the rest of the way, as he was certain it would be stolen or damaged otherwise.

Lusaka has been spared the urbicide of other African cities, where open warfare and persistent violent conflict have made rubble of the cityscape – even in contexts where the most horrific violence is imagined to be rural (Daley 2007: 118–21). Yet it has deep wounds in other ways: HIV/AIDS, crime, injustice, inequality, and displacement. Naomi Banda talked with me about the demolitions in her peri-urban area of Kalikiliki in 2002. On 5 December, the police came with a bulldozer to destroy the homes on the hill on the opposite side of a stream from Mtendere. 'The people attacked the one who they said had called the council in, and chased the council and police away.' More than ten police were injured. They came back in firing live ammunition, and three people died, one a fifteen-year-old boy. Two died in hospital, one in the street. 'This is a rough part of town, but this, it was like a war. Because Zambia has never had a war, when people heard the shots they came running to see what it was, and that is why the people died.'

Kalikiliki and this squatter extension of it are in a zone that was formerly a white settler's farm, like Ng'ombe. 'People used to pass that way going to work at Agriflora [a now defunct hydroponic flower factory] but there were robbers and bandits too. Sometimes you could just see dead bodies there so maybe they said let's put some houses there to calm it down.' Naomi's last remark took me a while to think through. To her, the open spaces between compounds were the spaces of danger. Filling them in with homes, however chaotically, would 'calm it down.' David Harvey (2000: 182), in *Spaces of Hope*, asks us to think about creating 'possibilities of spatial form' that might foster 'a wide range of human potentialities.' Geographer Patricia Daley (2007: 235) responds to Harvey, at the very end of her book *Gender and Genocide in Burundi*, with the assertion that 'finding spaces of hope [will] require actual engagement with emancipatory politics' and the 'rehumanization of African people.' One way that must happen is by de-centering discussion of urban experience to be able to encompass and rehear what people like Naomi Banda are saying about their cities, even when that means a chaotic spatial form to a residential area if that will 'calm it down.' Conceptions of order, security, or calmness in the most marginal areas of African cities may run counter to outsiders' expectations or common understandings. Chapter 5's discussion of wounded cities, with its focus on Mogadishu, seeks spaces of hope in a de-centered discussion that valorizes Somali voices, particularly in literature. That de-centering and revalorization of the discussion also lead to the recognition that there can be no real rebirth for a wounded city without cosmopolitanism and imagination – bringing me to the book's final theme.

Cosmopolitan city

The northern spine road heading east from the governmental center of Lusaka to its well-to-do eastern suburb of Kabulonga is a distinctive marker of the layout that emerged from the colonial plans of the 1930s. The wide boulevard passes the northern side of the presidential palace and the southern side of Lusaka Golf Club along the way to Kabulonga, which was, like Roma, a formerly separate, whites-only township until 1970. Kenneth Kaunda, Zambia's president from 1965 until 1990, pulled Kabulonga into the City of Lusaka, and then further consolidated control over the territory by abolishing the city council in the 1970s. The Kaunda regime marked its alliances through naming and renaming places and streets; this road came to be known as Saddam Hussein Boulevard, in honor of the late Iraqi president, in the run-up to the Non-Aligned Movement's conference in Lusaka in 1970.

Kaunda's regime was forced into holding multiparty elections in 1990 in which his United National Independence Party was trounced by the Movement for Multiparty Democracy (MMD), led by Frederick Chiluba. Chiluba was an unwavering US ally, and he had the MMD government change the constitution to proclaim that Zambia is a 'Christian nation.' He was not about to keep Saddam Hussein on the city map at a time when the United States and its 'coalition of the willing' were fighting to remove Iraqi forces from Kuwait. Hence Saddam Hussein Boulevard was renamed, amazingly, *Los Angeles Boulevard*. Soja (1989: 222) once proclaimed that 'Los Angeles is everywhere.' Lusaka makes his case.

More seriously, the story of the naming and renaming of Los Angeles Boulevard suggests some ways in which the 'cosmopolis' Soja discusses can be found in many different ways in cities like Lusaka across Africa. Lusaka is connected to the rest of the world, it is a 'worlding' city (Simone 2001a, 2001b). The flowers produced in its hydroponic factory-farms might show up on dinner tables in Holland the next day. One of Lusaka's more prominent residents, when he found out that I came from Kansas, told me that Wichita, Kansas, was his favorite city – the place where his airline, Zambian Airways, bought its small planes before it went bankrupt. One could be instantly connected with anywhere else after getting online in the Internet café that was adjacent to LA Fast Foods by the Haile Selassie Road intersection with LA Boulevard from 2002 onward. Farther west along the road, one passes the Millennium Village that

Libyan president Mu'ammer Gaddafi created for the summit where the Organization of African Unity became the African Union, in Lusaka in 2000; it was built so as to have a glitzy house in it for each president of a member state to use during the summit. (Kaunda created a similar 'village,' Mulungushi, to house delegates to the Non-Aligned Movement conference – see Collins 1986: 128 – and it is now a gated community.) Past the other end of LA Boulevard, once it becomes Kabulonga Road, one can see the tattered remnants of the flag of the Republic of Somalia fluttering above the compound where someone who somehow manages to be Somalia's ambassador to Zambia resides.

But it is not just in elite ways that we might claim that Lusaka is everywhere, or that everywhere is in Lusaka. Lusaka hosts thousands of refugees, former refugees, and resettled residents from the Democratic Republic of Congo, Zimbabwe, Angola, and Mozambique. Whether victims or agents within these conflicts, none of these Lusaka residents is a Lusaka resident *sui generis* – they are there after fleeing conflicts in which the major powers of the Cold War and power brokers of the new scramble for Africa played key roles. The United States, the Soviet Union, the People's Republic of China, Brazil, Portugal, Belgium, France – these powers are all, in a sense, *in* Lusaka, embedded in the causation of its refugee population's growth over the last forty years (Gray 2009).

Some 93 percent of Zambia's foreign exchange earnings come from the export of copper and copper products, making Zambia one of the top five producers of copper wire in the world. Copper, cobalt, diamonds, other gems, and coltan from Angola or the DRC find their way into the world market through Zambia every day illegally, often through Lusaka either by train or plane. Every cell phone in the world is stabilized with coltan and operated through copper conductors. There is probably a bit of something that passed through Lusaka in your pocket right now, if not in the phone, then in the coins, or the ring on your finger (Fraser and Larmer 2010).

What is more, many people in Lusaka are very aware of and connected to the world and the region, how it impacts their lives. Migration – be it rural to urban, urban to rural, urban to urban, circular, temporary, or whatever we call it – has been fundamental to all of the peoples of Zambia for at least five hundred years. One of my Zambian colleagues explained his country's effectiveness in hosting so many refugees by saying, 'that is because all of us were refugees.' Be it the Tonga originating in the southern Congo basin in the first millennium CE, the Luba and Lunda coming from there in the fifteenth and sixteenth centuries, the Nguni in the nineteenth century, or the Bemba and Lozi whose cultures were so transformed by the regional migrations and militarization of that Nguni incursion, most Zambians have legitimate roots somewhere outside of Zambia, should they wish to claim them. And of course the twentieth and now twenty-first centuries have if anything intensified the connectivities, with Zambians studying and working in South Africa (remember the WNLA!), Zimbabwe, Tanzania, the DRC, the UK, the former USSR, the USA, China, India, and elsewhere in ever greater numbers.

There are many words that might capture the related phenomena of the above paragraphs. Although *cosmopolitanism* is not without its critics, I start Chapter 6 with the idea that it is the best working term for the moment. The philosopher Kwame Anthony Appiah (2006: xiv) takes us back to the root of the term, cosmopolitan, in fourth-century BCE Cynicism: 'citizen of the cosmos,' whereby a citizen 'belonged to a particular city' and at the same time to 'the world ... in the sense of the universe.' He argues for cosmopolitanism not as the answer to the world's problems but as a challenge, 'a gauntlet thrown down' in the struggle with the increasing velocity and volume of interconnectivity the world is experiencing in the twenty-first century, which we typically refer to as globalization. Helpfully, James Ferguson has already deployed the term in his *Expectations of Modernity*, albeit about the modernist cultural bloc of the Zambian Copperbelt, rather than Lusaka. 'Cosmopolitans,' to Ferguson (1999: 215), were the Copperbelters of the 1980s and 1990s who had embraced the styles of dress, music, housing, and life more generally associated with 'the world out there.' A great many cosmopolitans moved to Lusaka from the Copperbelt as its copper industries declined in those years, another form of 'an attempt to perform in a society in freefall' by seeking out the 'surprising, shocking, foreign, strange, or transgressive,' another gauntlet thrown down (Myers 2005: 131). One finds versions of Ferguson's cosmopolitans across the continent in the early twenty-first century. But it is a gauntlet that one might just as easily throw down in Lusaka, to draw attention to the reality that globalization and cosmopolitanization are central to urban life even in this rather mundane city.

When the deputy chief of mission in the US embassy invited me in to talk about my research in January 2003, we had a very pleasant chat about a wide range of matters. At one point he exclaimed that he had heard that Lusaka really had more than two million people, and not the official census population of 1.1 million. 'Two million people,' he said, 'but where are they all?' I was too stunned to answer him coherently, and I honestly don't remember now what I said. Had I had my wits together, I might have said: they are on the move, all around you. Many, like James, are on the move walking to work, or for the possibility of work. Others are busy farming maize from the little strips of land between the walls of the estates in your neighborhood and the streets and other 'unimportant, peripheral, and marginal' zones because they have so little food and so little access to land for farming anywhere else (Simatele and Binns 2008: 1).

It may be, as Katherine Gough (2008: 243) contends (in a recent publication about the differing capacities for mobility among youth in Lusaka), that 'overall the picture emerging from Lusaka is rather bleak,' particularly 'in a context of spiraling economic decline and rising HIV/AIDs rates.' Many people are still 'getting stuck in the compound' (Hansen 2008: 3). Yet there are spaces of hope in sometimes surprising places. Godfrey Hampwaye (2008: 189) argues that 'at the level of urban government the traditional top down character has gradually given way to the formal recognition of decentralization as a means to empower local authorities in Zambia to affect change.' Certainly, schools, roads, infrastructure, markets, and other features of the cityscape have improved in the last decade as a result.

In 2003, I went to church with a friend, Steven Mumbi, at Oasis of Grace Tabernacle Pentecostal Holiness church, in Mtendere's Area C. Steven is a taxi driver who sings and leads a twelve-person music youth group – rocking gospel in a charismatic church. The experience was an ecstatic reminder of the importance of churches in so much of what people are and want in compounds. Steven gave me a CD of his gospel band's music, powerful, inspiring, passionate, and soulful music that brings me back to that day every time I play it.

After church, Steven drove me through Mtendere in his taxi. Mtendere is divided into quarters, known as A, B, C, and D, with road access throughout. Kalikiliki, the tough place across the ravine, is not laid out by plan; instead, its houses hop around the streambed and up the slope in a scatter, and it proved harder on Steven's taxi. 'With these compounds, the lower you go the more rough the place is.' Steven meant this 'low' in both economic and topographic terms, but he also spoke with admiration about some of the creative architecture, and creative piracy, one can find there in the 'low' places. 'I could leave this car there for ten minutes and it might be stolen, but I could go to Matero [another compound] the next day and buy it back – piece by piece!' We then went through PH I, the corrupt housing scheme of former President Chiluba, eerily unlived in for the most part, in which huge amounts of government money went into making a new middle-class planned neighborhood between Mtendere/Kalikiliki and the Great East Road.

It seems to me that this was a day when I saw the conceived, perceived, and lived spaces of Lusaka, to use the language of Soja's interpretation of Lefebvre, together, kilometer by kilometer – a post-colonial, informal, unruly, and wounded city, yet a cosmopolitan place full of imaginative, generative, and connective synergies internally and across the globe, in spite of the rest. We may still be in the midst of the 'years when there was a harshness in the land that had little sympathy for the weak,' as the Zambian novelist Binwell Sinyangwe (2000: 30) put it. Yet there is a creativity to the responses and resistance to that harshness that may go beyond mere endurance, as in Mulenga Kapwepwe's 2004 play (cited in Djokotoe 2004: 15), *Like Choosing between Eating and Breathing*, about sex workers in Lusaka. The emancipatory politics necessary to re-create or re-vision African cities within African studies and urban studies alike would certainly require many of the re-visions Daley (2007: 236–8) calls for in Burundi – a 'revalorization of the African human, ... a democracy that reflects and protects the human, ... alternative forms of masculinities and femininities, ... regionality and regional citizenship,' and 'the elevation of African agency.' Ultimately, such a re-vision would be a revaloriza-tion of the creativity, even in critique and resistance, manifested in so much of everyday life in urban Africa in these cosmopolitan times.

Conclusion

In this chapter, I have worked from the premise that Lusaka is an ordinary city, but one that might turn our imagination inside out, might potentially be an example of trends and themes for many cities in Africa and perhaps in the world. It is living with the con-sequences of colonialism's temporal aftermath and spatial legacies. Chief among these is the dominance of informality. At the same time, in struggling to overcome colonialism's legacies, Lusaka has experimented, at least on paper, with de-centralized and participatory forms of urban environmental governance, for example in solid waste management. The programs that have led this effort, externally funded and driven, are facets of why Lusaka can be considered a place well connected with the rest of the world. Some of its woundedness is clearly linked with the character of some of the connectivities. Its cosmopolitanism and connectivity have consequences. Yet Lusaka is also an imaginative city, generative of dynamic cultural practices.

I've used a series of vignettes patterned somewhat after Soja's six discourses of the post-metropolis, albeit not in an everything-compared-to-Los-Angeles mode. One test of this book is this: can we start from a city like Lusaka to offer themes that resonate in other cities in Africa, and potentially other cities in the world? Each of the next five chapters seeks to answer this question across a range of other cities on the continent. The other test of this book lies in the question of whether, by – as Robinson put it – 'decentering the reference points' in urban studies and African studies, we can have what Soja sought: 'practical usefulness in changing the world for the better.' To take on the real implications of Soja's phrase for creating an agenda for African urban studies, though, it is vital to remember Pieterse's (2008a: 106) model of a 'relational' understanding of cities and its 'sensibility of agonistic pluralism.' The chapters which follow travel the intersections between colonial and postcolonial urban design visions, formal and informal settlement, collaborative and contestatory governance, violent and non-violent urban imaginaries, and local and transnational conceptualizations of urban culture to embed this relational pluralism into my conclusion's exploration of 'changing the world for the better.'

TWO
Postcolonial cities

Introduction

Figure 2.1 is a photograph of me, standing in Nyerere Square in downtown Dodoma, the capital city of Tanzania. Behind me to my left is a statue of Tanzania's first president, Julius Nyerere. In the background, there is a billboard promoting Nyerere's ideas with his smiling visage, sponsored by Vodacom, a multinational cell phone company. The public square was empty, as it nearly always is. A few blocks away, an open space that Dodoma's planners would have filled with a ministerial office teemed with people packed into row upon row of plastic-covered market stalls, buying and selling cheap, imported basic goods, slipping and sliding through the mud-and-garbage-strewn paths.

Among his many bold achievements, Nyerere is remembered for having led the government's decision to relocate the national capital from Dar es Salaam to Dodoma in the 1970s. The move had its own pragmatic geographical and administrative logic. Dodoma is in the middle of the vast country, whereas Dar es Salaam not only lies on the Indian Ocean coast, but toward the northern end of that coastline. Nyerere (1972) based his blueprint for governing the country on a plan of 'decentralization' that supposedly would work outwards from the new central seat of power. But the move was also meant as a powerful postcolonial symbol of Tanzania's new order. In 1967, in the Arusha Declaration, Nyerere's government had made *ujamaa* the philosophy which would guide national development. Often translated as 'socialism', *ujamaa* literally means family-hood. *Ujamaa* articulated a vision for 'the elimination of exploitation, the control of the major means of production by peasants and workers,' and other elements of an African democratic socialism (Hess 2006: 120). The Arusha Declaration more broadly stressed the related principle of self-reliance, whereby collectivization of agriculture was expected to produce a sufficient basis for inward-looking development (Nyerere 1967). Under this framework, the government deliberately de-emphasized urban

FIGURE 2.1 Nyerere Square, Dodoma, Tanzania (*source*: Parmukh Singh Hoogan)

areas to deconcentrate and ruralize industrial growth (Darkoh 1994). The main urban area of Tanzania, Dar es Salaam, was for several long decades the main victim of this de-emphasis, largely because it 'remained for Nyerere a reminder of a colonial legacy,' and instead, Nyerere sought to 'construct his own personal vision of an African socialist state' in a new capital city nearer to the country's agricultural heartlands (Hess 2006: 123).

Dodoma's designed layout and plan were in keeping with the ideals of *ujamaa* philosophy. The 1976 Master Plan had 'proposed nothing less than the first nonmonumental capital city' (Vale 2008: 179). What the city now calls Nyerere Square was to have been Ujamaa Square. It would not have had a towering statue of Nyerere in it; the Master Plan envisioned a large sculpture of an acacia tree, to commemorate the traditional gathering place of Tanzanian villagers and townspeople in the shade of a tree (ibid.: 181). It probably would not have been his idea, either, to see his own face used to promote a cell phone company or, as it is on other billboards, a lottery – he virtually invented the KiSwahili invective for unjust economic usury, *ubepari*, a word that is typically translated as 'capitalism' – in a capital city whose very design stressed the 'avoidance of elitism' on every inch of the map (Capital Development Authority 1976: 71).

Making a truly different postcolonial city, in the ongoing circumstances of donor dependency, neoliberal economic policies, and resource limitations, would inevitably elude the Tanzanian state. The curious mixtures and inconsistencies that Dodoma today encapsulates (such as the empty people's plaza not far from a crowded informal market) make it a worthwhile case for examining the widespread efforts in postcolonial Africa to make 'new towns' that attempted to find a 'new approach compared with classic descriptions of urban phenomena,' as Henri Lefebvre (in Burgel et al. 1987: 27–38) once put it, in an interview about twentieth-century European new towns. In this chapter, I examine contemporary Dodoma, along with Abuja, Nigeria, and Lilongwe, Malawi. These are just three of the more notable examples of postcolonial Africa's created capitals. Gaborone, Nouakchott, and Yamoussoukro, the capitals of Botswana, Mauritania, and Côte d'Ivoire, respectively, were all also essentially postcolonial creations.

I choose to focus my attention on these cities in part because, in relation to postcolonial work within African studies or the discipline of geography – my two disciplinary homes – abstract 'theoreticism' has limited the 'purchase of its intellectual products' (Robinson 2003: 275). Spatial imagery abounds in postcolonial studies, but often the tangible and material matters beyond the images are left out of the discussion (Blunt and McEwan 2002: 1–2; Loomba 1998). Such criticism can be leveled at Achille Mbembe's (2001) brilliant but difficult book *On the Postcolony*, for example. Although the book is full of insights on postcolonial political geographies of power, some of which I put to use in this book, it is often obfuscating in its abstract theoreticism and more suggestive than understandable about space and spatiality.

Mbembe's (ibid.: 170) model of 'the colony' as a 'series of hollows' is at once intriguing for someone like me who grew up just uphill from a coal-mining hollow in Pennsylvania, and maddeningly unclear. Mbembe's first hollow is 'physical space ... made up of monotonous vistas, vast horizons in a sort of silence, calm, deceptive peace: indolence, the dead time of life. These vastnesses, with the heat that beats down and stifles them, make the colonizer nervous' (ibid.: 179). This evokes the empty-land myth of colonial discourse rather imaginatively, but the discussion which follows gets muddled. In Mbembe's hands, the elaborate and terrible beauty/disgust of colonial exploitation of Africa is rendered complete, extreme, seductive, orgasmic, phallic, outlandish, and impossible to outrun in the 'postcolony.' It is hard to know where to start interpreting the book, but Mbembe (ibid.: 237) does meander around, in his conclusion, to what he claims is the 'object' of his book: 'to define the quantitative and qualitative difference, if any, between the colonial period and what followed: *have we really entered another period, or do we find the same theater, the same mimetic acting, with different actors and spectators, but with the same convulsions and the same insult? Can we really talk of moving beyond colonialism?*' (emphasis mine). At the very end of this passage, Mbembe arrives at questions that really matter and challenges that remain unanswered in African studies: can we really talk of moving beyond colonialism? To provide some paths to answers, though, in my mind requires more tangible assessment than what Mbembe provides.

Staying within the language of postcolonial cultural studies, it is still possible to see paths toward that more tangible assessment. Working to move beyond colonialism will involve revalorizing 'indigenous management strategies' and embracing the cultural heterogeneity of African cities as a strength (Ndi 2007: 23; Demissie 2007a). These concerns with indigenous African citiness and the heterogeneity of it are crucial to Chapter 3's discussion of informality, for example. But in revalorizing that citiness it is important to move 'beyond tradition' if 'traditional' indigeneity is conceptualized as refracted through the colonial experience and consequent reshaping of its meaning (Bissell 2007: 37). Moving beyond colonialism definitely involves, quite literally, *moving*: coming to grips with diasporic understandings of African cities, as I discuss in Chapter 6, even while recognizing the warping triggered by nostalgia in many such renderings (Kehinde 2007). Cinema, literature, and photography are among the representational tools for postcolonializing African cities, but there are also still more tangible tools deployed, in architecture and urban planning in particular (Samuelson 2007; Fu and Murray 2007; Demissie 2007b).

There are plenty of professional place-makers among African urban planners and architects seeking to develop and implement imaginative, alternative, postcolonial urban visions. A new generation of African architects and planners is busily engaged in re-envisioning the continent's cities. The first order of business for some of these practicing architects and planners is tracing – writing, and in some cases rewriting, the varied and deep histories of architecture and urban planning on the continent, particularly to retrace colonialism's legacies (Elleh 1997, 2002). Others have experimented with possibilities for developing an Afrocentric architecture out of that history (Hughes 1994). Still more are engaged in re-envisioning the training processes in architecture and planning schools on the continent to think through African processes of planning and sociocultural influences on building and urban design. This has in turn led to collective and collaborative research that enables African architects and planners to both compare what is happening in one another's cities and to work toward non-Eurocentric visions of cities.

The African Centre for Cities (ACC) at the University of Cape Town (UCT), along with Cape Town's Isandla Institute, is engaged in fostering a rethinking of African urban development outside the box of Western mindsets, beyond colonialism (in the manner of postcolonial studies). The ACC and planners at UCT, along with planners at Dar es Salaam's Ardhi University, have been generous and generative forces behind the creation and maintenance since 2002 of the Association of African Planning Schools (AAPS), which has made impressive efforts aimed at 'revitalizing planning education' in its thirty-one member schools on the continent (http://www.african-planningschools.org.za/). Nine of the schools are in South Africa, but the other twenty-two are spread across Africa's cities from Cairo to Harare, Kumasi to Nairobi. Fred Lerise and Tumsifu Nnkya from Tanzania, who are among AAPS's most active and collaborative planning scholars, have, for one example, merged scholarly endeavors to link up key planning issues across the continent with activist, engaged collaborative efforts to rethink planning in Dar es Salaam, sometimes behind the scenes, as in their assistance to community groups in the informal settlement just beyond their university campus.

The ArchiAfrika network is another such example of applied re-visions that one might conceive of as postcolonial. ArchiAfrika's fascinating collaborative projects build bridges between architects in private practice, popular sector or civil society institutions in African cities, international donors, and governments, fostering research and then feeding research outcomes into actual plans and buildings.

ArchiAfrika's newsletter publicizes and promotes projects across the continent, publishing both technical reports and interviews. One recent example of ArchiAfrika's interviews, conducted by Rachel Jenkins (Gana 2009) with Libyan artist and planner Hadia Gana, brought attention to urban planning processes for Tripoli that are extremely difficult to research even in the current ongoing, if slight, opening to outside scholarship. In Libya, it is an eclectic mix of trained and untrained planners (engineers, architects, and artists) who have produced a vision for the primate city, *Tripoli 2025*. Associated with the blandly labeled Engineering Consulting Office for Utilities (ECOU), Gana is actually a ceramicist; her engagement with ECOU is central to efforts to revitalize indigenous Libyan building crafts, but she has been a part of the Tripoli 2025 collective and a group seeking to create urban villages within Tripoli. All of these loosely affiliated, fluid organizations emerged with the interest of making the new urban development projects that have come with Libya's petrodollars more 'compatible with the way Libyans live … a human-centred approach' (ibid.).

Yet Gana evaded Jenkins's question of whether the Tripoli 2025 plans were 'spearheaded by strong political and socially idealist leadership,' giving a funny but totally evasive answer about Dutch waffles and the architect Zaha Hadid. This evasion suggests that networks like ArchiAfrika can only do so much alone to effect changes toward a postcolonial city. Similar hints of political limitations appear in Archi-Afrika reports on architectural preservation planning in Dar es Salaam (Moon 2009), or on the impressive architectural accomplishments of Nairobi's Maranga Njoroge (2009). Njoroge himself summed up the strengths and challenges of new networks like ArchiAfrika very well:

> Organizations like ArchiAfrika … facilitate discussions and forums and idea generation of like-minded architects. These forums fire up ideas that when translated into action will leave an impact. The major hindrance in the way to progress is majorly political both from the macro to micro level. Governance and policy are parameters that architects have to work within. When unfavorable, then there is a high degree of conformity and compromise among architects.

Njoroge diplomatically suggests here the 'conformity and compromise' architects must accede to within the largely 'unfavorable' governance 'parameters' of postcolonial African cities. The Archi-Afrika network has done much to promote respect for vernacular or popular African architectural styles, innovative sustainable or green building techniques from indigenous origins, creative collaborative community rehabilitation, and fine alternative building designs. Yet it still operates within contexts that vary dramatically in their capacity to allow for meaningful socio-political changes. The AAPS's projects and the prospective future continental programs of the African Centre for Cities likewise face a similar contextual variation that makes their ambitions difficult to actualize.

There are other forms of postcolonial urban practice, to be sure, but for me Africa's new capital cities still embody the grandest and most tangibly postcolonial geographical theories put into practice, and we can use them as a lens on Mbembe's question of whether we can 'really talk of moving beyond colonialism.' I share with Cheryl McEwan (2003: 341) the sense that we ought to approach post-colonialism with our eyes on 'material problems that demand urgent and clear solutions,' and those material problems clearly include the gross inequalities, social and spatial, which African cities inherited from European colonialism, problems these cities were ostensibly created to militate against.

'Postcolonialism and geography are intimately linked,' Blunt and McEwan (2002: 1) wrote. This is first and foremost because *colonialism* and geography were so intimately linked, nowhere more clearly than in Africa. Most urban studies or human geography research that identifies itself as postcolonial studies in Africa in fact concentrates on excavating histories and legacies of colonialism, in part simply because these were and are so extensive (Demissie 2007a; Ndi 2007). This meant that after independence, African countries had to come 'after' colonialism – in the sense of attacking or contesting its legacies – geographically (Loomba 1998: 12; Blunt and McEwan 2002). Across the continental map, African countries took different approaches in attempts to remake their urban areas to mark them as having moved beyond colonialism. As in Dodoma, but in diverse forms, we find in these other cities odd juxtapositions of something unique and different beyond colonialism with legacies and continuities from the colonial era. Egypt sought to create an 'implausible' array of new towns and satellite towns in the desert to deconcentrate urban development away from Cairo and Alexandria (Florin 2005). In Botswana's case, the colonial power, Britain, had ruled what was then termed the Bechuanaland Protectorate from an office building in Mafeking, South Africa, so the new government obviously had to build itself some domestic place from which to rule the country (Best 1970). It was less obvious that Côte d'Ivoire needed a new capital city, or that this capital should be the home village of its then president, Felix Houphouet-Boigny (Yamoussoukro), or that the capital city of a country that was at best 15 percent Catholic would need a Catholic cathedral modeled on, but larger than, St Peter's Basilica in Vatican City (Vale 2008: 152). Before we can analyze any of the oddities or normalities of such postcolonial urbanism, though, it is worth reviewing what it was about colonialism and urban space that seemed so in need of remaking to the new rulers and many citizens of independent Africa in the 1960s and 1970s.

Colonialism and African cities

Perhaps the largest research area of African urban studies is concerned with the impacts and legacies of colonialism on the continent's cities. From this vast literature, certain key themes emerge. The first is the diversity of African experiences of European colonialism. Most of the continent experienced formal European rule, but the particular colonial power, its length of impact and its capacity or desire to develop urban areas or transform pre-existing ones, varied. The British and French empires eventually dominated the continent, but Spain, Italy, Germany, Belgium, the Netherlands, and Portugal also held colonies in some fashion for periods ranging from eight years (the Italian occupation of Ethiopia) to nearly five centuries (the Portuguese in Cape Verde or São Tomé and Principe, as well as parts of Angola and Mozambique). Some colonies were merely zones for the extraction of agricultural goods, with a limited European urban impress, while others witnessed European construction of large cities for white settlers and industrial investors.

Of course, cities existed in many areas of Africa prior to the 1500s, and a few (Cairo, Tunis, Ibadan, Jenne, or Kano, for example) were comparable to many European cities in size prior to the rise of European power, while other areas were essentially devoid of larger-scale urbanism (Myers and Owusu 2008). Liberia was technically never colonized (although it certainly was an American colony economically, its elites were African-American settlers, and its two largest urban areas, Monrovia and Buchanan, are named for US presidents). Italy's brief occupation of Ethiopia led to only a small transformation in Addis Ababa's central business district (CBD). The Dutch settled in Cape Town in 1652, the French began their settlement colony in Algeria in the 1830s, trading hubs with attendant hinterland spheres of influence existed all along the continental rim from the early 1500s, some of which were declared colonies, and so on. The story is a little different anywhere we start it.

The prevailing trend, though, is that formal colonial rule began to stretch firmly across the map and into the interior after the Berlin Conference of 1884/85 that officially established European spheres of influence, and the most significant urbanizing for our contemporary interests came with that expansion. The conference also coincided with the explosion of industrial capitalism in Europe, with its demand for African raw materials, and competition between the colonial powers over markets and materials. We can thus tease out patterns that are at least comparable across most colonies. The first of these patterns, and the second theme of the colonial cities literature, is what the historian Catherine Coquery-Vidrovitch (2005a: 4) has termed a 'shared ... historical rhythm': the most significant investments in the creation of urbanism on African soil coincided with the era of formal colonial rule, roughly from the 1880s to the 1960s.

Consequently, the biggest urban spatial impact of European colonialism lies in the location of so many of Africa's eventually major cities along the coast or in close proximity to sites of resource extraction, and the functional retardation of African cities into roles as either entrepôt/warehouse towns, bureaucratic capitals, or both at once, rather than as organically grown industrial manufacturing engines of value added. Cities where colonial rule facilitated the growth of industry and manufacturing as the basis for urbanization were the exception, rather than the norm. Some cities that pre-dated the rise of Europe were able to capitalize on colonialism to grow larger (e.g. Mombasa, Kenya, or many North African cities), but others were bypassed and replaced, ultimately superseded and occasionally falling into ruin. In several cases, the colonizers followed some administrative-geographical logic in locating a capital, rather than a strictly economic one (Lusaka, from Chapter 1, is one such example), but this made the urbanism an even odder imposition in the space economy than, say, a terminal port-as-capital (Freund 2007).

This latter form is still an enormous legacy. Even in 2010, for forty-six of the continent's fifty-three independent states, the primate city in the urban hierarchy is the colonial capital, primary port, or port-capital. Fully twenty-eight of the fifty largest cities on the continent were cities of those historical types in 2010. As Table 2.1 shows, the

dominance of the largest of these urban types has actually increased
on the continent since 1980, rather than decreased (UN-Habitat 2008).

TABLE 2.1 Africa's largest cities: population (in millions) for the twenty
largest cities on the continent

1980		2010	
Cairo*	7.349	Cairo*	12.503
Lagos*	2.572	Lagos*	10.572
Alexandria	2.519	Kinshasa*	9.052
Casablanca	2.109	Khartoum*	5.185
Kinshasa*	2.053	Luanda*	4.775
Cape Town*	1.900	Alexandria	4.421
Johannesburg	1.656	Abidjan*	4.175
Algiers*	1.621	Johannesburg	3.618
Abidjan*	1.384	Algiers*	3.574
Kano	1.350	Addis Ababa	3.453
Durban	1.214	Kano	3.393
Ibadan	1.186	Nairobi*	3.363
Addis Ababa	1.175	Dar es Salaam*	3.319
Khartoum*	1.164	Cape Town*	3.269
Ekurhuleni (East Rand)	1.107	Casablanca	3.267
Luanda*	0.962	Ekurhuleni	3.157
Dakar*	0.957	Dakar*	2.856
Accra*	0.863	Durban	2.839
Nairobi*	0.862	Ibadan	2.835
Dar es Salaam*	0.836	Accra*	2.332

Note: * Cities that served as colonial capitals, primary colonial ports, or
both. Data for Johannesburg's consolidated metropolitan area in 2010 would
yield a much larger population, of more than eight million.
Source: UN-Habitat (2008: 174–7)

Thirteen of the other twenty-two largest cities are in Nigeria and
South Africa, pointing to another, related, element of the colonial
legacy: most African countries other than Nigeria and South Africa
have what mainstream Western geographers would consider to be
poorly developed urban hierarchies, so that very high rates of primacy and the absence of significant secondary cities are still rather
common. In much of the continent, colonial regimes attempted to
restrict migration to cities from the countryside or even to exclude
Africans from the legal right to live in cities. This was certainly a factor in many of these poorly developed urban hierarchies. So were the

dislocation, disjuncture, and enclave status of leading cities; capitals and ports sometimes grew functionally more connected with the metropole than with the cities in that colony. Movement controls were lifted at the end of colonialism, leading to huge upswings in urban populations in the first decades after independence. Yet it is only in the last ten years or so that higher rates of urban population growth are occurring farther down the hierarchy and growth is slowing in the primate cities (Potts 2009, 2011). Infrastructure connectivity between cities within countries still lags far behind what the sizes of the cities might suggest, to say nothing of the still-weak connectivity between cities in different countries even when they are near to one another (e.g., despite some fanciful current planning dreams, there is still no bridge across the Congo river between Brazzaville and Kinshasa, twin capital cities of the two Congos, ruled separately by France and Belgium until 1960; de Boeck 2010).

In the abstract, high primacy ratios are not immediately disastrous for a country's development, but what makes the twin challenges of primacy and a thin urban hierarchy more daunting in many African countries is that the causes for rapid growth are commonly seen to be not directly attributable to economic growth and industrialization, with exceptions here and there (Becker et al. 1994; Bryceson 2006). Under colonialism, rural-to-urban migration seems to have been fueled as much by the pull factor of perception as by actual opportunity, and by the push factors of rural landlessness, herdlessness, involution,[1] poverty, and lack of employment. The end result in many countries was large numbers of the rural poor becoming the urban poor. This conundrum only became more extreme in the independence era in many countries.

Colonialism's other urban legacies concern internal form and spatial structure. These legacies in African cities are well known and widely studied (Celik 1997; Home 1997; Myers 2003; Nast 1994; Rakodi 1986; Western 1985; Winters 1982; Wright 1991). One is the segregation and segmentation of the urban landscape, and another is the related high degree of inequality. Often, the most obvious dimension of the segmentation was racial segregation, with separate

---

1 Agricultural involution is the concept developed by Clifford Geertz in Southeast Asia, whereby smallholder farmers progressively subdivide inherited plots over generations so that all descendants have unviable plot sizes.

areas for business or residence restricted to Europeans, Asians, and Africans, respectively, in many colonial cities, justified by rhetorical concerns with health (Swanson 1977). Where white settlement or investments were more limited, such as in many parts of western or Equatorial Africa, then this segmentation existed in modified form. In Maiduguri, in northeastern Nigeria, where so few whites settled even as administrators, the colonial plan of the city still excluded all Africans except servants from the small 'European Residential Area' and the small Syrian trader population was confined to its own zone of shops in a special business area (Kawka 2002: 42–4). In any case, this is a legacy one often sees in the dramatically 'distorted' divisions between 'high status centers ... and a spreading, sometimes immense, dirt-poor habitat that is poorly served and under-integrated' (Coquery-Vidrovitch 2005a: 5).

Since the largest colonial cities were such owing to their political (and often, to a lesser degree, economic) significance, they became laboratories, incubation sites and potent physical symbols of mechanisms of colonial power (Demissie 2007a). In attempting to 'replicate a quasi-metropolitan culture in every physical respect,' colonial regimes took on the task of a normative reordering of African spatiality (Lloyd 2003: 107). As centers of power, with growing African populations living in conditions of deprivation, these cities were crucial arenas for the administrations' drive for order and control to be expressed in architecture and spatial planning. Urban form thus reflected at least four ideological concerns. These were: (1) separating out who could and could not be in the city; (2) devising a map for who belonged where among those allowed to be urban; (3) providing for and reinforcing spatial expressions of the hierarchy of colonial rule; and (4) enabling the accumulation of resources by the colonial regime, the metropolitan power, and elites associated with both (Mitchell 1988; Berman 1984; Myers 2003; Robinson 1990). That set of intertwined strategies seldom worked as it was meant to in any colonial city, but it established patterns and processes that left independent African countries interested in overcoming colonial legacies or decolonizing urban space with an apparently daunting task (Hamdan 1964).

South Africa presents perhaps the most extreme example of this on the continent. Apartheid South Africa built upon the urban geographies of Dutch and British colonialism before it. Robinson (1996: 2, 1990) has shown how what she referred to as the 'location strategy' deployed by apartheid grew out of colonial tactics. Yet both the colonial and apartheid systems of spatial control were far from 'perfect.' They were rooted in a state that was deeply conflicted, inefficient, fragmented, and easily distracted, resulting in inconsistent and ineffective attempts to impose urban order, for instance in her case study of Port Elizabeth (Robinson 1990, 1996). Grahamstown presents another example of this sort of ambivalent, half-undone, and imperfect system of control. Although segregation dated at least to the 1840s, the ferocity of its imposition waxed and waned with the whims of different colonial or national regimes in relation to local governments. Apartheid's Group Areas Act of 1950 was not enforced in the city until twenty years after its passage, in 1970, thirteen years after the government had announced its intention to do so. 'Life for black Grahamstonians was tough,' to be sure, amid 'appalling slum conditions' (Davenport 1980: 9). But lackadaisical and chaotic implementation and enforcement of apartheid legislation meshed with 'government incompetence,' political disputes between central and local authorities, and of course widespread community opposition to dilute the absoluteness of apartheid's geographies there (ibid.: 47).

It is important, then, not to overplay the draconian authoritarianism embedded in the urban strategies of either the apartheid state or its European colonial antecedents across the continent. Colonial regimes established much of the playing field for urban policy, in terms of building rules, land administration, housing strategy, spatial organization, and the like; there are no doubts on that (Njoh 2003). Colonialism's legacies still fester in other dimensions of Africa's urban stories: the dominant role of central governments at the expense of urban or municipal councils; the strong orientation toward blueprint master planning for modernist visions; or the co-optation of 'traditional' rulers into urban local government. Yet quite often, the enforcement of laws or codes, or the implementation of plans and schemes, lagged far behind the intended order. The trouble was, though, that ordinary African residents were not empowered to remake or overturn the unenforced and unimplemented ideas; they simply endured in the interstices between what the Europeans wanted from the urban order and what the cities might have been without colonialism.

Postcolonialism and African cities

Most African countries obtained independence from Europe between 1956 and 1977, with a few earning it ahead of the first date

(Egypt and Morocco), and a few after that (Namibia, Zimbabwe, and Eritrea). The most difficult state to place on this timeline is, of course, South Africa, since the country earned independence from Britain in 1910 but some 85 percent of its population earned liberation only with the complete and formal end of the apartheid regime in 1994. For some, it is only with that last date that we can truly say that mainland Africa was free of formal colonial rule, but even a rejection of that logic only pushes the formal end of colonialism back a year (if we consider Eritrea's independence from Ethiopia, the occupying power after the end of Italian colonialism, in 1993) or four (to Namibia's independence from South Africa in 1990). Supporters of the Polisario Front in Western Sahara (the former Spanish Sahara, occupied since the mid-1970s by Morocco) might even make a plausible case that colonialism is not yet formally over, at least in their corner of Africa. Regardless, all of this means that colonialism, while a fading memory in places like Sudan (independent in 1956) or Ghana (independent in 1957), remains a relatively recent story, pertinent to and within the lifetimes of citizens over age fifty in virtually every African city.

The fact that independence is a bit more than a half-century old at most and that the urban legacies of colonialism are profound are important starting points for any critique of the postcolonial trajectories of African cities. Add to these the poverty of most African cities relative to their counterparts in Europe or North America, and it is not so surprising to learn that cities have not come very far in attempting to overcome the colonial past. Changing the colonial inheritance of planning laws, building rules, the economic structures of the world economy and the national urban hierarchy, political processes at the urban and national levels, spatial divides, and the character of racism – if these are even possibilities, they are not going to occur overnight.

Be that as it may, if African cities have indeed been attempting to subvert or eliminate the colonial legacies they inherited over these postcolonial decades, then fairly often it must be said that one is hard pressed to see the result. In city after city, formerly white or elite areas are increasingly full of exclusive and infrastructure-rich gated communities and fortress compounds, and the 'dirt-poor habitats' at the other end of the segmented plan of the colonial order are even more overcrowded and destitute. Postcolonial regimes have often improved upon the strategies of colonial administrations, becoming even more exclusivist, authoritarian, and segmented (Bissell 2007). Thirty years of structural adjustment programs and poverty reduction strategy papers imposed on African cities essentially by the former colonial powers have meant that 'high unemployment, escalating poverty and widening inequality have actually worsened' (Demissie 2007a: 7). If postcolonialism is in this sense 'something fairly tangible,' then it is just as tangibly lacking in the sense of being identifiable as something new, different, or better than colonialism for African cities (Yeoh 2001: 456).

Just as apartheid South Africa represented an extension of colonialism's geographies, the post-apartheid era in many ways parallels the postcolonial era for other cities across the continent. Apartheid was famously geographical, and therefore the post-apartheid New South Africa's efforts likewise are inherently so. As Deborah James (2007: 1) puts it, in a discussion of post-apartheid land reform that nonetheless fits well with urban policy reforms: 'what was at stake in the public imagination was nothing less than the complete redrawing of the map of South Africa.' This redrawing has ended up being highly problematic on many levels. The most obvious shortcoming is that the stark racial segregation of the country's cities remains just as stark, or even more so. But even in less tangible ways, the efforts to undo apartheid's legacies fall short. One example is in attempts to democratize grassroots planning, where one might have expected the post-apartheid regime to build upon progressive tactics of the liberation movement to remake the poorest areas of cities, but instead a more mixed picture emerges, particularly on questions of social justice beyond basic redistribution (Visser 2001). Janet Cherry's (2000: ii) dissertation on the politics of transition in the Port Elizabeth township of Kwazekele, built on her many years of radical activism as well as formal research, shows that 'representative democracy' was rather rapidly 'successfully consolidated' there, but at the cost of declining direct participation in civic action. This is a striking decline, when one considers the meaning of the place-name for this self-help housing scheme, Kwazekele, in isiXhosa: 'the place which we built by ourselves' (ibid.: 66). She traces the sense of self-reliance inherent in this name to the settlement's beginnings, but finds the street and area committees that essentially ran the neighborhoods of Kwazekele during much of the 1980s to have been 'both empowering and intolerant' (ibid.: 96). The decline of the civics movement does not bode well for residents' capacity for building on a grassroots vision of post-apartheid politics that would move past such local intolerance while holding on to the sense of empowerment. She cites an anonymous forty-five-year-old man in Kwazekele who remarked, 'there are lots of promises being made which have not been fulfilled, and the future is filled with uncertainty' (ibid.: 186). One finds similar critiques of failures of participatory urban development in post-apartheid South Africa's Integrated Development Plan (Harrison 2006b) or the state's engagement with social movements (Ballard et al. 2006).

Postcolonial studies, as a field, seeks to 'open up the notion of agency' (Power 2003: 126) to not simply include such social movements in, say, remaking built environments, but to attempt to create a 'conceptual frame which works to destabilize dominant discourses' (Yeoh 2001: 457) and 'decolonize the mind' (Ngugi wa Thiong'o 1986). Many engagements of postcolonial studies aimed at creating counter-discourses reside in the arts: in film, photography, sculpture, and painting, for example (McEwan 2009: 156–61). My discussion of Nuruddin Farah's fiction on Mogadishu in Chapter 5 relies on his very postcolonial discursive tactics, such as his unsettling of subjectivity. Artistic and discursive postcolonialism is far from a hopeless cause, and it remains an important means for reconceptualizing the representation of colonial subjects or colonized cities (Robinson 2002b: 116–18). This reconceptualization effort still seems to have 'promised more than it has delivered' (Driver and Gilbert 1999: 7), at least in terms of reconceiving the state's relationships with the people in cities.

So if we are looking for postcolonial urban thought, in the sense of thinking that truly attempts to move past colonialism, the places to look are probably not necessarily in government planning offices or the posh campuses and gated compounds of expatriate donors. Instead, it may be found in the 'ingenuity with which African urban residents have developed novel strategies' for confronting the 'structural and social crisis confronting them' (Demissie 2007a: 8) in places like that crowded informal market in Dodoma. The problem, though, as the Port Elizabeth example suggests, is that we must be cautious of blindly championing some sort of postcolonizing of the city from below given both the potential for non-democratic or repressive city-building to dominate the grass roots and the challenges for the capacity of those grass roots to take on recolonizing or neo-colonizing states. The three case study cities of this chapter provide ideal examples of these dynamics, which also then tie into Chapter 3's discussion of informality and Chapter 4's analysis of governance.

In focusing below on the socio-spatial dimensions of these three planned capitals as attempts to move beyond colonialism, I move from the least postcolonial case, Lilongwe (in that it has most closely followed colonialism's tactics and strategies), to that which at least attempted to move the farthest away from colonial approaches to planning (Dodoma). In so doing, I attempt to follow what I think of as a postcolonial intellectual practice of learning from the scholarship of Malawian, Nigerian, and Tanzanian geographers and urbanists as much as possible.

Lilongwe Rather than being a place of an alternative vision moving beyond colonialism, Hastings Kamuzu Banda's Malawi fits the imaginative model of a 'postcolony' provided by Mbembe (2001: 102), a place 'characterized by a distinctive style of political improvisation, by a tendency to excess and lack of proportion' that is 'also made up of a series of corporate institutions and a political machinery that, once in place, constitute a distinctive regime of violence.' Lilongwe, Banda's planned capital, is a physical manifestation of the improvization, excess, and machinery of his regime of violence.

As in Dodoma, prior to the decision to move the postcolonial capital there, Lilongwe was a small district administrative center. It had been created in 1904 by the British administration of the colony then known as Nyasaland. In contrast to the other two case studies in this chapter, in Malawi, the decision to relocate the capital to Lilongwe from the colonial capital in Zomba came in the first weeks of independence. As in Dodoma and Abuja, though, geographical centrality was fundamental to the relocation argument as the postcolonial regime articulated it (Kalipeni 1999; Englund 2001). Lilongwe also lay at some distance from the areas of white settlement in the colony. Like many settlement colonies on the continent, Malawi had a developed core, and infrastructure built to serve that core, close to white settlement and European interests in the southern end of its elongated shape (Myers 2003). To the extent that Malawi could be said to even have an urban hierarchy at independence (given that the country's population was less than 5 percent urban in 1964), that hierarchy was overwhelmingly dominated by Blantyre, some forty kilometers west of Zomba in the south's Shire highlands. Developing Lilongwe would give Malawi a second larger city in the country's mid-section (CCDC 1972). In these ways, on the surface, this capital shift was a move away from the colonial legacy.

In virtually every other way, though, the capital plan for Lilongwe was not a grand leap from colonialism. Lilongwe's planners were white South Africans from a private Johannesburg firm at the height of apartheid, supervised by a European (Connell 1972). Banda created the Capital Cities Development Corporation (CCDC) with a loan from the apartheid regime (Myers 2003: 139). The CCDC's plan of the city replicated most of the ideological goals of the colonial city discussed above, where zones of residential density, starkly set off from one another by physical and natural boundaries, separated who belonged where by class (Mjojo 1989). What the geographer Deborah Potts (1986: 26) referred to as a 'virtually clinical degree of orderliness' was meant to segregate functions in the city in a direct continuation of colonial policies. The tallest point in the city, Capital Hill, was used for the grand new ministerial offices, and Banda built a garish presidential palace outside the city on another hill.

The argument that Lilongwe fostered the enablement of elite accumulation in line with colonial capitals is less certain. The geographer J. Ngoleka Mlia (1975: 389) argued that national pride and the rise to political power of Central region outweighed any expectations for Lilongwe to become an economic growth pole. However, the political prominence of Central region and its Chewa peoples had its corollary in economics, with the 'Chewa-ization' of the elite, who came to control much of the land around Lilongwe while holding shares in its new, fledgling industries (Kaspin 1995: 605). Hence even colonialism's agenda for accumulation from its urban areas seems to reappear in Lilongwe in postcolonial garb.

I have written previously about the 'odd, unlived-in feeling' Lilongwe exuded in the late 1990s for me (Myers 2003: 144). Twenty-five years ago, Potts (1985: 51) wrote of the sense of 'artificiality' in the place. But this is the planned city that Potts and I critiqued. Lilongwe's majority population lives outside of the plan. Informal settlements emerged all around the edges of the original planning area of the capital, and together with the 'traditional housing areas' allowed within the planning boundary these house most of Lilongwe's urbanites (Potts 1994; Kaluwa 1994; Englund 2002). This is to a degree the 'dirt-poor habitat' side of the postcolonial version of colonial segmented space that Coquery-Vidrovitch has discussed. But it has also grown so large that this other city dominates the city built to model Banda's clinical orderliness; its ways have overwhelmed that order and reshaped it through the residents' 'tenacity ... in the absence of official supervision,' such that *this* is really the postcolonial city

(Englund 2002: 152, 143; Englund 2001; Myers 2003; Kalipeni 1999). As the first capital buildings came online in the early 1970s, Lilongwe had scarcely 20,000 people, and it has nearly a half-million now; a good deal of this growth followed the democratic ousting of the Banda regime in 1994 and in effect the abandonment of the plan he had for the city (Chamley 2006).

The capital plan and its implementation evidenced the 'inability' of the Malawian state or elite 'to capture the soul of popular consciousness' in its majority areas (Myers 2003: 158). Despite the veneer of democratization in Malawi, the two post-Banda presidents have each displayed authoritarian tendencies. The current one, Bingu wa Mutharika, even reoccupied Banda's presidential palace, which his predecessor, Bakili Muluzi, had at least turned over to the parliament (Vale 2008: 152), and Bingu began to explicitly model himself on Banda, erecting an elaborate mausoleum at the dictator's gravesite in Lilongwe with four pillars to honor the cornerstones of the old regime: unity, loyalty, obedience, and discipline (Chirambo 2008: 155). Yet where Banda had no problems evicting squatters and demolishing informal settlements that contravened his master plan, the subsequent quasi-democratic regimes have had less leeway or less compulsion to enforce such order. A recent wave of eviction orders in 2005, for example, never reached implementation owing to vocal, organized opposition from the grass roots that would have been unthinkable in the Banda era (Chamley 2006: 49). Lilongwe's Centre for Community Organization and Development, the Malawi Homeless People's Federation, and other local activist organizations, poets, musicians, and artists, challenge the state and elite visions, and as a consequence of Malawi's increasingly vibrant, often intensely contested public sphere, they reshape the city in the process (Lwanda 2008). Unfortunately, the social capital that inheres to the mushrooming settlements that now house most of Lilongwe is 'highly dynamic ... volatile ... and fragile, constrained' by the severe poverty that defines them, meaning their capacity to give birth to a genuinely workable or reproducible postcolonial alternative to the model capital is extremely limited (Rohregger 2006: 1154; Roe 1992). I explore this conundrum facing many African cities, beyond the postcolonial capitals, in greater detail in Chapters 3 and 4.

Abuja If Lilongwe represents an example of a postcolonial state attempting to expand upon colonialism's regimented order and repression in favor of a new elite, then Abuja can at least be taken as a moderate attempt at a *post*colonial urban vision. The decision to create a centrally located federal capital came in 1976, scarcely five years after the formal end of Nigeria's civil war, at a time of increasing oil revenues and optimism about the country's possibilities (Mabogunje 2001; Ikejiofor 1997). Abuja seemed to be at that time a potent symbol of national unity which had the capacity to rise above ethnic and political differences (Vale 2008). By the time of the official capital relocation in 1991, optimism had faded from the scene and political conflict was on the rise. Yet by 2010, Abuja, with more than 1.8 million people, had become a city of 'paradoxes and disparities' (Adama 2007: 13): not a total failure, not a city completely compromised by its authoritarian aura, but also, like Lilongwe, not really the city envisioned by its planners, and for some similar reasons.

This planned city was envisioned in an ambitious, grand design. An American planning firm headed the team that produced the Abuja Master Plan, working in conjunction with Doxiadis Associates and the planners of the UK new town of Milton Keynes (Vale 2008: 157). The layout actually had more in common with Washington, DC, or Brasilia, rather than Milton Keynes, in keeping with the two different moments when Nigeria's leaders explicitly sought to model its political system after that of the USA (ibid.: 165–8).

Even with these American elements and purported attempts to build on what were claimed as Nigerian indigenous urban traditions, the new city replicated several spatial-ideological features of colonialism. It did not take long for the segmented map of a colonial city to emerge, along class lines rather than racial ones (Elleh 2001: 75). It also upheld the monumental ideological tactics associated with colonial urbanism. Its National Assembly sits on the highest hillside available (the top of the highest point, Aso Rock, being too rocky for construction), and eventually its presidential palace took to higher ground as well. Since it was created to be a federal capital, its central 'business' district was a central government district, reproducing the colonial pattern by which urban growth was disconnected from organic economic development processes. Capital accumulation by Nigeria's elites and political leaders clearly expanded to fit the new capital city, though, particularly in the contracting for its construction, where these elites gained significant economic advantages (ibid.). Even the supposed idea that Abuja was 'virgin land' when it had a pre-existing town and several thousand years of smaller village settlements, adding up to tens of thousands of residents already in its midst, replicated colonialism's spatial myths about Africa's interior (Vale 2008: 162).

It was several years after the government of Nigeria made the capital relocation decision before construction began. Of the three phases of building planned in 1979, geographer Onyanta Adama (2007: 46) shows that by the mid-2000s essentially only phase one had been undertaken. Even Nigeria's then vice-president acknowledged the relocation to have been 'dogged by serious flaws, anomalies and distortions' (Kalgo and Ayileka, in Adama 2007: 51). Perhaps the largest flaw was that of the failure to develop housing to keep pace with the growth of the city as the capital relocation intensified, as this led to the extensive development of unauthorized housing areas outside of the parameters of the plan (Mabogunje 2001; Morah 1992). Even for the public housing that was constructed, researchers found widespread dissatisfaction among residents (Ukoha and Beamish 1997). The staggering speed of the city's growth, from under 100,000 in 1986 to more than 370,000 just five years later, practically made these problems inevitable (Ikejiofor 1998). Abuja then quintupled in size in the next decade, and it continues to grow at a pace far greater what any of its planners anticipated or any of its managers can handle (Imam et al. 2008).

Actually-existing-Abuja is a city ruled by 'disorganized order' (Onyekakeyah, in Adama 2007: 15). Some of that disorganization occurs because of the inconsistency by which the government has dealt with the 845 pre-existing indigenous settlements in the Federal Capital Territory, whereby some villages have been wholly resettled, others partially so, and still others left intact in the heart of the city (Adama 2007: 52). Adama (ibid.: 54–8) studied one village, Nyanya, that is now home to all three settlement types – the indigenous settlement, the government's 'New Layout,' and a labor camp that is something of a mix of planned and unplanned. The evident contempt of Nigerian officials for the idea of low-cost self-help housing – over 40 percent of the officials surveyed by Morah (1993: 252) considered a plan for this sort of solution to Abuja's housing crisis to be a Western plot to keep Nigeria 'backward' – fed further disorganization. The contempt of many of these same officials for the places like Nyanya, too, has led to ruthless attempts to enforce Abuja's Master Plan to the detriment of its poor majority, whose houses get demolished and whose rights to the city get restricted. Lawrence Vale (2008: 174) cited the then Minister for the Federal Capital Territory, Hamza Abdullahi, for example, proclaiming in an interview that it was 'impossible for slums to develop here in Abuja' because 'there is what is called our land-use plan and this is our bible … There is absolutely no room for anybody to just start building substandard structures.' It is no surprise to see the response from the city's majority: 'to shut Nigerians out of their own capital, like the "natives" were kept out of the old African colonial capitals, is unacceptable,' as novelist Ike Oguine (2007: 29) put it.

Yet there are some possibilities for re-envisioning Abuja, and one might see this city as one that has moved beyond colonialism in ways that are more tangible than those in Lilongwe. Nigeria remains a country confronting ethnic and regional conflict in numerous areas at once, and Abuja does provide a genuine opportunity to build a unitary pluralist vision, however much its centrality might mark it as 'the eye of the hurricane' (Vale 2008: 161) or the dominance of northerners in Nigerian politics compromises the vision (Ikejiofor 1997). Lagos remains a choking megacity that is difficult to govern, to say nothing of the capacity to govern Nigeria from it, and Abuja still presents itself as a somewhat less choking, viable alternative (Oguine 2007). However deep the flaws of Nigeria's democratic political system, it is consolidating, and the bursts of constructive investment in Abuja have coincided with civilian rule (1979–83 and 1999– in particular) rather than with military rule (Adama 2007: 89). There is certainly vibrant scholarly debate on Abuja within Nigeria's own considerable urban studies universe (Abumere 1998). The growth of the democratic regimes' interests in developing Abuja make the idea of using the new capital to spur development in the previously underdeveloped Middle Belt of Nigeria at least possible. Adama (2007: 90) makes the case that 'relocation was welcomed by the majority of Nigerians,' and it continues to be, suggesting that Abuja moves beyond its authoritarian shadows as swiftly as it makes a postcolonial statement, in effect one in which a designed capital becomes an informal 'Afropolis' (Mbembe and Nuttall 2008: 1). Here again, there is more to contemplate in Chapter 3 on informality, however, in terms of re-envisioning African cities: can the creeping informalization of Abuja remake the city as an Africanized and postcolonial urbanism?

Dodoma If Lilongwe and Abuja are visions made problematic from their very start, by virtue of their emergence out of obviously authoritarian regimes, perhaps Dodoma deserves some deeper consideration. The city is one of the greatest physical symbols of *ujamaa*, and since *ujamaa* is one of the most significant 'alternative visions' of urbanism and human settlement that has emerged from postcolonial Africa, it needs to be taken more seriously than the other two as a postcolonial urbanism. The philosopher Valentin Mudimbe (1988: 94) called *ujamaa* 'probably the most pragmatic of all African socialisms.' The literary theorist Robert Young, in his *Postcolonialism: An Historical Introduction* (2001), argues that Nyerere's emphasis on 'self-reliance and the preferability of small-scale projects' as opposed to 'grandiose plans' has shaped the character of debates over development in Africa ever since. The irony here for Nyerere's deserved prominence in the political pantheon of postcolonialism is that Dodoma itself was something of a grandiose plan, despite its modesty by comparison with Lilongwe or Abuja.

Although the German-built railway that passed through Dodoma gave rise to the development of a settlement there in the 1890s, Dodoma was a rather small regional center until the 1970s (Kombe and Kreibich 2000). Tanzania's decision to relocate its capital there came in a vote by the Biennial Conference of the ruling party, Nyerere's Tanganyika African National Union, in 1973 (the party subsequently became Chama cha Mapinduzi – CCM – four years later, after uniting with the ruling party of Zanzibar). The Master Plan was commissioned the next year and published in 1976. As had been the case in Dar es Salaam in 1968, the professional planners who produced the Master Plan were Canadian, and certain idealized European (or actually North American) notions of what African socialist planning should be found their way into the plans (Armstrong 1987; Alexander 1983). Still, had it been fully implemented in its planned ten-year process, Dodoma's Master Plan would have created a model of African socialist urbanism (Kombe and Kreibich 2000; Hoyle 1979). The strongest African influence on it came through Nyerere, as the 'father of the nation.'

Dodoma's spatial plan was designed to 'enable the open space of the landscape to flow through it' (Capital Development Authority 1976: 69). In practical terms, this meant the design attempted to mimic an idealized notion of Tanzanian rural communal life (Nyerere 1967, 1968, 1970). The residential form of the plan involved building on the then one-party political system's ten-house cell social organization, in effect creating pod after pod of communalism, much like a dense collection of the rural settlement structures at the heart of the governing philosophy, *ujamaa* villages (Omari and Lukwaro 1978). As Hess (2006: 124) has written, 'the architecture of Dodoma was intended to embody Nyerere's belief in the equalization of urban and rural development,' emphasizing 'the village as the means to "the brotherhood and equality of man."' In between the pods, since planners avoided placing the communal areas on higher-quality farm and pastureland, the idea was to foster agricultural development for food self-sufficiency, along with afforestation and recreational green spaces (Lupala and Lupala 2003).

The original idea was to transfer the capital gradually from Dar es Salaam to Dodoma over the course of ten years (Hayuma 1981). Almost thirty-five years after the publication of the Master Plan, the transfer is yet to be realized in most respects. To be sure, Dodoma has grown from a dilapidated, dusty settlement with fewer than 50,000 people at the time of the Master Plan to a city of more than 300,000. Unlike Lilongwe or Abuja, it has grown at a slower pace than the plan envisioned, although as with the other created capitals, most of the growth areas have been out of character with the vision. Again most have been informal settlements, expanding in the opposite direction from the plan (Kombe and Kreibich 2000). Many observers have noted the common trend of parliamentarians to stay in Dodoma only as long as necessary to attend sessions of the parliament – 'no sooner has the session ended than everybody picks up the files and moves back to Dar es Salaam' (Ng'maryo, cited in Hess 2006: 125).

As a consequence, it could be easy to dismiss Dodoma as a failed postcolonial urban vision along with Lilongwe and Abuja. It is certainly not the green city of urban communal foresters, farmers, and herders Nyerere might have idealized (Lupala and Lupala 2003). It has some vestiges of the segmentation by income that dominates Lilongwe or Abuja, even if it lacks the monumentalism (save for the Nyerere sculpture) or obvious elitist capital accumulation (Hayuma 1981). The Tanzanian-German planning research team of Wilbard Kombe and Volker Kreibich (2000: 186) charted out the expectations and achievements of the Capital City Transfer Program, and their chart documents notable gaps. Most significantly, the government itself did not really move its seat of operations – parliament meets there most of the time, but essentially none of the ministerial headquarters is there, and neither are the main offices of the president or prime minister. Despite the slower than expected growth, government housing construction fell far short of what had been planned. Amenities, infrastructure, and services that the Master Plan expected – a new hospital, six new dispensaries, twenty primary schools, new hotels, and so forth – either had not materialized nearly a quarter-century after the plan or were far more limited in number or scope. Moreover, the planning practices of the Capital Development Authority (CDA) were often repressive toward residents and building control, hardly in step with ideas of 'negotiation, dialogue and consensus building' which one might think could form the basis of a city built to symbolize 'family-hood' and 'self-reliance' (ibid.: 135).

Yet perhaps we should not be so quick here. Kombe and Kreibich (ibid.: 126) are critical of the CDA's pace of plot allocation between 1982 and 1998 for self-built but surveyed and serviced residential developments, since only 29,967 of 42,816 applications for plots (or 70 percent) were honored. Yet that is a much higher planned land allocation pace than one encounters in that same era in Dar es Salaam or Zanzibar, for example – cases where the percentage of applicants successfully allocated land in many years lies below 10 percent. Kombe and Kreibich's (ibid.: 132) fascinating study of the Chang'ombe informal settlement in Dodoma also reveals the ways in which community leaders, including ruling party activists and ten-house cell leaders, 'worked tirelessly as a pressure group to mobilize [informal] settlers against' attempts by the CDA to evict them. The active collaboration and collusion of the majority of settlers with local party and government leaders created 'spatial orderliness' in the 'informally regularized' settlement during the first ten years of its development (1976–86). Kombe and Kreibich (ibid.: 147) argued that there had been a steady decline in community cohesion, and a corresponding rise in 'apathy' toward socialist goals among residents, both of which followed a 1986 central-government directive that limited the CDA's capacity for demolition and enforcement of strict building controls. The orderly and regularized dimension of Chang'ombe's subsequent expansion decreased, but Kombe and Kreibich (ibid.: 147) nonetheless saw great potential at the grass roots for 'collaborative initiatives' in future planning.

In the years since their study was published, the formal capital relocation re-emerged as a serious idea, particularly under the leadership of Nyerere's protégé, Benjamin Mkapa, during his second term as president (2000–05), and then continuing with the election of Jakaya Kikwete as Tanzania's president in 2005. Despite predictions that multiparty politics, which emerged in Tanzania after 1992, would lead to the capital relocation being 'scrapped altogether' (Kironde 1993: 435), in fact since opposition politicians first came to parliament in 1995 they have often joined with ruling party activists to push the government to speed up the process of relocating the capital, particularly in the last decade, with an emphasis on nationalist and nation-building rhetoric. As a result the government's budget and aid moneys have gone toward, for example, substantial upgrading of Dodoma's trunk road connection to Dar es Salaam to the east. Increased road traffic and improved bus service ensued, along with major trucking. The quality of other roads lagged behind, but up-grading and improvement had at least begun for roads to Arusha, Iringa, and Mwanza by the end of the first decade of the twenty-first century. In 2008, Dodoma finally had plans to receive a commercial air service from Dar es Salaam. The University of Dodoma took over the CCM's large conference center on the outskirts of town in that same year, with plans to expand to upwards of 40,000 students by 2018. A new parliament building was completed and pressed into service. Local hotels, guest houses, and restaurants increased in number and quality, along with other service industries and small factories. It seems that Dodoma is becoming more than a 'singular precedent for the amalgamation of moral vision and architectural planning' (Hess 2006: 126): it is becoming its own city. The way in which that city's residents live their lives is hardly in tune with the socio-spatial ideals of *ujamaa*, but one might argue that the residents often work toward their own *ujamaa* (as in its literal translation: family-hood) framework of development. Dodoma may be heading for an era of more participatory, decentralized, and democratic planning, whatever the government plans, but even there one senses a much greater degree of popular ownership of the idea of the capital transfer and active efforts to push the agenda (Kitilla 2008). Although the Dodoma capital project was, like those of Lilongwe or Abuja, a state-led vision from the outset, the less authoritarian governing ideology and the strength of community action make it the most likely of the three settings for something much closer to a genuinely postcolonial African urbanism.

Conclusion

Africa had many cities prior to the rise of European power on the continent, but formal colonial rule unquestionably reoriented urbanization, urban forms, and urban functions to meet its needs. Even if we are now more than a half-century past the date of independence in many African countries, contemporary cities on the continent still cope with colonial legacies in sociocultural and political-economic terms.

If we consequently conceive of African cities as being postcolonial, in that they are amid both the temporal and conceptual aftermath of colonialism trying to find ways to deal with or subvert those legacies, in most cases the evidence is fairly weak for claiming successes in doing so. The urban hierarchies of most former colonies remain highly imbalanced, and the political and economic dependence that characterizes many larger cities does not seem to be withering away all that dramatically. Postcolonial regimes have struggled to subvert the internal urban form, segmentation and inequality inherited from colonialism, as post-apartheid South African cities have struggled in attempts to overcome apartheid's urban spatial legacies.

Even in the cases of cities that independent governments built to speak back to colonialism, such as Lilongwe, Abuja, or Dodoma, we can see colonial tactics and strategies replicated or adapted by states and elites. As with the circumstances of all cities on this most diverse and vast continent, these cases vary, so that Dodoma suggests more of a state-led alternative to colonial visions of urban order than the other two. But truly postcolonial citiness seems to have more potential to emerge in the informal settlements that increasingly dominate all three of these planned capitals. A 'relational' and 'pluralist' understanding of African cities, à la Pieterse (2008a: 106), suggests that we need to know much more about the interrelationships of informal settlements with formal visions of urban order if we are to develop an agenda for 'practical usefulness in changing the world for the better' in African cities (Soja 2000). Thus I next take my search for alternative visions for urban theory and practice to these informal areas in the next chapter, before moving to the realm of governance in Chapter 4.

THREE

(I)n(f)ormal cities

Introduction

In 2007, on the last day of interviewing residents in one of Zanzibar's most impoverished and densely built informal settlements, called Uholanzi (Holland), my research assistant, Ali Hasan Ali, and I were trudging down a narrow ravine toward our government minder, walking ahead of us. We were tired. It had been a long, hot day of tense interviews in KiSwahili, traipsing up and down the settlement's ridges and ravines. We were interviewing residents about land and housing issues, gathering their views on government-led land reform processes and their settlement's development. We were finding that virtually no one in Uholanzi followed the formal government rules for land and housing development, nor did very many people hold out hope for the reform programs. We had, for days on end now, heard a lot of anger, frustration, and despair.

On our right, at the ravine's bottom, was a very small structure with walls made from burlap and plastic sacks sewn together and nailed onto a wooden frame, the thatched roof standing no more than a meter and a half off the ground. I asked Ali what it was. He looked, shrugged, and gave a weary answer: 'a chicken coop.' Our minder stopped, turned to us with a wry smile, and said: 'I think we have one more interview. This is the home of people.'

A week later, accompanying Ali on a walk outside his home in the nearby informal settlement of Mwera, where I was staying, he shook his head and told me that he could not stop 'thinking of those people we met who lived in the chicken coop. I can't believe people live in conditions like that, in my own city. I have lived my whole life in Zanzibar. I know this is a poor country. But it makes me ashamed that people live that way, just down the road.'

It is a truism that many urban residents in Africa live in what are called 'informal settlements.' A principal aim of this chapter is to unpack this characterization. That tired afternoon with Ali, and the walk a week later, taught me critical lessons for this unpacking. First, informal settlements are often very different from one another, and they are characterized as such by their residents; they vary dramatically within and between cities across the region (Myers 2010a). Second, informal settlements are the 'homes of people,' at the beginning and the end of the day, and everyday realities are often normalized for residents, regardless of the poverty, hardship, or grief that that form of 'normal' might be. And third, a lot of people, like Ali that day, shake their heads and do not know what to do about informal settlements.

In this chapter, I discuss the terms, origins, and scope for informal settlements in African cities. In this first part, I started writing with a set of basic questions in mind. What is an informal settlement? Is this the best phrase to use for the phenomenon in question? Where did informal settlements originate? Just how widespread is the informal African city now, and how do we know this?

The second part of the chapter addresses what is done to, for, or with informal settlements in African cities. In that section, the questions get more complicated. Is an informal settlement something other than the Davis-like *Planet of Slums* nightmare scenario? In relation to Soja's question regarding the practical usefulness of theory for changing the world for the better, should informal settlements be eliminated, upgraded, formalized, or championed, and, if any of these development paths make sense, how so? There is no one answer for these questions for a continent as vast as Africa, let alone for one country, to say nothing of variations in the answers in one particular city over time and space. In the third section of the chapter, I explore some of the variations in the conditions of existence in informal settlements with a focus on three case study settings, Cape Town, Accra, and Dar es Salaam.

Defining (i)n(f)ormal settlements

To understand what informal settlements are, we have to begin by defining their relationships with larger questions about informality. The economically oriented phrase, the informal sector, came to prominence in African urban studies in the 1970s, with its African-studies origin often credited to the work of Keith Hart (1973) in Ghana on Accra's 'informal economy' (though recognition of its existence by other terms did not really escape British or French colonial administrators or scholars from the 1930s onward, as the discussion of colonial Lusaka in Chapter 1 brings out). Like many other researchers, Hart saw the informal sector as an *autonomous, unregulated, often illegal, small-scale, low technology arena* for jobs many people would use as a stopgap en route into formal sector employment – meaning *registered, regulated, legal, waged, and often larger-scale, higher-technology, legal work*. This bifurcation of the economy found its spatial equivalent for many observers in a neat separation of informal from formal residential settlement areas in cities. In an idealized bifurcated form, the first of these would have unserviced impermanent houses in irregular patterns on unregistered, unsurveyed land lacking title deeds, and the second would have serviced permanent housing in planned and surveyed layouts on registered land with title deeds.

For African urban studies, the other widely noted early moment in a historiography of informality is the International Labor Organization's report on research in Nairobi (ILO 1972). The ILO report codified certain language that has predominated in the scholarly understanding of informality since. Its characteristics for identifying informal sector activities included 'ease of entry, reliance on indigenous resources, family ownership of enterprises, small scale of operation, labor-intensive and adapted technology, skills acquired outside the formal school system, and unregulated and competitive markets' (ibid.: 6). The ILO report harbored a similar assumption about the spatial manifestation of the duality in settlement patterns.

Much of the debate on urban informality shifted to Latin American urban studies in the ensuing decades (AlSayyad and Roy 2004; AlSayyad 2004). Some Latin Americanists, notably the Brazilian geographer Milton Santos (1979), essentially argued for the connections extant between informal and formal sectors, by writing of them as lower and upper circuits in the economy at urban, national, and international scales. Some took this argument about connectivity still farther, to claim that the formal sector depended upon keeping certain facets of the informal sector going in order to further extract profits from the majority economy, tying their arguments to structuralist theories (Portes et al. 1989). The geographical manifestations of such formulations varied, but generally it is apparent that by rejecting a clear separation of formal from informal and stressing their interpenetration, Santos and others at least implied a potential blurring of the spatial segregation of formal and informal settlement areas. But the emphases of both ways of conceptualizing informality – as a separate sector, or as one of two interlocking circuits – still kept the conceptualization in rather narrow economic confines.

More recent writing on the informal sector in urban Africa has argued for 'reconsidering' informality more broadly, beyond small business or employment (Hansen and Vaa 2004; Lindell 2010). More economistic conceptualizations miss the wider ways in which housing, land, infrastructure, and services, as well as politics and social organizations, develop informally, and the ways in which state agencies, and other formal institutions, act informally or act to produce informality (Konings et al. 2006; AlSayyad 2004; Roy 2005). The built environment and political and cultural spheres serve as the tangible emphasis in this chapter, focusing on informal settlements as a manifestation of one element of informality more broadly.

Regardless of which sphere researchers prioritize, it seems to be generally agreed that there is a strong trend toward *informalization* in African cities, meaning an overall growth in and growing breadth to informal activity, notably in the growth of informal settlements and the informalization of formal settlements (Harrison et al. 2008; Grant 2009). The 'new waves of informalization' in the economy are typically reliant on 'forms of work beyond the purview of state regulation' and on an increasing 'precariousness of work' (Lindell 2010: 1–2). The new waves of informalization are most observable in everyday social life with the apparently rising importance of unregistered social networks in the built environment, livelihood strategies, social reproduction, cultural organization, or political mobilization.

It is worth remembering, as we consider this contemporary notion of increasing informalization, that what we call informal settlements in urban Africa can have very long histories. Many African urban areas grew informally from the beginning, if we think of political theorists' separation of how societies operate into informal and formal institutions and the general lack of legible (written) forms of the latter in many pre-colonial African cities (Knight 1992). Commonly in Atlantic West Africa, such settlements were not considered 'squatter settlements' or 'slums,' in part because informal rules governing their development were so well understood and enforced via indigenous practices (Konadu-Agyemang 1991: 140).

Moreover, if we conceive of informal settlements as existing only in relation to, and as the opposite of, something we deem formal settlements – those bound by formal (written) laws governing housing and land use – then clearly European colonialism had a significant role in their creation. As I noted in Chapter 2, given the diversity of colonial experiences for African cities, one must be cautious about overgeneralizing, but it was common for urban areas in British, Belgian, Dutch,

French, German, Italian, and Portuguese colonies to have within them a fundamental dichotomy between colonizer and colonized zones that ran parallel to distinctions made between 'modern' and 'traditional' economies and cultures (Drakakis-Smith 2000: 125). Sometimes, each part of the city took on its own built-environment manifestation. Bidonvilles, the tin towns or shack settlements of France's North African cities, had emerged outside of formal towns by the 1920s. Even where formal housing predominated, such as in Zambia's Copperbelt, one in five mining families lived in 'unauthorized compounds' by the time of independence in 1964 (Freund 2007: 81–3).

Colonial regimes tended to look to what we now speak of as informal settlements as dangerous and disorderly zones of resistance and detribalization, and policies existed from the beginning of their emergence geared toward their elimination. As we saw in Lusaka in Chapter 1, colonial regimes were as often ambivalent – colonial officials profited from 'unauthorized' development, or tolerated informal indigenous practices if they benefited the regime. With independence in the 1960s, and then particularly in the 1970s, some national and urban governments – at least on paper – attempted to champion the development potential of informal activity, by harnessing it, and thus formalizing it. In the last decade, the drive to formalize informal settlements has become almost a religious movement in development circles (Manji 2006).

The capacity for and efficacy of harnessing informality for formal development goals are questionable. Some elements of informality exist to evade the formal institutions of the state and the private sector, and profiting from them depends on this continued evasion, e.g. various forms of corruption or tax and license avoidance. Given that areas of cities dominated by informal arrangements are typically marginalized and poor, it makes sense that planners and urban professionals still abound who dedicate their careers to the eradication of informality as a way to eliminate poverty. Sometimes that eradication is largely rhetorical, involving adroit recategorization or a mantra about formalization. But at other times, the push is real and quite tangible – as in the bulldozing of informal settlements for political ends (Harrison et al. 2008: 228–33; Kombe and Kreibich 2000; Myers 2005).

However, because informal city life is, by its very nature, 'unregistered, unmonitored' and unruly, there is a 'severe lack of statistical data' to document and analyze regarding its size, form, functions, or other characteristics, whether one wants to champion it, formalize it, or bulldoze it out of existence (Bryceson 2006: 9–10). That means that for all the difficulty one encounters in defining the meaning of informality or informal settlements, assessing the scope of either is if anything more difficult. This problem bedevils the recent report compiled by the United Nations Habitat program, entitled *The State of African Cities 2008: A Framework for Addressing Urban Challenges in Africa*. Its data for informal sector activity and for what it terms 'slum' conditions are both fascinating (for the range of data that seems to be made available on African cities) and problematic (for enduring concerns with data sources, and gaps in what data are discussed), as the data in Tables 3.1–3.3 suggest for cities of interest to this book.

These data are presented here – as they are in the UN report – to suggest some general characteristics about these urban economies and societies, because these are, in global terms and in national terms in most African countries, the data which shape the policy elites' discussion of informality. I note from the outset of my discussion of these data that not all informal settlements are necessarily slums, not all slums are informal settlements, not all aspects of the informal economy are confined to informal or slum settlement areas, not all urban employment is male, and so forth. The UN's definition of a slum does sound something like a typical characterization of an informal settlement: 'a contiguous settlement where the inhabitants are characterized as having inadequate housing and basic services; a slum is often not recognized and addressed by public authorities as an integral part of the city.' And in estimating slum conditions, UN-Habitat takes five criteria of household life into account, measuring as a 'deprivation' any lack of: *access to improved water supply*; *access*

TABLE 3.1 Percentage of male city residents employed in informal sector by shelter deprivation status

City	Overall	Non-slum household	Slum household
Douala	93.2	88.9	97.7
Accra	35.8	31.3	47.6
Nairobi	2.8	2.9	2.4
Niamey	54.7	47.4	58.3
Lusaka	6.9	8.3	5.9

Source: UN-Habitat (2008)

TABLE 3.2 'Slum components' for selected cities: the percentage of the population for each city with access to ...

City	Improved water	Improved sanitation	Finished main floor	Sufficient living area
Douala (2004)	86.9	75.5	88.1	90.4
Accra (2003)	88.5	81.9	98.8	n/a
Nairobi (2003)	93.3	81.5	87.4	81.7
Lilongwe (2004)	92.9	52.3	65.1	83.1
Niamey (2006)	94.7	65.5	72.4	66.2
Abuja (2003)	81.8	63.6	100	68.2
Cape Town (1998)	95.8	82.4	93.7	90.9
Port Elizabeth (1998)	97.2	70.6	83.4	79.2
Dar es Salaam (2004)	81.1	58.5	93.8	84.1
Lusaka (2002)	97.2	66.4	97.5	n/a

Source: UN-Habitat (2008)

TABLE 3.3 In the countries of the cities shown in Table 3.2, percentage of the urban population listed as being slum households in slum areas

Country	Percentage slum households in slum areas
Cameroon	41
Ghana	32
Kenya	57
Malawi	80
Niger	95
Nigeria	75
South Africa	21
Tanzania	80
Zambia	56

Source: UN-Habitat (2008)

to improved sanitation; *security of tenure*; *durability of housing*; and *sufficient living area*. These deprivations are often characteristics – though not uniformly – of informal settlements. Hence although there is nothing like a perfect statistical correlation, let us attempt to roll with the premise that the slum conditions as measured by these deprivations are reasonably close to a proxy for informal settlements by the UN's estimations – that is, in fact, what quite a few scholars do, including Davis (2005) in *Planet of Slums*.

Although the report more generally concludes that about two-thirds of all urban Africans live in slums and about half are employed primarily in the informal sector, Tables 3.1, 3.2 and 3.3 do not im-mediately suggest that broad generalizations are helpful. According to the UN report's data in Table 3.1, almost all working urban males are apparently employed in informal sector activities in Douala whether they live in slums or not, while men in Nairobi almost never are, again whether they live in slums or not. Accra and Niamey, both of which present data close to the continental norms, appear to conform to what might be logical expectations, in that more slum-dwellers are employed in the informal sector. But the Lusaka data suggest the inverse – that non-slum-dwellers are more likely to have informal employment than slum-dwellers. The ultimate conclusions one might draw from data of these types are elusive. It is patently unbelievable that so few employed men in Nairobi or Lusaka work in unregulated, unregistered, or unlicensed enterprise – even with Nairobi's recent activist interventions to build collaboration between informal sector workers and city government, informality dominates this city far more than the UN data's supposed 2.4 percent of the (male) labor force suggests (Mitullah 2010: 188).

At first glance, the UN data in Table 3.2 suggest that things are not so bad in these cities, since relatively large percentages of the population do not suffer deprivations in the categories listed (four of the five categories which count in the UN's definition of a slum). The UN considers a household to be a slum household even when suffering one of the deprivations, though, giving rise to its much larger numbers for overall percentages considered to be slum households in slum areas listed by country in Table 3.3. (The overall percentages for slum households or slum areas for individual cities are given only sporadically in the report, and are not presented in the report's statistical appendix.)

There are worrying problems with how the slum conditions are defined or reported in the *State of African Cities* report. Most obvi-ously, the fifth category is missing from the UN's statistical data set – namely, security of tenure. In many countries an overwhelming number of urban households lack formal, legal security of tenure in the form of a deed or title to the property, but this is 'not as easy to measure or monitor' as the other four deprivations (Pieterse 2008a: 31). This leads to the hidden dynamic in the UN report of just how the fifth category is calculated into the mix with the other four 'deprivations.' There are also real questions about just how crucial a Western law-defined registered land title is to African urban residents or to the generation of slum conditions, alongside questions of who decides what a sufficient living space is, or that a dirt floor automatically belongs to a slum household. The recent update of the UN-Habitat (2010) report on African cities makes some improvements – for instance, it focused, from its subtitle onward, on three crucial issues that overlap with my concerns in this book – namely, governance, inequality, and urban land markets. Yet it still suffers from unevenness and inconsistency in data collection, reliability, and deployment: the emphasis on urban land markets notwithstanding, the new report still has no city-by-city comparative data on informality in land markets or security of tenure (ibid.).

Still, while quibbling with many of its numbers, one can come away from either of the *State of African Cities* reports with some evidence for what seems like a reasonable assumption: *a great many African urbanites live in informal settlements, in cities where informality plays a key role in the built environment, as in economics, politics, and society.* One can also reasonably conclude that the scope and proportion of informal settlement and informal sector activity varies across the continent's cities, as does the relationship between informal economic activity and informal settlement. At least for these reasons and for its detailed discussions of policy dynamics, the report might be a valuable resource and starting place for analysis of informal settlement.

Theorizing and planning for (i)n(f)ormality

At the same time, the inexactitude of definitions and the paucity or inconsistency of data, as well as the apparent pervasiveness of informality within formal ways of doing things in urban Africa, give rise to a line of thinking that rejects the language shaping the discussion entirely. 'Rather than opposing the "formal" and the "informal"', Achille Mbembe and Sarah Nuttall (2008: 8) write, 'we need a more complex anthropology of things, forms and signs in order to account for the life of the city in Africa.' They go on to argue that 'the informal is not outside of the formal' and that the 'processes of formalization and informalization work together' (ibid.: 9), though in a less formulaic, economistic way than Santos's vision of upper and lower circuits. They argue that what ought to be the focus of research is 'how they work together and how this working together ends up producing city forms and urban economies' (ibid.: 9). This seems to me a reasonable insertion into the debate, one that questions what many see as 'outdated dualities' like formal versus informal and instead stresses seeing urban informality as 'an organizing logic' growing more prominent in the contemporary era of globalization, liberalization, and the restructuring of urban governance (AlSayyad 2004: 26).

But Mbembe and Nuttall are writing about a city that, as any data sources will tell us, has more of a formal economy, and the formal wealth that comes with it, than any other city on the continent – Johannesburg, which they describe quite problematically in the first sentence of their book as 'the premier African metropolis, the symbol par excellence of the "African modern"' (Mbembe and Nuttall 2008: 1). How broadly can we apply their argument? Are the informal and the formal interpenetrating and working together in quite the same way in Johannesburg as they are in Accra, Tripoli, Nairobi, Dar es Salaam, or Douala? Is the 'African modern' which results from the blending of informal and formal in Johannesburg really so easily comparable to these or other African cities? I have my doubts. Johannesburg's African identity itself is an ambivalent thing. Proclaiming 'the Africanness of Johannesburg' is part of 'the search for a political and cultural legitimacy for the elite' who manage the city, but the proclamation clashes with a simultaneous agenda to mark Johannesburg as a 'world class city' that is trying to distance itself from the problems of 'Africa' (Robinson 2006: 144). The highly 'partitioned urban landscape' (Murray 2008a: 155) that emerges and is reinforced as a result has themes in common with other cities on the continent, but I hesitate to proclaim it as 'the premier African metropolis' given how particular its story clearly is.

There is, though, a common tension one can see and sense in most African cities, whether we sit in Johannesburg or in a city to its north, south, east, or west. This tension exists between modernist ideas of how cities should look and work – the formal city – that sometimes make little sense, and an alternative, fluid, ambient – informal – city that is getting by on its own, if perhaps barely so. The degree to which the city is angled toward a formal, modernist vision and toward an informal one – or an 'Afropolis,' as Mbembe and Nuttall (2008: 1) want to call it – varies in each city, as does the geography of the proportioning.

The outcomes vary in terms of how formal and informal visions 'work together and how this working together' produces space and the space economy of the city. Where there is more clashing than 'working together,' some posit this as an outcome of 'conflicting rationalities' or planning mindsets (Watson 2007: 72). Formal planning, 'grounded in the rationality of Western modernity and development,' holds to one notion of 'proper' communities, while the marginalized majority in informal settlements work from a different notion of what a city should be, based around their attempts 'to survive, materially and culturally, in ... alien places' (ibid.: 69). By this line of thinking, two contrasting sets of concepts and practices that are deeply and essentially different crash into each other in those cities, in urban planning, both in the building and managing of environments through land subdivision and its regulation, housing construction, infrastructure and service provision, and the like, and in the attachment of sociocultural meaning and value to such places.

Some scholars don't see these conflicting rationalities as being 'insurmountable,' stressing that the capacity of the urban poor to engage with formal planning processes 'is usually limited by the material resources at their disposal rather than "cultural" factors' (Robins 2006: 99). It is hard to separate out an argument about deeply different cultural rationalities from an old, tired debate about a clash between traditions and modernity. Mbembe and Nuttall remind us of the 'inherently contradictory, unfinished nature of cities' (Shepherd and Murray 2007: 9) and the central role of informal settlements in them. They use this reminder to argue for work that can articulate the 'virtues of curiosity and astonishment' that emanate from appreciating the 'practices and imaginations of citiness' in the 'other scripts' that lie 'beneath the visible landscape' in informal areas (Mbembe and Nuttall 2004: 357, 363; Mbembe and Nuttall 2008). In more practical ways, I think another way of getting at their point might be to argue for trying to understand 'how urban dwellers in Africa develop their own mechanisms of production and create their own urban forms [and] ... developmental norms' (Locatelli and Nugent 2009: 7). In most cases, these mechanisms, forms and norms involve a strategic and ever-changing mixture of modernist and non-modernist rationalities, of formal and informal, that is not necessarily as 'hidden' as Mbembe and Nuttall imply.

The question then becomes whether these other scripts for citiness or mechanisms for producing urban forms and norms, via nimble reframing of harsh reality into survivability, are anything more than tools for barely surviving. Is it possible to consciously make and shape informality through alternative channels where 'subaltern reason' can guide planning to 'connect with the survival strategies of the poor' (Harrison 2006a: 326)? What is the best manner of approach, in practical terms – should modernist, state-driven planning learn the other scripts and read the city through them, should the modernist vision be magically made to disappear, allowing the informal ways of planning the Afropolis to essentially be the way the cities grow in its absence, or should African cities seek some form of 'hybrid governance' based on 'mutual acceptance' of duelling or interpenetrating rational orders (Trefon 2009: 31)? How plausible is such a conceptual drive toward 'forging collaborative initiatives between the formal and informal processes' and mindsets (Kombe and Kreibich 2000: 148; Myers 2010a)?

Let me talk about the family of Ali Hasan Ali, from the beginning of this chapter, to illustrate what these rather abstract questions mean more tangibly. Ali likes to write his name with different spellings – Aly instead of Ali, Hassan instead of Hasan – and he is far more widely known by his nicknames – Zungu and George are the most common. Ali says he is a fisherman, though he has not been to sea for several decades. When not working as an assistant with me, he makes his living as an agent for fishing boats in negotiations with fishmongers at the portside fish market in downtown Zanzibar – in either case, his employment lies outside of the formal economy, tangential to it. He and his wife, Zuhura Abdulrahim Mohamed, obtained the plot informally for their house in Mwera, via a dense network of friendships and allegiances that had been set in motion during his work as my field assistant in my dissertation in 1991/92. Zuhura has coordinated the multi-stage, decade-long construction process for this permanent house, using an ever-changing set of off-the-books *fundi* (craftspeople) out of a similarly dense, constantly evolving social network. They have lived in Mwera for a decade, but neither Ali nor Zuhura would say they are from Mwera. Ali comes from the Malindi, Vikokotoni, or Kikwajuni neighborhood in the inner city, depending on the context in which one asks him, and he is variously Arab, Comorian, Muslim, or mixed-race as his first line of self-identification, again depending on the context. Zuhura likewise is Comorian one day, Pemban the next, a revolutionary one day, royalty the day after that (her father was a famous figure in Zanzibar's 1964 socialist revolution, and her grandfather an even more famous figure with the government overthrown in that revolution). She grows many food items for the family in her kitchen garden, alongside herbs she grows to sell or give as gifts. I could go on and on with their example; my point is that they live their lives in an ambient, fluid, flexible other script for citiness that some may see as deeply different from that of a Western-trained urban planner, for instance. Is it a script that must forever clash with the official order? Can it be replicated, or made to be the script that takes the place of modernist, rational, planning mindsets? Or is it possible to find a way to bring the differing rationalities into dialogue with one another?

All of these questions run together with those embedded in debates in African studies more broadly about 'alternative modernities' (Deutsch et al. 2002; Ferguson 2006, 2008; Gaonkar 2001; Geschiere et al. 2008). Like the ideas generated from attempts to articulate alternative or multiple modernities in relation to Africa, the ideas of alternative planning as generated from indigenous informality and creativity can be quite inspiring and stirring. As Konings et al. (2006: 3) put it, 'the majority of the residents in disadvantaged African neighborhoods have not passively watched conditions deteriorate ... they appear to behave as active agents, devising alternative strategies to shape their livelihoods.' Yet many of these ideas as put into practice in cities have their origin in a response to what Ferguson (2008: 10) refers to as the *abjection* of Africa – its 'humiliating expulsion'; he reminds us that the word's 'literal meaning also implies not just being thrown out, but being thrown *down*.' What we may have in these alternative ideas are small, creative urban practices that are, if you will, applied attempts by the abject poor to lay claim to 'equal rights of membership' in a global urbanity that is not only 'spectacularly unequal' but highly uneven in its capacity to acknowledge – let alone accept – such claims (Ferguson 2006: 175; Myers 2010a). Ali and Zuhura make good use of the limited opportunities around them, but the power dynamics in Zanzibar are such that their marginalization increases regardless. The Zanzibar state may work in informal channels, but its land reform programs and the modern order they belong to want subjects who spell their name the same way every time, have a fixed address at a registered plot, where they build a house using licensed contractors, paid for out of income from salaried jobs on which they also pay income tax. Ali and Zuhura do not consciously *choose not* to be those subjects – the system threw them down and out to a place where that is their only choice.

Is informality fundamentally limited by its apparent origins in the sort of abjection Ferguson sees? How, when, and for whom does it become an alternative vision of the city? Informality does ensure that 'new possibilities emerge, at times in surprising places' (Mbembe and Nuttall 2008: 6). But because of pervasive informality certain cities are rendered virtually ungovernable and desperately deprived, living with a 'spectacular architecture of decay' (ibid.: 7; de Boeck and Plissart 2004). For some neoliberal theorists and donors, the informal sector is the 'incubator of ... entrepreneurial ingenuity' (Myers and Murray 2006: 14). For others, the whole 'crisis of African cities' can be 'attributed to the "informality", "illegality", and "anarchy" of their economies' (Locatelli and Nugent 2009: 7). Still others see informality as a complex combination of creative and destructive tendencies (Simone 2004). The heart of the concerns with what informality means or what to do about informal settlements centers on land; land issues are a valuable means of illustrating issues related to informality because the uncertainties surrounding rights to occupy, control, and build on land are fundamental to why informal settlements are so often considered a problem for states and citizens.

Residents in a city's informal settlements generally lack formal legal security of tenure, and so this might, at first pass, be a clear way one can distinguish between a formal city (where residents have registered titles for their landed property) and an informal one (where they don't). Urban theorists and practitioners have long debated the importance of security of tenure, but the prevailing argument today within the development rubric that dominates most of sub-Saharan Africa, neoliberalism, is that residents need secure legal tenure rights to gain an economic foothold. Registered title deeds formalize, order, and regulate the city, eliminating one of the UN's five fundamental slum-defining 'deprivations.'

The neoliberal development paradigm has many different flavors within it, but the buffet of policies almost always includes the drive for security of individuated land tenure in order to 'unleash the entrepreneurial power of the poor,' as former US Secretary of State Colin Powell (2002: 6–7) put it. The 'greater prominence given to property rights in the development agenda' (Mooya and Cloete 2007: 148) is manifested in the wide influence of Hernando de Soto's book *The Mystery of Capital* (2000) and programs aimed at land titling for the urban poor (Payne 2002). The key argument of de Soto and others on paper is that formalized and secure property rights reduce poverty. The contention begins with arguments against informal or common property regimes. Neoliberal thought argues that when property rights are poorly or vaguely defined, properties are used wastefully, with high transaction costs, and when they are held in common, they are overexploited (Alston et al. 1996). The urban and peri-urban poor's best assets are often their properties, the reasoning goes, and therefore securing their individual control over them allows the poor, cast as 'heroic entrepreneurs,' to gain the greatest value from them (ibid.; Manji 2006). The increased market activity created by lower transaction costs and more secure property rights, it is claimed, will eventually filter down into greater economic activity and greater income for the poor, if it takes place through 'facilitative institutional arrangements' (Mooya and Cloete 2007: 155). Therefore the key to bringing to life the 'dead capital' of the informal landholdings of the urban poor and raising them from the depths of poverty is formalization of property ownership, with government as merely a helpmate in land management (de Soto 2000: 29; Myers 2008a, 2008b).

The World Bank and many donors have fallen in lockstep with de Soto. Relatively uniform land reform laws and programs have been rammed through across the continent to implement de Soto's thesis, despite the fact that empirical evidence behind his claims proves thin in many settings (Gilbert 2002; Home and Lim 2004; Varley 2002; Myers 2008b; Manji 2006; Ikejiofor 2006). This includes my case study cities in this chapter, all three of which have been home to de Soto-inspired land reform.

In Cape Town, with what Robins (2006: 104) calls de Soto's 'strikingly seductive idea' – the magic of title deed – it seemed 'plausible and desirable' to post-apartheid South African planners to expect that building proper houses through public–private partnerships in the Reconstruction and Development Programme and then turning them over to people with title over them would provide collateral for loans that would then lead to investments to improve those properties and sell them. But the obstacles have proved huge. Owners of these houses have seldom found buyers. Furthermore, 'the lengthy struggle of many township residents for urban rights and access to a house during the apartheid period means that, even if they have title deeds, they are unlikely to want to sell' because 'houses are often part of a family's social and political biography' (ibid.: 104).

Accra offers an extensive and far-reaching example of de Soto-led urban land reform (Grant 2009; Manji 2006: 4). At the same time, it is also the site for several effective research critiques of de Soto's thesis, and intriguing alternative planning in informal settlements (Abdulai 2007; Abdulai et al. 2007; Larbi et al. 2003). Abdulai (2007), for example, showed that 'the real obstacle' to land market formal-ization is the generally low income levels of Ghanaians vis-à-vis the high interest rates charged by financial institutions, and not land registration. He found that any 'documented evidence of property ownership ... and the income-earning capacity of the prospective mortgagor' are the 'critical requirements' for a working system, but the poor don't have enough income – their property 'is likely to have low market value due to inappropriate location.' Larbi et al. (2003: 355) argued for a 'redefinition of formal property rights to effectively incorporate indigenous rights and the lowering of planning and building standards.' They admit that indigenous land markets 'tend to be disorganized, with conflicting and often unrecorded ownership claims and unclear boundaries,' but find that the responsiveness and dynamism of these markets meet 'the changing needs of society' more than the formal neoliberal system (ibid.: 356).

Hernando de Soto himself visited Dar es Salaam in 2005, where the 'message of formalization was fully articulated' in subsequent reports and policies – the visit was even preceded by a symposium organized by the United States embassy featuring various local perspectives on reading *The Mystery of Capital* (Brown and Lyons 2010: 42; Myers 2005). The government had already issued a new National Land Policy in 1995, directly in line with neoliberal thinking, despite the findings of a Presidential Commission of Inquiry into Land Matters that had favored the preferences of peasants and the urban poor for very different policies (Manji 2006: 44). Legal scholar Ambreena Manji's (ibid.: 68) contention is that Tanzania's new land laws had as their main objective 'the creation of a suitable environment for invest-ment in land by large-scale foreign buyers and the setting up of an efficient system for a market in land.' That the laws have not created an efficient and regulated land market in urban areas is apparent in analyses of Dar es Salaam by Tanzanian planning scholars (Kombe 2005; Kironde 2006). Land-grabbing by foreign interests is becom-ing prevalent in some rural settings; the de Soto-inspired Property and Business Formalization Program in Tanzania (known more by its KiSwahili acronym Mkurabita) results in the twin outcomes of gentrification and the further displacement of the poor from the inner city in Dar es Salaam (Muhajir 2011).

In contrast to the logic of land reforms that aim to formalize the informal systems, 'in their daily struggle for survival urban dwellers develop their own rationality and logic of behavior, which often do not comply with externally imposed visions of the city' or wouldn't be enforceable in 'modern courts of law,' but they sustain 'people's livelihoods in a context of widening material poverty' (Lindell 2002: 30). In these informal systems, 'access to land is neither haphazard nor spontaneous but instead follows certain procedures that are usually well known and adhered to by the actors involved. The key actors in the process actually appear to borrow pragmatically from different normative orders' (Konings et al. 2006: 6). The systems are often highly reliant on informal social networks which are themselves built from kinship and friendship. As geographer Ilda Lindell (2002) points out, though, ordinary residents have a very different capacity for exercising informal rights. Even in informal systems, increasing proportions of urban residents struggle to access land for building houses (Konings et al. 2006: 6). Significant tensions arise (or persist) between natives and strangers, or between classes or genders or races, in many cities (Lindell 2010: 10–13; Konings et al. 2006; Grant 2009). Certain efforts emerge to reach across these divides in institutionalizing, organizing, or deploying informal systems in the interests of the poor majority, but these are still rare (Mitullah 2010). Thus, in the land question, as in the broader questions about informality, the way forward, or the path toward Soja's 'practical usefulness in changing the world for the better,' is far from clear. Pure reliance on the de Soto thesis is deeply flawed, an idealized fantasy at best: even if we assume that regularization of tenure is pro-poor, most states do not have the central or local government institutional capacity to facilitate that regularization in a fair and equitable manner. It seems equally problematic to abandon urban land processes to informal systems that, even when not as polluted by a competing formal system, are unreliable sources of equitable poverty reduction. Some form of hybrid governance over urban land would appear to be the most viable option, but the route to it or capacity for it is bound to vary by city and context.

Informality does not seem to inevitably disappear in the urban land development process under neoliberal reforms – the outcomes are highly variable (Lindell 2002). With that variability in mind, in the remainder of the chapter I examine informal settlements in Cape Town, Accra, and Dar es Salaam. It is not my intention to rewrite the histories of any one of them, but instead to sketch out comparative answers to these questions: (1) What constitutes an informal settlement in these three cities? (2) What is everyday life like in the settlements? (3) What are the planning dynamics around informal settlements that have predominated in contemporary times? In my conclusion, I then use the short answers to these three questions to engage with the broader concerns of the chapter, with the possibilities for enacting Pieterse's notion of relational cities and for deploying hybrid governance of formality/informality.

Informal settlements in Cape Town, Accra, and Dar es Salaam

Although data from UN-Habitat are again frustratingly incomplete and maddeningly inscrutable on informal settlement in these three cities, they do provide us with a few general hints at features of distinction. Looking at Table 3.4, it is a reasonable observation that informal ways of doing things – in terms of making a living, finding

TABLE 3.4 Changes over time in deprivation status for households in Cape Town,[a] Accra, and Dar es Salaam: percentages of households with access to …

City	Year	Improved water	Improved sanitation	Finished main floor	Sufficient living area
Cape Town[a]	1998	95.8	82.4	93.7	90.9
Accra[b]	1993	99.8	67.5	99.5	77.6
	1999	97.7	70.9	99.7	80.3
	2003	88.5	81.9	98.8	n/a
Dar es Salaam[b]	1992	90.5	47.8	80.0	77.1
	1996	85.4	54.1	87.9	83.4
	1999	90.1	57.5	86.5	n/a
	2004	81.1	58.5	93.8	84.1

Notes: a. The UN included data only for 1998 for Cape Town. The South African Cities Network's 2006 *State of South African Cities Report* lists the following relevant data for Cape Town over time: 1. In 1996, 19.5% of households were considered informal households; by 2004, that percentage had dropped to 17.5%. 2. While there was a 14.17% increase in households without access to formal housing in Cape Town between 1991 and 2001, the report lists a 4.45% *decline* in such households between 2001 and 2004. b. The UN report lists no overall percentage of Accra households in informal settlements; it lists 64.9% of Dar es Salaam households as slum households.
Source: UN-Habitat (2008)

land, or building a house – are *pervasive* in Dar es Salaam, *common* in Accra, and a *notable minority trend* within everyday life in Cape Town. Estimates for the proportion of the population residing in informal settlements in Dar es Salaam range from 65 percent to more than 80 percent. Despite extensive research, comprehensive and reliable data are not available for Accra, but local researchers' estimates fall between 32 percent and 40 percent. The South African Cities Network reports show a slight but steady decline in the percentage of Capetonians living in informal areas from 19.5 percent in 1996 to 17.5 percent in 2004 and 16 percent in 2009, and however much these data may undercount the population of Cape Town's informal settlements, it is entirely defensible to characterize it as a less informal city, overall, than either of the other two. In three subsections below, I sketch what defines informal settlements and the character of everyday life in them, as well as the nature of debates over planning responses to them, in the three settings.

What is an informal settlement? Understanding what an informal settlement means in Cape Town is inextricably bound up with the racialization of space from the origins of the city with Dutch settlement in 1652. The first attempts at formal segregation began in 1901. Cape Town's black African population was historically comparably small, and the apartheid regime, the white minority regimes before it, and the colonial governments before that instituted various measures to attempt to keep it that way. Apartheid's Group Areas Act, Pass Law, and Coloured Labour Preference Area (which included Cape Town) were meant to discourage Eastern Cape isiXhosa-speaking blacks, or any other blacks for that matter, from migrating to the city. The apartheid regime even made it unlawful to build any housing whatsoever for blacks at the Cape from 1972–79, leading to a steady rise in illegal squatting since people still migrated anyway (Western 2001: 625). Geographer John Western (1996 [1981]: 288) estimated that Cape Town's black population in 1980 consisted of 120,000 'officially enumerated' residents and another 90,000 illegal squatters (96 percent of whom were Xhosa). The government's subsequent strategy of 'Orderly Urbanisation' in the early 1980s did establish an increasing number of formal housing units for blacks in the three racially segregated townships reserved for them, but it proved incapable of controlling the 'influx' that its 'influx control' policies were designed for (Saff 1996).

Blacks comprised nearly 32 percent of Cape Town's population of just under three million people by 2001, marking the culmination of dramatic change for the city demographically over the last half of the twentieth century (Western 2001; Van der Merwe and Davids 2006). This growth is concomitant with the increasing informalization of Cape Town, and many of the spontaneous settlements, land invasions, and shantytowns that dot the cityscape have their origins within the last three or four decades (Western 1996 [1981]; Lemansky and Oldfield 2009; Dierwechter 2002). By 1993, there were forty-two informal settlements, with more than 200,000 residents (Saff 1996: 238). The settlement of Crossroads was among the most powerful symbols of 'grand apartheid,' and its story epitomizes the story of informality in Cape Town (Western 1996 [1981]: 287). First, given that so many informal settlements originated in the apartheid era, they are both deeply racialized and highly politicized. As a nearly entirely black African settlement into which the apartheid regime had relocated black squatters from the city's coloured (mixed-race) locations, townships, or shack settlements beginning in 1975, Crossroads spoke to the ghastly injustices of apartheid's spatial engineering. While coloured and black African squatters often settled together in shack areas through the mid-1970s, by 1975 the local government was attempting to consolidate all black squatters into Crossroads.

Second, Crossroads symbolizes much of what has transpired in the informal cityscape, with significant post-apartheid government efforts to formalize the settlement smashing into settlers' reinformalization efforts and spontaneous settlements in the face of severe shortcomings in housing provision, leaving most informal areas as oddly juxtaposed agglomerations of 'partial formalization' (Oldfield 2002). Although there are Informal Residential Zones in a variety of smaller spots around the greater Cape Town area, the largest and most famous informal areas, like Crossroads once was, are those located adjacent to the former black townships of the Cape Flats. As the place name implies, the Flats are low-lying, frequently flooded lands between the Atlantic and Indian Ocean sides of the Cape region, east of Table Mountain and south of the Cape Ranges. Crossroads today is a typical Cape Flats area where regularized and platted neighborhoods of standard-issue housing contrast with shack infilling that maps typically identify as hatched areas adjacent to the massive and sprawling new planned areas, but a closer look reveals many reinformalizations of the formal housing areas, too (Robins 2008).

Where informality in Cape Town is tied into a history of racial injustice, apartheid, and inequality, in Accra its story is connected much more to questions of belonging and indigeneity. The scope and scale of informal settlement are larger here than in Cape Town, and smaller than in Dar es Salaam (Grant and Yankson 2003: 70). Accra has grown in the years since its selection in 1877 as the new capital of Britain's Gold Coast colony into a city of at least two million people, mostly on land settled or hunted historically by the Ga peoples (Gough and Yankson 1997).

Ga claims to the land of Accra's informal settlements mark out Accra as a distinctly different case than either Cape Town or Dar es Salaam. Until economic liberalization in the mid-1980s, indigenous landholders and the state, collectively, managed to accommodate the growing urban population's housing needs without 'slums' (Konadu-Agyemang 1991). Income inequalities grew within Accra's Ghanaian population after independence, but the fervent push to adopt neoliberal economic policies severely exacerbated these inequalities. The newly expanding private sector failed to meet the huge backlog of housing units needed in the city (ibid.: 541). The 'acute housing problem' that emerged in the era of liberalization led to the expansion of low-quality informal residential structures, particularly in peri-urban areas historically recognized as Ga lands (Grant and Yankson 2003: 70; Grant 2006).

Although there are, as in Cape Town, formal areas where 'housing conditions have deteriorated' and semi-permanent rental-room add-ons have essentially informalized neighborhoods around the whole city, the more striking story is that of 'slum/squatter' areas full of nonpermanent dwellings which have arisen, particularly on the western side of the city and along its northbound rail line (Grant 2009: 115). Probably the largest and most controversial of these squatter areas is the Agbogbloshie/Old Fadama settlement squeezed between the Korle Lagoon and Accra's CBD. Richard Grant's (ibid.) portrait of the twin settlements, dubbed 'Sodom and Gomorrah' in the Ghanaian popular press, serves as an example of how different informal settlements look in Accra when compared with Cape Town. The first notable distinction is that, unlike in Cape Town, where urban data are plentiful and updated frequently even if they are not completely perfect, Grant (ibid.: 115–16) found 'virtually no data on Accra slums,' and 'no current accurate surveys or statistics' about Sodom and Gomorrah. He gauged that more than 40,000 people lived on the

146 hectares of frequently flooded lowland when he conducted his research, with about 15,000 in the somewhat formalized Agbogbloshie area and the majority in the more informal area, Old Fadama.

Historically, Ga families claimed all the land around the Korle Lagoon, which they considered sacred. British colonial planners were limited in efforts to plan the development of the lagoon area, creating only two small settlements – Agbogbloshie (from the Ga language, 'site of the Agbogblo shrine') for the Ga, and Fadama (from the Hausa, 'floodplain') for northern Ghanaian migrants (ibid.). In the former case, titles were issued by the colonial government honoring rights granted by Ga chiefs. Although Ghana's first independent government claimed the area around the lagoon, issued itself a certificate of title to the area, authorized several industrial development projects, and reclaimed some land by dredging the lagoon, their only very limited efforts to use the land led Ga traditional chiefs toward a 'renewed claim to the land' in the 1990s (ibid.: 120). That renewed Ga claim arose just as the population of the informal settlement of Old Fadama exploded. From a nearly empty swamp in 1990, it became a bustling multiethnic settlement of more than 25,000 people within a decade.

A 'select elite' among the Ga actually claim all of the land of Accra, through the GaDangme Council (GDC), an alliance of Ga leaders with elites of the smaller Adangme ethnic group, formed in 1999 to fight both government and squatter claims to Sodom and Gomorrah (Yeboah 2008b: 436; Grant 2009: 125). The GDC sees all other residents of Accra as 'trespassers' despite the extreme challenge of identifying who, exactly, has Ga or Adangme rights to which portion of Accra in the first place (Grant 2009: 126; Yeboah 2008b: 441). The Ga's decentralized landholding system traditionally relied upon communal ownership through which a lagoon god's priests, local chiefs, and family (House) leaders oversaw the allocation of rights. The colonial and postcolonial governments took rights to much of contemporary Accra through 'compulsory acquisition,' with two-thirds of Ga land in the city under the management of the government's Land Commission, but 'most land claims are shrouded in cadastral secrecy' (Yeboah 2008b: 437–8). The GDC, Ga lagoon priests, local chiefs, and family heads were 'plagued by perennial litigation' among themselves above and beyond any conflict with the state or the trespassers (ibid.: 441). This has meant that informal settlements like Sodom and Gomorrah have grown around Accra over the last twenty years in circumstances which lack clarity over rights to the land underneath their nonpermanent or permanent houses. In Sodom and Gomorrah, this led to an ongoing bitter three-way legal scramble between the GDC, the government, and the informal settlers, many of whom have organized themselves into powerful nongovernmental organizations. This legal scramble manifests itself in three cityscapes of Accra – the formal, globalizing city, the informal-indigenous city, and the informal-stranger city – that rest uncomfortably amid each other.

Defining an informal settlement in Dar es Salaam is perhaps an even more difficult task than doing so in Cape Town or Accra. Dar es Salaam has an estimated population of more than three million people, and it is often listed among the most rapidly growing major cities in the world, but data are far more problematic for this city than for the other two (Kondoro 1995; Maira 2001; Myers 2005). Also, in much of Dar, visible distinctions between formal and informal areas are hard to discern because of the preponderance of the latter, and because of their relative lack of dire squalor to juxtapose with equally less common gated communities or posh estates (recognizing that here, too, both squalor and splendor are increasing). Like Cape Town and Accra, Dar was essentially a colonial creation, and its spatial structure does remain nominally divisible by the colonial racial-spatial categories masked as distinct zoning areas on colonial plans: Zone A for low-density residences (read: whites), Zone B for middle-density (Asians), and Zone C for high-density areas (Africans). In Swahili parlance, one speaks of the *rangi tatu*, the 'three colors' of the city's geography, as Uzunguni, Uhindini, and Uswahilini – literally, the places of the whites, Asians, and 'Swahili' (Africans), respectively (Smiley 2007, 2009). However, the first two of these may no longer really be defined in racial terms; 'Uswahilini' informal neighborhoods actually predominate in both; and severe inequalities, while growing over the past few decades, have less of the graphic and extensive spatiality of either Cape Town or Accra (Brennan and Burton 2007: 4; Smiley 2009; Moyer 2006: 167–8, 2004).

Despite being the majority presence in the city from its beginnings in the 1850s, Africans faced legal barriers to their permanence there under German (1885–1916) and British (1920–61) colonial rule, as well as obvious inequalities in investment in infrastructure, housing, and services for Uswahilini (Burton 2005; Kironde 1994). Yet the colonial city's controls never worked as planned, and the lived space

of Uswahilini produced and was produced far more by the consciousness and practices of its residents. Under the *ujamaa* socialist regime
discussed in Chapter 2, nationalism and single-party rule played a
prominent role in those beliefs and practices in Dar's African areas
(Brennan 2002; Geiger 1997). But the steady drone of disappointment
with nationalism's practical policy outcomes in Dar as the main city
of independent Tanzania meant that even in the explicitly socialist
era (1967–85) the urban landscape witnessed a 'long-running struggle'
over 'the informalization of urban space' (Brennan and Burton 2007:
6; Tripp 1997).

The informal settlement appropriately named Rangi Tatu typifies
much of the process of informalization in Dar es Salaam. The sisal
farm of a German settler by 1910, this peri-urban land was national-
ized under *ujamaa* in 1967 and turned into an *ujamaa* village in the
1970s (Kombe and Kreibich 2000). That small planned settlement
has been overwhelmed by the urbanization of Rangi Tatu in the last
thirty years. The vast majority of new urbanites here bought land
to build houses in much the same way as the residents of Uholanzi
in Zanzibar with whom Ali Hasan Ali and I spoke in 2007: illegally.
Wilbard Kombe and Volker Kreibich (ibid.: 68) showed that 50 percent
had no record of their transaction, 40 percent had a local, informal
written document with no legal weight, and fewer than 10 percent
had obtained their land in the formal manner and obtained title deeds
to it. Yet there is little concern with 'security of tenure' among its
people, with little or no perceived threat to their right to occupy their
dwellings. It seems evident that Rangi Tatu now looks like much of
the rest of Dar, where somewhere between 65 and 75 percent of the
people, at least, are estimated to reside and to survive informally,
outside of regulated formal channels.

What is everyday life like in an informal settlement? It is a common notion that Cape Town is becoming more of an informal city
by the day. Researchers document an increasing casualization of labor
(with increases in part-time, seasonal, temporary employment) in the
post-apartheid era, so that the city's still noticeable 'formal economy
is surrounded by extremely high levels of unemployment, poverty and
underdevelopment' (Jordhus-Lier 2010). One obvious manifestation
of this apparent informalization comes in the settlement structure.
'Built outside the law,' as Owen Crankshaw and Sue Parnell (1998:
441) put it, shack settlements 'are vividly opposed to the order and

regularity of state-built formal housing and, within the constraints of poverty, they reflect the individual aspirations and styles of the residents.' Shack settlements are densely packed, overcrowded, underserviced, and sometimes volatile (Robins 2008; Lemansky and Oldfield 2009). The formality of coloured townships has, notably, not been a remedy for pervasive poverty or systemic violence. While the shack settlements share with formally developed townships in 'the grim everyday social, economic and political realities experienced by the majority of South Africa's citizens,' they also manifest local African capacity for social organization and reliance on rural–urban ties, whether in politics, service provision, or organized crime (Robins 2008: 2).

Like most South African cities, albeit perhaps more dramatically so in topographical terms, post-apartheid Cape Town is still a 'starkly polarized city' with 'poverty-stricken and overcrowded settlements' in the Flats and around its edges, and an affluent, mostly white core and near-core suburbs hugging Table Mountain (Turok 2001: 2349; Lemansky and Oldfield 2009: 636). Accra, too, is very much becoming a tale of two (or maybe three) cities. On the one hand, the last quarter-century has seen the rise of a nouveau riche. High-quality, low-density peri-urban residential sprawl, gated communities full of foreign investors or high-flying transnational Ghanaians, or those with sizable remittances from abroad are prominent features of the spatiality of liberalizing Accra where at least some people would seem to be living quite well (Yeboah 2003; Briggs and Yeboah 2001; Grant 2009: 29; Konadu-Agyemang 2001).

At the other end of the spectrum, in the expanding array of informal squatter settlements around Accra, everyday life is increasingly grim. Whether one considers the rapidly informalizing old formal areas under 'traditional' control or the new informal squatter areas, this Accra is dramatically different from that of the gated communities and fancy privately developed neighborhoods. There is severe overcrowding, and a high proportion of the residents live in nonpermanent houses with little infrastructure or services in 'deplorable destitution' (Yeboah 2008b: 440). Geographer Ian Yeboah (ibid.: 440) speaks of walking into one informal area as stepping 'into a litter of garbage and human excrement.' Local media wrote of Sodom and Gomorrah (Agbobloshie/Old Fadama) as a 'no-man's land' of 'invaders' and a 'hideout for armed robbers, prostitutes, drug pushers and all kinds of squatters' (cited in Grant 2009: 122). Yet these highly fractious, violent areas were able to form a common organizational front to combat the GaDangme council and the Ghanaian government attempts to evict them, evidencing Grant's (ibid.: 127) claim that both Old Fadama and Agbogbloshie had had 'robust social and political orders since the early stage of their formation.'

This sense of a normative ordering from their origin onwards is clearly there for the informal settlements that characterize the greater part of the cityscape of Dar es Salaam. In her study of place-making among the residents of Dar es Salaam's 'shanty town' of Uwanja wa Fisi ('Field of Hyenas'), Eileen Moyer (2006: 167) notes that neighborhoods like it, such as Rangi Tatu, 'are home to a large majority of Dar es Salaam's residents,' and they are 'places teeming with activity.' They may be defined by informal rules, in many ways off the grid of the state's understanding, but 'there is no doubt that they are true neighborhoods.' Such sites are keys to a sense of self and belonging, rootedness, and community, even if fleeting. Moyer (ibid.: 168) notes that in the explosion of building since the 1980s, 'the houses in Uswahilini are an engineering wonder ... perched on the edge of rivers and on the sides of steep hills with the ground sometimes visibly eroding away from under them.' Outsiders might see Uswahilini as 'a place where ordinary rules of order and discipline do not apply, where the world is turned on its head' (ibid.: 171). Yet its rules of order have become normalized. An otherwise seemingly authoritarian regime has eschewed intervening much in the sprawling growth of Rangi Tatu, for example, leaving officially 'unrecognized' community organizations to contend with the pervasive 'conmen' orchestrating its expansion (Kombe and Kreibich 2000: 67–9). If informal settlements are the shack scourges that dot Cape Town and house about one fifth of its residents, or the squalid squatter settlements like Sodom and Gomorrah that are home to less than two-fifths of Accra citizens, to most Dar people – three- or four-fifths of the population – informal settlements *are* the life of the city.

What are the key debates over planning responses to informal settlements? The most visible aspects of planning dynamics to deal with informality in Cape Town come in the form of the massive Reconstruction and Development Programme (RDP) for housing construction and the equally ambitious Breaking New Ground (BNG) housing program that replaced it. As part of a commitment to creating 'a better life for all' in the New South Africa after apartheid, the successive African National Congress governments have worked with municipal and provincial governments to eliminate shack housing, by gradually replacing under-serviced nonpermanent informal areas with formal, serviced neighborhoods with permanent 'core houses' on regular, surveyed, titled plots. The outline of procedures contains rhetoric that explicitly seeks to create distance from the apartheid era. The SACN's 2006 *State of South African Cities Report* (2006: 2/27) noted that in Cape Town 'the Western Cape Provincial government has made provision for an "Informal Residential Zone" to be included in all municipal zoning schemes, and which ceases to exist as soon as the settlement is upgraded.'

In spite of appearances – especially for residents or planners from most other African cities – that suggest the RDP/BNG housing is an amazing and progressive step by planners genuinely aiming to literally make a statement about a 'better life for all' in bricks and mortar, these related programs have endured withering criticisms from urban scholars and politicians, from their residents and even from some of the very planners involved. While no African governments, with the possible exceptions of those of Libya and Egypt, have even been in a position to contemplate building so many homes for the poor in their cities over the last twenty years (and no private sector housing construction sector on the continent comes close to South Africa's in potential capacity to partner with government in doing so), many elements of the critique of this, the continent's most ambitious effort to tackle the problems of informal settlement in the last quarter-century, hit home in examining Cape Town.

To begin with, the program has fallen far short of housing demand (Oldfield 2002). Second, the old 'ghosts' of segregation, poor government–society relations, and social tension just don't disappear (Robinson 1998). Cape Town still has relatively weak institutions of local government, conflicting relations between ethnic and racial communities and municipalities, poor public participation, discord between and within communities, and high levels of crime and violence (Van der Merwe and Davids 2006: 28). The recipe for curing apartheid's hangover has been elusive. In developing a national agenda for urban strategies, South Africa's African National Congress government has tried a mix of neoliberal policies with others – Robins (2008: 5) sees a heady stew of 'privatization and economic liberalization policies' with what he refers to as 'discourses of *ubuntu* communitarianism and ... programs typically associated with the African development

state.' The RDP housing program is the most obvious place one can
see that heady mixture, and it is not always a pretty picture. Many
Cape Town residents resisted moving into RDP houses because they
were considered too small – in isiXhosa, RDP houses were nicknamed
Veza ('show foot' ... because one shows a foot out the door since
the house isn't long enough; Watson 2007). RDP areas often suffer
from problems with unemployment, poverty, service delivery, disease,
and violence that make them functionally indistinguishable from the
shack settlements they are meant to replace, and residents seem to
go about turning the RDP areas back into informal residential zones
by reintroducing nonpermanent structures and informal, unregulated
business transactions, including for land and housing. What has gone
wrong?

For some analysts, the explanation lies in the 'clash of rationalities'
argument discussed above, between the planners and government on
the one hand and the informal shack dwellers on the other. Vanessa
Watson (ibid.: 69) argues that planners in South Africa, whether
progressive or conservative, see informal or shack housing 'as unacceptable and in need of replacement by formal housing projects,'
with the goal of 'extending the grid of formalized and regulated
development.' The planners' counterparts in the shacks are mostly
Xhosa residents who long for a rural home (*ikhaya*) and find more
of the accustomed rural sociability in the shacks than in the RDP's
gridded neighborhoods (ibid.: 69; Watson 2003). Watson's (2007: 73)
Crossroads case study showed that 'the splitting of extended families
into individual, formal housing units is breaking social and family
networks' and destroying social capital built up in 'stretched households' of shack settlements which connect rural and urban relatives.

Robins (2006, 2008) disagrees that a 'clash of rationalities' is at
the root of the problem with RDP housing. His strongest response
to Watson comes in a study of a public–private partnership RDP
scheme in the middle-upper-income Cape Town suburb of Milnerton.
The idea was to turn the shack settlement of Marconi Beam there
into 'an orderly low income suburb,' known as Joe Slovo Park (JSP).
After a decade, though, 'instead of the anticipated neat rows of
brick houses with grassed front lawns,' Robins (2006: 97) found that
JSP was 'barely distinguishable from the informal settlement that
had been demolished to make way for' it, as it reverted 'back to its
original "unruly" state.'

This case, Robins admits, speaks to a 'disjuncture' between

planners' ideals and the actual lived reality, but he resists character-
izing it in Watson's (2003: 395) terms as a case of 'clashing cultures
and conflicting rationalities.' In the JSP case, the poor faced extended
families' needs. They found that extending the core house in brick
was too expensive, so they could either extend it with iron sheets or
other nonpermanent material, or move back to the informal settlements. So JSP got reinformalized 'as a result of chronic poverty and
limited access to income' – what Robins (2006: 106) calls the 'more
mundane material legacies of apartheid.'

Robins also argues, *contra* Watson, that the shack dwellers' differences with planners are not 'insurmountable,' because 'people living
in Crossroads, and elsewhere, are ... capable of switching registers,
repertoires, and identities depending on the specific contexts, audiences, and political objectives' (ibid.: 100). In a related publication,
he analyzes the case of the South African Homeless People's Forum
(SAHPF), and specifically the Victoria Mxenge (VMx) Federation
in the Cape Town neighborhood of Phillipi. The SAHPF partnered
with the increasingly well-known and well-connected transnational
activist organization Slum Dwellers International to build grassroots
empowerment and improvement. He shows that despite the SDI's
consciousness about 'deep democracy,' the VMx Federation had
'established a centralized style of leadership that tightly controlled
federation resources in fundamentally anti-democratic ways' (Robins
2008: 78). He uses the case as a reminder that civil society has
'its democratic and emancipatory face, as well as its illiberal and
authoritarian underbelly' (ibid.: 79). It is an example of a mixing
and matching on the part of shack dwellers that would not be possible
if deeply different cultural rationalities prevailed in all cases.

For planning to produce viable solutions to the problems shack
settlements represent for residents and planners alike, both Watson
and Robins argue for a transformation of consciousness. In the current
complicated dynamics, deliberative, progressive, and participatory
planning might look good to outsiders, but people in Cape Town's
informal neighborhoods like Crossroads 'stand to lose much by enter-
ing these deliberative spaces and abandoning patronage politics and
popular demonstrations' (ibid.: 83). As a consequence, standoffs
and standstills predominate in the city's efforts to find solutions to
informal settlements' conundrums.

Most planned residential neighborhood developments in Accra
involved significant government engagement and investment until the

1990s and 2000s. Although new planned housing areas still began with government purchases of Ga lands, in the new era the government has worked with private development companies to create a middle- and upper-class housing market (Grant and Yankson 2003: 73). As real estate prices were 'pushed beyond the affordability of a significant proportion' of Accra residents, more and more people were forced to rent, and, increasingly, to settle in illegal squatter settlements (Konadu-Agyemang 2001: 528). The planning responses to these mushrooming informal settlements provide a fascinating mixture of state-led modernist tactics and grassroots activism.

Ghana's government approached the Korle Lagoon and settlements around it with several global agendas at play. The lagoon has been, for two decades, the site of an ecological restoration project that has received major international funding (Sam 2002). As part of Accra's participation in the UN-Habitat's Sustainable Cities Program, the city's Strategic Planning Framework marked out the lagoon and its surroundings as green space for recreational use. The terms of the government's loan for the ecological project 'require the removal of settlers,' whose neighborhood it considered 'an eye sore as well as a major source of pollution' (Grant 2009: 125, 122). The indigenous GaDangme Council, for its part, also advocates the removal of the settlers, but at the same time it considered the government to have encroached on Ga land rights, for which it sought significant compensation.

In many cities in Africa, particularly, say, twenty years ago, a situation including these two groups of actors with these agendas would spell the end of the informal settlement and its forced removal. Intriguingly, the settlers themselves organized across ethnic, class, and religious lines to combat eviction, thus far successfully. Grant (ibid.: 126–35) details the means by which Old Fadama leaders collaborated with Ghana's Centre for Public Interest Law, the Geneva-based Centre on Housing Rights and Evictions, and, indeed, the Cape Town office of Slum Dwellers International to work for the cessation of evictions and foster a sense of solidarity across the squatter areas of Greater Accra. By 2005, he found evidence of positive shifts in the squatter areas' relationships with local and national government agencies, despite persistent 'internal community obstacles' (ibid.: 133). Hence Accra seems to hold the potential for developing negotiated, hybrid governance via radical relational politics, along the lines suggested by Pieterse's model. The possibility is still quite strong that such negotiated hybrid understandings toward informal settlement may be undermined, but there are numerous examples of the health of Accra's potential for activist democracy.

Despite socialist rhetoric that dominated planning in Dar es Salaam from 1967 through the mid-1980s, the city experienced a 'continuation of colonial style planning under a colonial style planning law' (McAuslan 2007: 175). Yet that also meant that urban planning in the postcolonial era functioned as ineffectually as it had under colonialism to impose its order on the majority. In Rangi Tatu, the government 'maintained a blind eye on the invasion on planned, surveyed and allocated plots' in the area despite its nominal capacity to fully control the urban development process (Kombe and Kreibich 2000: 76). Attitudes toward the informal economy by elites and government in Dar have fluctuated over time (Brown and Lyons 2010). Since whites and Asians comprise less than 3 percent of the city's population, this is a fluctuation that plays out 'between two very different strata of [African] society,' described by the city's long-time legal consultant Patrick McAuslan (2007: 173) as 'the urban elite – the politicians, the public servants, the small but visible private sector economic elite' posed against the 'ordinary people, for the most part poor, struggling to find somewhere to live, something to work at and some income to survive on.'

Yet these are highly ambivalent elites, often still quite sympathetic to the urban poor. Kombe and Kreibich (2000: 41) see an elite planning apparatus that says 'do and don't at the same time' in Dar es Salaam. Sometimes the regime is 'sympathetic and tolerant' toward informal areas, building on rhetoric of inclusivity and the participation of civil society that meshes with global agendas like that of the United Nations Habitat Sustainable Cities Program with its stress on community 'enablement,' and on *ujamaa*'s inspiring collaborative grassroots dimensions (ibid.: 41; McAuslan 2007: 177; Myers 2005; Brown and Lyons 2010). Yet despite the rhetoric about 'openness, fairness and impartiality' in city planning, much of the time what occurs is 'a heavy-handed, insensitive and bullying approach to the exercise of powers against the urban poor' (McAuslan 2007: 178–9). Brown and Lyons (2010: 42) cite as an example the March 2006 order from the prime minister's office for major municipalities to evict petty traders – an order delayed for six months by public outcry, but eventually carried out, with the result that more than 200,000 informal traders were prosecuted and evicted by mid-2007.

McAuslan is particularly stunned by the failures for significant progressive outcomes from the do-and-don't tug of war in the face of Dar es Salaam having received praise as the pilot city for the UN-Habitat's Sustainable Cities Program: 'despite more than 6 years of efforts by a specific Habitat project which was in fact used as a model for the Habitat Agenda, attitudes to planning and the urban poor on the part of the political and administrative elites in the Government had not changed one iota' (McAuslan 2007: 181). The government still wants to control the processes of land allocation, under the banner of equality and poverty alleviation, yet Lusugga Kironde (2004: 10) has documented that it surveyed and allocated plots to scarcely 3 percent of the more than 240,000 residents who submitted applications for land between 1990 and 2001. Even a recent 'success' in scaling up to the allocation of some 20,000 plots in a three-year period barely made a dent in demand (Kironde 2006). The Mkurabita project, under de Soto's tutelage, did formally register slightly more than half of its target goal of properties in the city (219,000 of 400,000) in a five-year period, but nearly 100,000 new informal households are estimated to have arrived in the city during the same period (Muhajir 2011). The tiny formal private sector in residential construction concentrates solely on the equally tiny elites' housing needs, as the Mkurabita project has been most successful in registering elite and gentrifying areas. The net result is the endurance of a woeful housing shortfall and a city where the informal tactics of residents, like the 25,000 or so who live in Rangi Tatu, produce the spatiality and sociality of urbanism, without the capacity for 'changing the world for the better.'

Conclusion: toward hybrid governance in a relational city?

The multiplexity of African cities is nowhere more in evidence than in the discussion of informality – what it means, where it is or isn't, and what to do about it. Even if it is hard to define, document, or delimit its reach and scope, we can still say that informality means different things in different cities and start to grasp some dimensions of this. In Cape Town, the conversation has to include the racist past, in Accra, the question of indigenous land rights, and in Dar, *ujamaa* socialism, to make the meaning of an informal settlement in each respective city intelligible. People's lives in informal settlements vary too. The planning dilemmas take off in different directions in each, again following the varied histories of state–society relations. In all cases, at the surface, cities seem to face choices among some kind of

Afropolis where informality would essentially be the organizing logic; a de Soto-land of formalized informality; or – the likeliest scenario – hybrid understandings that more comfortably weave together the already interpenetrating organizing logics. As we have seen, though, these organizing logics are not the same in the three 'informal' cities we have looked at here.

The last, hybrid option would certainly be Ali Hasan Ali's choice. To Ali, the first direction would lead to a city where many more people live in chicken coops in the gutters below gated mansions. The second path might hide the chicken coops in ravines like those in Uholanzi. The most likely way is a hybrid way to make the city *relational*, where the Uswahilini areas relate to the de Soto-land planned globalized spaces, or to the rest of the city. In Ali's (2007) very straightforward words about his own informal settlement of Mwera:

> It would be better if there was cooperation between government and unauthorized landholders to facilitate planning ... We want there to be cooperation between the government and the landholders in order to put a good plan in place. This depends on the education of citizens to understand planning, and the improvement of the government's relationship with the people.

Such a simple set of renegotiations is unlikely to occur in Zanzibar in the way Ali might hope. But it is not an impossibility. It is doubtful that, scarcely ten years ago, migrant community leaders of Accra's informal Sodom and Gomorrah area would have imagined finding allies as far away as Geneva and Cape Town in advocating for their rights to their land and houses. Many residents of Cape Town's Crossroads area, some twenty years ago, would probably not have imagined that a government program formed by their liberation movement's African National Congress leadership to create 'a better life for all' and the better houses to go with it would be deemed by many residents and experts to be unpopular and unsuccessful. Residents of Rangi Tatu's *ujamaa* village in the 1970s are unlikely to have imagined that the city would engulf their settlement in quite the disorderly manner that it has. My point is that informality and informal settlement do not have inevitable, predictable, reproducible fates in any African city.

Showing how formal and informal understandings 'work together and how this working together' (Mbembe and Nuttall 2008: 9) varies significantly across the continent and even within its individual cities over time and space has been a key element of this chapter. We have seen that easy, one-size-fits-all analyses, like those of de Soto (or Davis for that matter), are inadequate. We might need new terms for the apparently fading dichotomy of formal and informal, given how interwoven they are. Yet these terms are still so pervasive, and so much a part of shaping the discourse, that it is hard to throw them away. Differences and distinctions still do exist, even if they are not insurmountable in some inevitable way. Clearly a history and legacy of abjection appears in the story of informal settlements, but that is not the end point of the narrative, as it seems to me the Accra example of Sodom and Gomorrah may eventually prove.

The increasing informalization widely noted in many cities, including the three on which I have focused, seems to me to really be another way of saying the cities are becoming poorer and more unequal. Certainly, there does not seem to be one clear set of mechanisms to reduce poverty and inequality, whether by formalizing informal areas or processes, allowing the informal systems to completely take over, or working toward hybrid governance, but this last trend would seem to hold the most participatory, emancipatory, relational potential.

Getting there will mean much more discussion of politics. This chapter has had a more socio-economic geography focus, while skirting political issues in the city. These concerns are at the heart of the next chapter. In Chapter 4, I continue to operate somewhat in the terrain of informal settlements, but with my focus on the questions of urban governance, service delivery, and justice.

FOUR
Governing Africa's cities

Introduction

My first experience in sub-Saharan Africa came just after a 1982 coup attempt in Nairobi against the government of Kenya's president at the time, Daniel arap Moi. When the coup failed, Moi's government crushed his opponents with a vengeance. The elite western suburbs of Nairobi seemed undisturbed for the months I was there, save for the minor inconvenience of a dusk-to-dawn curfew in the city center. Meanwhile, wholesale evictions and demolitions characterized the response to the coup in the poor and under-serviced informal settlements where the city's overwhelming majority resided, the government justifying its actions in the name of environmental health (Otiso 2002; Myers 2008b). More than twenty-five years later, Nairobi erupted in political violence again, after a highly corrupt national election in December 2007 returned Moi's former vice-president, Mwai Kibaki, for a second term as Kenya's president. This time both the death toll and the numbers of urban population left homeless were far higher than they had been in 1982. A year after that violence, President Kibaki launched a major, US$412 billion initiative to make Nairobi a world-class global city by 2030 (Gathanju 2009).

I begin this chapter with these events for several reasons. First, they bring up the politics of *governance*. Like postcolonialism and informality, the words at the heart of the last two chapters, governance is a very contested and complicated term central to debates and discussions about urban Africa. The word started out meaning something about the 'manner of governing,' but it has come to be linked with decision-making processes that are not limited to the state, 'measures that involve setting the rules for the exercise of power and settling conflicts over such rules' (Hyden 1999: 185; Hyden et al. 2004; Hendriks 2010; Davies 2008). The last three decades have seen the steady rise of a discourse of '*good* governance' in African cities, ideologically deployed in both the rhetoric and practices of democratization, privatization, decentralization, and liberalization. The eruption of Nairobi in August 1982, coupled with the post-election violence there in early 2008 and the bold plan for making it into the West's idea of a modern world-class city, suggests a growing gap in the city, and in many cities of the continent, between the rhetoric of good governance and the political and economic realities most residents face in their daily lives. Nairobi has one of the world's leading think tanks on urban policy, UN-Habitat, in its Diplomatic District of Gigiri, and (both because of Habitat and for reasons outside of its influence) it has seen major large-scale experiments with its governance regimes come and go for three decades while its famous slums, such as Mathare and Kibera, grow larger and more deprived (Hendriks 2010; Njeru 2006; Mitullah 2008; Murunga 1999, 2007; Kinuthia 1992). What *good* is this good governance Nairobi residents are experiencing? Should African cities like Nairobi move toward the 'hybrid governance' of Chapter 3 (through finding common ground between formal and informal rules of the game) in the face of this kind of glaring political-economic gap, and if so, how would they move in that direction? Why does it seem that there is a 'deep difference' between the state, elites, and the urban poor majority, a difference that turns to brutality?

Second, the most tangible discussions of good governance in African cities have been in regard to the delivery of *urban services* (sanitation, water, electricity, solid waste, land management, and the like). We have seen some of this already in Chapter 3. Following independence in most African cities, urban service delivery had been seen primarily as a responsibility that governments performed, however unevenly or inadequately, through the 1980s. In the years since, African cities have been at the forefront in the world for energetic efforts to privatize the delivery of basic urban services. In Nairobi and elsewhere, these efforts appear to have increased the inequalities of service delivery to levels of disparity exceeding those of the colonial era (Kinuthia 1992; Murunga 1999; Otiso 2002).

Finally, this leads me to the question of socio-environmental *justice* in Nairobi, and in urban sub-Saharan Africa. The years since 1982 have seen the blossoming of a vast literature dedicated to questions of sustainable urban development (SUD) in sub-Saharan Africa, and a slew of policies for implementing SUD that have largely emanated from Nairobi's posh suburban UN offices, under the banner of good governance. President Kibaki's multibillion-dollar initiative for Nairobi is couched in the language of SUD (Gathanju 2009). By contrast, in most of sub-Saharan Africa these decades have brought much less critical attention, particularly in terms of scholarship or policy, to questions of urban socio-environmental justice, in terms of equity and fairness in the distribution of outcomes, opportunities and capabilities in the city (although there are some exceptions, notably in South Africa, as I discuss below). I find this absence strange considering the starkly obvious and interconnected social and environmental *injustice* evident in many African cities, such as Nairobi in 1982 or 2010, given growing inequalities between elites and the severely poor, along with the inequitable distribution of negative environmental consequences of development.

In this chapter, I first discuss governance, service delivery, and justice as they have been debated in African cities. I highlight how good governance and justice concerns play out in service delivery in a few settings, and then in a longer case study on Zanzibar. Ultimately, I am testing out the routes to the relational city of Pieterse's (2008a) diagram, and suggesting that we may need to change the map of discussions about governance in urban studies toward nuanced empirical analysis to get us there.

Urban governance

The term governance is used many different ways. In urban studies, it is most commonly understood as a term for getting at the shifting power dynamics of decision-making in an era when the roles of states are in flux. Just how these power dynamics have shifted has generated considerable debate. Much of the debate centers on the degree and character of change in the role of the state, with the theorized 'shift from government to governance,' whereby the nation-state has been hollowed out 'as functions are dispersed to supranational entities, localities, and non-state actors' (Davies 2008: 24; Stren 2003). As a number of scholars have noted, debate on governance and service delivery in African cities can be broken down into competing positions on this question about the state.

Neoliberal good governance For one camp, the conventional World Bank version of good governance is assumed to be the goal. To those holding this view, governance has been and is at present severely flawed in most African cities, a point with which many scholars would find it hard to disagree. The World Bank view argues that urban governance is therefore in need of reforms that bring it in line with neoliberal ideals: in sum, the more that urban service provision is governed by market forces, the better. In fact, this is not so much an argument as it is a deeply held assumption that most Western experts and local elite policy-makers have been 'steeped' in so long that this is seen as 'the only pathway to development' (Yeboah 2006: 50). For at least twenty years, the rhetoric has been loud and strong in Africa advocating this shift away from government or state-dominated urban management. Foreign donors and local leaders alike have heavily emphasized strengthening the private sector, opening the door to transnational capital, enabling democratic, municipal governments, and empowering community groups at the same time by creating new networks and partnerships for urban development across the whole landscape of city management, from land (Brown 2005) and water (Yeboah 2006) to transport (Rizzo 2002), electricity supply (McDonald 2009) or solid waste services (Adama 2007).

Good governance, as the idealized agenda for cities in Africa put forward in different but related ways by the World Bank Cities Alliance, the United Nations Habitat program, and Western donors, has come to the fore simultaneously with the neoliberal development agenda. The neoliberal good governance approach is essentially that which I discussed in Chapter 3, as in de Soto's approach to land. In reference to Western urban neoliberalism, geographers Jamie Peck and Adam Tickell (2002) distinguished between what they termed 'roll-back' and 'roll-out' neoliberalism. Using the US/UK experiences as examples, the former was characteristic of the Reagan or Thatcher 'roll-back' of state engagement in urban management and service provision, while the latter is associated with the Clinton/Blair reintroduction of state institutions in 'Third Way contortions' that created 'neoliberalism with a human face.' Urbanists Neil Brenner and Nik Theodore (2002: 362) note the ways in which these two versions of neoliberalism stop and start, and go back and forth in terms of which has the lead in any given context. In European cities, Patrick Le Galès (1995: 60, cited in Stren 2003: 17) noted a 'greater diversity in the organization of services, a greater flexibility, a variety of actors, even a transformation of the forms that local democracy might assume' as urban neoliberalism took root, in line with Brenner and Theodore's argument.

To the World Bank in Africa, though, good governance certainly started as a one-size-fits-all idea, 'presented as a commonsensical notion that requires no definition' (Blundo and Le Meur 2009: 7). African cities have seen an increase in the significance of private sector, civil society, or other non-state actors in service delivery in the last two decades, with what seems to me like a surprising lack of widespread active and organized popular opposition (other than in South Africa). Roll-out neoliberalism would appear to have had the upper hand for most of the last two decades, albeit with many variations in institutional maps of implementation. In other words, the Cities Alliance/Habitat/Western donor line of approach has involved making and remaking state institutions that can work in partnership with a new array of private sector and civil society entities in facilitating the delivery of urban services, but exactly what institutions or entities, and exactly how the implementation processes have evolved, vary on the ground.

These neoliberal approaches to good governance, sustainable urban development and urban environmental management have risen to prominence for a number of reasons, but the most important one is donor dependency, and a related dependent mindset among local planners and decision-makers (Yeboah 2006). Rarely, if ever, do initiatives coming from African urban communities recognize this form of neoliberal planning or management as being in their best interests. Most are heavily donor-driven, and local engagement is elite- and state-dominated (Nnkya 2007). The origins of the plans, in many instances, can be traced to the World Bank's Urban Management Program, which was a crucial force in the creation of the United Nations Habitat's Sustainable Cities Program, which in turn introduced many cities to the new governance regime in the first place (Dahiya and Pugh 2000; Myers 2005). Certainly, state-delivered urban services that had been reasonably effective in the 1960s and 1970s were faltering in cities across the continent in the 1980s amid structural adjustment programs, and city and national governments as well as citizens were seeking improvements (Mitullah 2008). In most cities, though, the residents themselves had very little to do with the policy decisions made, even in the most politically democratized (i.e. in electoral terms) countries (Yeboah 2006; Fredericks 2009).

This is particularly ironic because many neoliberal governance reforms in Africa are, on paper, built around decentralization, collaborative visioning, and stakeholder democracy (Mitullah 2008). The participatory rhetoric that sounds so good within these programs often ends up being a form of that roll-out neoliberalism with a human face; to wit, the World Bank urban agenda – state withdrawal, privatization, and private investment coupled with new or re-engineered government institutions to facilitate the transition – was central to solutions offered by the 2002 World Summit on Sustainable Development in Johannesburg (Middleton and O'Keefe 2003). There and elsewhere, the stakeholders, the vision plans or action plans, and even the political decentralization efforts are ironically highly centralized in donor and state-elite hands (Hendriks 2010; Mitullah 2008). Any possibility of neoliberal SUD *actually* prioritizing themes such as the 'freedom to participate in national and local decision-making processes' depends a great deal 'on the particular balance of socio-political forces which must be determined in each concrete case' (Kipfer 1996: 122). There is surely variation, but in most sub-Saharan African cities, the balance is tipped against the interests of the urban poor majority. Two decades of neoliberal good governance have done little to rebalance that equation in most cases; many argue that inequalities and injustices within African cities have increased under neoliberalism. Some even argue that 'good governance' is in effect a replacement for real democracy – what matters to it is the effective maintenance of control and a welcoming stance toward foreign direct investment (Abrahamsen 2000). In any case, donors clearly sought to 'depoliticize the reform process,' which in practice actually made 'reform' into a heavily politicized set of 'dance steps' (Murunga 2007: 277). The donor-driven character of much urban policy and urban research in sub-Saharan Africa keeps the neoliberal governance approaches to the fore in the dance, regardless of injustice or the absence of urban democracy in decision-making.

The neoliberal good governance argument brings out one critique emanating largely from a historical materialist framework, often in the form of a broadside against all that is wrong with the neoliberal approach (e.g. Bond 2002). A second critique includes scholars taking variations on what for lack of a better catch-all term I will call a post-structuralist line, looking for ways to deconstruct the hegemonic 'good governance' narrative while imagining the indigenous 'informal' governance in new ways (e.g. Simone 2004). I've drawn a bit on both of these critiques above in criticizing neoliberal good governance, but let me discuss each approach in more detail for its possibilities in offering an analytical alternative to neoliberalism.

Materialist critiques of neoliberal good governance Materialist critiques of neoliberalism follow a line familiar from Harvey's *Brief History of Neoliberalism* or Davis's (2005) *Planet of Slums*. One of Harvey's (2005: 154) few sentences in that book in relation to Africa argues that neoliberalism has 'done nothing at all to generate positive changes.' The World Bank is Davis's (2005: 149) primary villain, and its structural adjustment programs are held responsible for Africa's vast urban crisis, in collaboration with local elites who avert their eyes as they 'move to gated communities in the suburbs.' But as the geographer Rosalind Fredericks (2009: x) puts it, Davis 'doesn't allow us to see the specific way that neoliberal reforms have worked in particular contexts, the idioms through which they are understood, or how these processes are contested and reconfigured in the process' and he 'tends to depict the urban African as a passive victim who has no role or recourse in dynamics occurring on a planetary scale.' Materialist urbanists whose career focus lies in Africa, as one would expect, have more fully developed and richly researched critiques, albeit still drawing inspiration from Davis and Harvey. This is most evident with Patrick Bond (2000a, 2000b, 2002). Bond (2000b: 37–8) has critiqued post-apartheid South Africa's neoliberal Municipal Infrastructure Investment Framework, for example, for correlating the number of urban services to be provided with 'households' ability to pay'; he contends that the new South Africa's urban governance reforms have 'cemented existing patterns of inequality through market mechanisms.'

Similarly, sociologist Greg Ruiters (2006) argues that South Africa's 'free basic water' (FBW) program, despite its avowedly pro-poor policy credentials (as the name of the program suggests, it involves allocating a 'basic' amount of water to each household for free), has had the contradictory outcome of extending state and elite control along with further impoverishment and endangerment of the health of the people most in need. Ideas of neoliberal urban governance, as the FBW program makes plain, were 'hybridized to fit into national liberation discourse' (ibid.: 293). FBW grew out of the pushback that the hardships of five years of roll-out neoliberalism created in the lives of poor urban supporters of the post-apartheid ruling party, the African National Congress (ANC). But its 'free' water came attached to other cost-recovery mechanisms (such as pre-paid water meters) instilling a 'market culture' and 'market environmentalism' – the poor still had no say in how much water was 'basic' to their needs, while the amount set by the state and the market was far below their own conception of needs – and the policy was all the while working toward creating a 'marketized social life,' Ruiters (ibid.: 297–302) argued. The comparable roll-out neoliberalism that has characterized electricity service delivery in the New South Africa has involved private sector partnerships with a decentralized version of a newly corporatized parastatal, Eskom. Geographer David McDonald (2009: 27–8) critiques the governance reforms of the neoliberal era in electricity along the same lines suggested by Ruiters for the water sector: policies are 'designed to create the image of a progressive, developmental state' while actually privileging 'the export-oriented sectors of the … economy and the elites who run it.'

It is not accidental that all three of these examples come from South Africa, as its cities have provided the canvas upon which the most well-known materialist critiques of urban neoliberalism in Africa have been painted, and it has the strongest range of plausible alternative visions of governance given the resources available to its effectively functioning and democratically elected state. I want to suggest that these and other similar critiques are quite useful, but potentially problematic. For now, let me stick to the problems that appear within South Africa itself. Crucially, the materialist critique may miss the ways in which local adaptations of neoliberal policies actually might lead to improvements in the quality of life or institutional landscape available to the urban poor (Ferguson 2007), or how neoliberalism imposed from above may result in an expansion of such state activities as the provision of subsidies and services to the poor and indigent (Parnell 2007). Robinson and Parnell (2011: 4), while referencing the South African materialist critique, draw on Aihwa Ong's (2006) work on Asian cities to make the case that all critiques of urban neoliberalism need to pay more 'attention to those people and places excluded from the ambit of neoliberal forms of rule.' This is a part of their ringing call for 'a progressive politics beyond a focus on neoliberalism and anti-neoliberalism … which is intellectually more ambitiously post-neoliberal' (Robinson and Parnell 2011: 8). By this, they mean that a great deal which matters to urbanists in South Africa happens outside of a relatively narrow concern with the grand agenda of neoliberalization, and that careful attention to contestations over governance and its outcomes in South African cities can be invaluable to broader understandings in urban studies. This seems a valid criticism applicable to materialist critiques of urban neoliberalism across the continent.

Post-structuralist approaches Post-structuralist approaches to the analysis of urban governance in Africa are quite varied, and it is difficult to emerge from reading a range of works one might categorize this way with one single line of critique or analysis. I therefore examine several key authors identified with post-structuralist arguments – and even this can be a challenge, since even strongly materialist scholars like Ruiters (2006) may deploy post-structuralist theory, in his case in the form of Foucault's ideas.

Of the many scholars most identifiable with the variety of post-structuralist approaches, Maliq Simone has dealt the most directly with questions of governance. Simone is both the most prolific and the most provocative urbanist working on Africa, so much so that it can be hard to keep up with his arguments as they evolve through multiple publications, as he seeks, in essence, to find a new language for discussing African cities (Simone 2010). But arguably his most pertinent piece for this chapter has to do with what he terms 'pirate towns' (Simone 2006). Simone (ibid.: 357) seeks to draw attention to 'the concerns and possibilities of piracy' as a notion that may help us 'come to grips with the radical remaking of urban life in much of Africa.' Pirate cities, in his interesting estimation of them, are those where 'order is essentially underfunded' (ibid.: 358). Ordinary citizens turn to piracy 'as a means of negotiating everyday urban life' in cities such as Douala, Lagos, Abidjan, Kinshasa, Johannesburg, or Dakar, in Simone's conceptualization essentially because the governance framework they live under has broken down. Neoliberal good governance is an empty shell, while materialist critiques are just critiques, offering no alternative governance framework; hence we get pirate governance. This could be, for a basic example, a way to make sense of how people in Nairobi's Mathare or Kibera obtain services (for land, water, electricity, or solid waste) through pirate operators in the absence of genuine state or formal private sector engagement in delivery.

Simone is hardly unaware of what a loaded term piracy is, and how easily its deployment can be usurped by the cause of continued stereotyped representations of failed African urbanism (I had that worry myself with Chapter 1's opening section). Yet he argues that 'the chronic sense of crisis necessitates more extraordinary actions in order for households and individuals to stay afloat,' and scholars need to attend to those actions even when they are outside the law (ibid.: 361). He acknowledges that 'concerted efforts continue to be made to govern cities through zoning, cadastre, property and administration,' but he finds that these efforts not only fall short; they also fail to eradicate 'the unruly yet dynamic intersections among differences of all kinds to which the city offers both setting and cause' (ibid.: 358).

Simone's elaborate prose requires careful attention, but sometimes leaves the reader with poetic uncertainty. For example, in illustrating his notion of piracy, he says that 'Douala has become largely a city for evacuation' (ibid.: 363). This is fantastic writing, an image that hits the reader and may never leave her. Claiming Douala to be 'a city for evacuation' proves a dramatic way of highlighting the increasing economy through which people seek to leave the city, but, like the evocation of piracy, it can also be misconstrued, as an overstatement on a nightmarish African urbanism that people are fleeing with abandon. Almost everything one reads about Douala is depressing but, clearly, not everyone has evacuated the city; it is instead a city that continues to grow in population (Malaquais 2006; Ndjio 2006a, 2006b). Some evacuees are making money abroad that is sent home; others send earnings from Douala to the rural settlements they come from (Mercer et al. 2008). It is perhaps more appropriate to think of it as a city 'on the move' in many directions at once (Malaquais 2006: 36).

One thing that post-structuralists clearly see as having evacuated Douala, though, is a responsible state. State power is there, but seemingly largely for privatized accumulation (Mbembe 2001). The notion of a state that could or would ever want to partner with a private sector or community groups in the interest of *serving* citizens, even just to project a developmentalist image, as materialist critics claim about the ANC's South Africa, seems decidedly absent in post-structuralist urbanist accounts of the city. Basile Ndjio (2006a) portrays Douala as a model necropolis, a city of death, based on Mbembe's (2003) idea of Cameroon's necropolitics. To Mbembe (2001: 146–7), the 'increased repression and intensified authoritarianism' in Cameroon over the 1980s and 1990s had the result that 'everyone has suddenly gone "underground"' – not necessarily to an underworld of death, but to what is in essence a realm invisible to the state and elites.

Scholars regularly return to Douala's massive informal settlement of New Bell as the (dead?) heart of the metaphorical underground necropolis (Konings 2006: 49; Ndjio 2006a, 2006b; Simone 2004, 2006; Malaquais 2006). Although it was eventually incorporated into the city from which colonial maps excluded it, New Bell's residents, like those of Kibera or Mathare in Nairobi, 'became part of a "floating population", always on the look-out for better options elsewhere and ignoring the city's fluid borders' (Konings 2006: 50–51). It is a poorly serviced maze of a neighborhood with extensive conflicts between its indigenous Duala minority and the migrant Bamileke majority (Ndjio 2006b). In Piet Konings's (2006: 53) terms, New Bell residents show 'a remarkable capacity for evading all efforts at state control' as they 'engage in a wide range of legal and illegal economic activities that have enabled the community to survive and, in some cases, even to thrive.' Art historian Dominique Malaquais (2006: 36), like Konings and Mbembe, uses transport as the vehicle by which to connect the state's governance failures and the community's survival tactics: 'within the city, the absence of a regular public transport system means that the business of moving about occupies the better part of people's days and nights.'

Ndjio (2006b: 67) sees New Bell as an ideal setting in which to ask some broader questions about urban society that are really at the core of governance-as-decision-making: 'who should (or should not) be allowed to live with us? Who should (or should not) be granted the legitimate right to enjoy full membership of our locale?' He argues that answers to these questions have become even more exclusionary in postcolonial New Bell and Douala. Cameroon's new 1990s constitution, for example, 'stratified citizenship by starting first with belonging to an ethnic group, district, or province before any national consideration' (Awasom 2001: 22). This by extension also meant that 'one's admission into a particular neighborhood ... depends largely – but not exclusively – on one's status either as an "autochthon" or "allochthon"' (more common terms in English would be 'native' and 'stranger'; Ndjio 2006b: 69). So the state may have evacuated governance in Douala, in the sense of promoting idealized neoliberal good governance seeking to create public-private-popular networks that better the lives of its citizens, but the state has been present enough to skew what Simone might take as the 'pirate' governance toward a micropolitics of difference versus belonging.

The grim tragicomedy that so often characterizes post-structuralist representations of African urban governance is elegantly articulated in de Boeck and Plissart's (2004) *Kinshasa: Tales of the Invisible City*. De Boeck and Plissart's Kinshasa is even more of a pirate cityscape than the Douala of Simone, Malaquais, Mbembe or Ndjio. 'Every city has its elsewheres,' they write, but 'Kinshasa often strikes one as a city that is, in and of itself elsewhere, invisible' (ibid.: 24). Because the Democratic Republic of Congo's postcolonial regime of Mobutu Sese Seko (1965–96, under whom the country was renamed Zaire for twenty-five years) gradually 'abandoned all efforts at urban planning,' the residents of its vast and sprawling 'shantytowns' were at the forefront of the city's attempt to 'reinvent itself' (ibid.: 32–3). What de Boeck and Plissart (ibid.: 34) then refer to as 'post urbanism' is the result: the 'city has bypassed, redefined or smashed the (neo)colonial logics that were stamped onto its surface.' They therefore find the 'standard vocabularies used by social and political scientists, economists, demographers and urban planners' to be inadequate in their deployment in Kinshasa (ibid.: 34). They use the fascinating example of gang territorialization within Kinshasa historically to illustrate the alternative governance that emerges, as youth rebels 'refashion the city … in their own terms, which are those of longstanding moralities, rooted in local rural pasts' (ibid.: 43).

Like Simone, de Boeck and Plissart write beautifully and passionately as they struggle to move the conversation beyond the 'neoliberalism good/neoliberalism bad' axis of the prevailing discussions of African urban governance for World Bankers or materialists. All three authors open up our understanding of daily dynamics that dominate the lifeworlds of the majority in Africa's unruly cities. Yet there are risks in the poetics of post-structuralist approaches. De Boeck and Plissart's poetic journey ultimately takes us back to places we have been to before, not just to Conrad's *Heart of Darkness* – admittedly de Boeck and Plissart (ibid.: 15) kick themselves 'for allowing this cliché to take over' – but also to the mystic notion of rural moral orders of the past. Despite the general gloominess that prevails in both *Invisible City* and in much of Simone's writing, one may worry in both cases about what Fredericks (2009: x) sees as their 'Afro-optimism that is conveyed in an overemphasis on radical openness and contingency.'

Governance outcomes

Neoliberal good governance advocates and their materialist critics often appear wedded to analyses that have inevitable trajectories. Despite the fact that many post-structuralist urban theorists in African studies are clearly breaking from that grid of inevitability, many readers struggle to interpret their alternative visions. While I am ultimately most sympathetic to this very loosely configured third grouping, we still need more tangible ways to see and analyze with fresh eyes the complexities of what is actually going on, on the ground, in African cities. The anthropologists Giorgio Blundo and Pierre-Yves Le Meur (2009: 2), in an innovative introduction to their recent edited volume

The Governance of Daily Life in Africa, aim at analyzing the actors involved in actually existing governance, 'the way in which the rules for such services are produced, debated, transformed and controlled' and how the urban services themselves are performed in African cities. This seems a helpful intervention, one that is quite similar to recent work by Fredericks (2009) on solid waste management in Dakar. Both Fredericks and the Blundo/Le Meur book would concur with geographer Anna Davies's (2008: 25) observation that debates on governance in urban studies, political science, and urban geography remain focused on conceptualization and abstraction, giving rise to a growing advocacy for more grounded, empirical assessments. In African urban studies, it seems increasingly evident that both the directions and outcomes of shifts from government to governance do vary, particularly in the sphere of service delivery (McDonald 2009; McCarney and Stren 2003). In moving toward empirical assessments of this variation, Pieterse (2008a: 162) suggests that we need to pay particular attention to the 'systemic drivers of urban development.' These drivers include the way decision-making processes work in local urban politics, how infrastructure is built, technology deployed, and landscapes shaped in creating and re-creating a city's spatial structure, and both how economic activity works and how local structures and agents work to address inequalities that result from it.

Nairobi is becoming a city for grounded, complicated analyses of governance and service delivery. The 'exclusionary governance' and 'unequal terrain of power relations' in the city that I first saw twenty-eight years ago have endured, and in some ways deepened, even in the post-authoritarian era, for some observers (Njeru 2006: 1054–5). Yet Nairobi is also a fascinating case for the ways in which its governance structures, institutions, and processes have transformed over the last thirty years (Nasong'o 2007). In particular, the period since the end of single-party rule in 1992, and then the electoral defeat of the party that had ruled Kenya from independence in 2002, signaled possibilities for openings in governance to provide for popular participation and more effective service delivery. From 1996 to 2002, the Nairobi Informal Settlements Coordination Committee (NISCC) operated as an attempted partnership between local and central government, with a technical advisory committee dominated by donors, a set of stakeholder working groups, and local NGOs, which had the expressed objective of poverty reduction. NISCC started as an outgrowth of earlier efforts by the Nairobi City Council funded by the UN. Yet

NISCC's creation was tied to the results of Kenya's 1992 multiparty elections, which gave that council an opposition majority. That new opposition council rapidly issued a call for a citywide convention in 1993, to gather views on 'The Nairobi We Want' (Hendriks 2010).

NISCC was later folded into the Local Authority Service Delivery Action Plan (LASDAP) network. LASDAP has a longer institutional history, tied as it is to the Local Authorities Transfer Fund (LATF), which was itself a practical implementation of the mid-1980s government policy shift toward decentralization, known as the District Focus for Rural Development (Mitullah 2008; Hendriks 2010). LATF sets aside 5 percent of Kenya's national income tax as a means to provide local authorities, such as the Nairobi City Council, with funds for service delivery. LASDAP is the mechanism for identifying where to spend those funds, a 'three year rolling plan for which citizens are consulted yearly to identify and prioritize their service and facility development needs' (Hendriks 2010: 64). In 2008, the national government established the Ministry for Nairobi Metropolitan Development, as further evidence of the intensification of efforts at urban governance reform in the post-authoritarian era (Gathanju 2009). The national government also cooperated with civil society groups in conducting the 2009 national census, the results of which gave momentary pause to alarmist rhetoric about the out-of-control growth of Nairobi's slums (UN-Habitat 2010: 168–9).

Yet all of these reorganizations, or efforts at the rescaling of governance, have repeatedly led to similar outcomes: 'citizen non-engagement,' where the reforms were 'not convincing to many citizens' or 'citizens turned away,' where most of the power is concentrated in the hands of corrupt councilors while 'collective action' from citizens has been 'absent' (Hendriks 2010: 70, 73). Civil society groups and nongovernmental organizations that engaged in the new 'rules of the game' in urban Kenya often became what political theorist Shadrack Nasong'o (2007: 51) calls MONGOs (as in 'My Own NGO'), mere vehicles for 'self-advancement and personal accumulation.' There have been some wards of the city where more activism has led to more genuine engagement with the new governance framework, but this is almost always in Nairobi's wealthier neighborhoods, where residents' associations are stronger and wealthier; in the rest of the city, 'local-level actors and residents continue to be disengaged from effective participation in service delivery' (Mitullah 2008: 62). Only 12 percent of LASDAP project moneys have been spent in the informal settlements, where some estimate that two-thirds of Nairobi's population resides (Hendriks 2010: 75). Even in the case of collaboration in the gathering of the 2009 census data, the new participatory governance seems deeply flawed. The census results appeared to severely undercount the populations of informal settlements (the official numbers show only 33.7 percent of Nairobi's population in them, and declines from 1999 in the population of several major slums, including Kibera, when other data suggest the complete reverse, such as voter registration rolls which increased for Kibera by nearly 25 percent from 2005 to 2010 alone); this can only further their marginalization in a city that registers one of Africa's highest Gini coefficients of income inequality outside of South Africa (UN-Habitat 2010: 168–9).

With the guiding hands of the World Bank, the UN, and major Western donors, and counter to their stated intentions, successive plans for new governance initiatives in Nairobi actually 'limit the roles of stakeholders,' narrow down who these stakeholders are (for instance, they are overwhelmingly male and either middle-class or elite), and actually further centralize control in the national government; nowhere is this more obvious than in the newly created national Ministry of Nairobi Metropolitan District (Mitullah 2008: 62). Once again, 'vertical accountability for citizen voice [is] limited' (Hendriks 2010: 71). As Winnie Mitullah (2008: 66) put it: 'effective decentralization requires people to articulate their aspirations and priorities in policymaking and implementation, an act which has largely been the preserve of the economic and political elites. Due to suspicion and indifference, many people are not willing to participate.'

In some urban African settings, though, people have managed to take the projects over. Fredericks's study of solid waste management in Dakar offers one such example. While both materialist and post-structuralist critics often offer worst-case-scenario cities in countries that are falling apart, her study focuses on a lively city in a country with a history of democratic politics from independence onward. Fredericks's dissertation contrasts the city's 2007 trash revolts with the 1989 Set/Setal movement, wherein youth organized to clean up the city. She writes to counter the narrative of African urban decline, seeing her two cataclysmic trash crises and contrasting movements not as part of 'chaotic periods of disintegration, but productive moments in which key political, economic, and social factors crystallize and new configurations of social relations are negotiated.' She effectively shows how 'certain people get positioned, and position themselves, to do the dirty work, with different rewards and dangers, across the uneven spaces of the city' (Fredericks 2009: 4). She shows how the youth of the earlier movement became so 'indispensable in filling the gaps left by the failing trash collection company' that Dakar's mayor, Mamadou Diop, 'masterminded their incorporation into a city-wide participatory trash system' that lasted a decade (ibid.: 81). After Senegal's newly elected government's privatization effort stalled for these community activist groups in the solid waste sector in the early 2000s, a muddled, in-between 'transitional phase' was marked by a second major garbage crisis (ibid.: 100). She left the city after fieldwork that documented this crisis, which she described as 'characterized by nebulous institutional arrangements, poor working conditions, and garbage build-up in the public space' (ibid.: 99). Yet youth engagements with the 'dirty work' showed the possibilities for, if not a solution to the crisis, a transformation of it into a moment for understanding more of the complexities of political engagement.

In contrast with settings like Nairobi or Dakar, South African cities arguably provide us with more detailed and deeper analyses of actually existing service delivery. In South Africa, the post-apartheid era brought with it the possibility for restitution and redistribution of the fruits of the city as the systemic drivers changed so dramatically. We have seen, in Chapter 3, the grandest dimensions of this in the RDP and BNG housing schemes, but as the urbanists Udesh Pillay, Richard Tomlinson and Jacques du Toit (2006: 1) have shown, over the first fifteen years of the New South Africa, the emphasis shifted from addressing issues of 'housing and urban form to governance and service delivery.' Urban policy thus targeted the redemarcation of municipalities to integrate service delivery and tax bases, the task of making local governments developmentalist, and the 'mass delivery' of urban services more generally, following from these earlier two policy themes (ibid.: 2). The processes in implementing all three were and are deeply politicized, notably with the Municipal Demarcation Board under the direction of its staunchly ANC-supporting chairperson (Cameron 2006: 99). And as we have seen with the critiques above from Bond, Ruiters, and McDonald, both the move (at least on paper) to a developmentalist local state and the mass delivery of urban services seem to have fallen short of even their advocates' expectations. The New South Africa's rhetorical commitment to participatory and collaborative urban governance also ran into the brick walls of a 'performance management culture' that placed great pressure on officials 'to attain targets within specified time frames' against a history of activist civic groups in opposition to government interventionist tactics (Harrison 2006b: 192).

Yet there is much to value in the South African cases when pondering governance and service delivery in other parts of urban Africa. For comparative purposes let us take, as an illustrative point of departure, the issue of urban electricity supply, and compare the processes and debates in South Africa with those in Tanzania, and particularly in Zanzibar. In 2008 and 2009/10, the city of Zanzibar twice endured months-long blackouts, the first when the undersea cable through which a mainland-based corporation supplies the island's government parastatal company with electricity (the parastatal is responsible for all power distribution in the city) experienced a surge that blew out the transformer at the receiving station, and the second when the replacement for that transformer blew for undisclosed reasons. While some friends noted that the coping mechanisms that they developed in concert with neighbors led to a reinvigoration of social ties, in practical terms the effects of these blackouts on the economy and quality of life of urban Zanzibaris were near catastrophic. Businesses and ordinary citizens privately expressed anger and frustration at the costs, human and financial, of the shutdowns, and several elderly Zanzibaris reportedly perished from the fumes of generators in their poorly ventilated homes. But the absence of transparent, democratic decision-making, open popular organizing, and evident influence of ordinary citizens on the government and its parastatal left people without any recourse for popular expression or expectations of amelioration. Few if any notable public demonstrations of dissent occurred and no one in authority in the political system faced any consequences in their employment. By contrast, during the same years, urban service delivery shortfalls, for electricity as well as water, sanitation, and solid waste, were absolutely at the center of vocal public politics in urban South Africa, resulting in the sacking of mayors or city managers in tandem with loud protest movements that occupied municipal buildings or confronted the state openly and even occasionally violently – and all covered in vibrant press accounts (Cull 2009; Daily Dispatch 2009; Jack 2009; Ngcukana 2009; Njwabane 2009).

Just including more people in active, contested democratic politics and decision-making, or allowing for popular influences on demands for services – simply put, *empowering people* – did not lead to immediate and evident improvement in the quality of life for poor urban South Africans. But the possibilities for such a positive trajectory are greater in urban South Africa than they are in Zanzibar. As Rebecca Ghanadan (2009: 401) argues, 'ordinary Tanzanians find themselves far removed from the technical and decision-making processes governing service changes,' and this is even more the case in Zanzibar when compared with the mainland. By contrast, in South Africa, 'public-sector unions, ratepayer associations ..., civic organizations and social movements ... have been inserting themselves into debates over electricity provision ... in ways that did not exist 15 years ago' (McDonald 2009: 20).

We have an era, then, where the dominant voices of donors, the state, and local elites sing the praises of more participatory, democratic governance and decision-making in urban service delivery. Materialist and post-structuralist critics, in different ways, see the ethos of this era as fatally flawed. More empirical analyses on the ground, with a focus on service delivery outcomes, also seem critical, while at the same time offering a cautious openness toward a new political era in African cities.

Justice

What makes South African cities so different from Zanzibar and other Tanzanian cities – and many other sub-Saharan cities – is the centrality of issues of justice (social and environmental) to the country's urban politics (not just in a theoretical sense but in practical policy dimensions, and in terms of contesting how to enhance human capabilities) over the course of at least a century. South Africa is the earliest and largest center for urban socio-environmental justice discussion, debate, and action in sub-Saharan Africa (McDonald 2002; Smith 2004; Debbane and Keil 2004). South Africa's constitution, environmental laws, and deliberative processes, at least on paper, place it well ahead of most other African countries. This is especially so for the degree to which justice rhetoric has become embedded in policy. It is true, as Patel (2006), Bond (2002), Ruiters (2002), and others have shown, that neoliberal sustainable development strategies predominate in practice. But post-apartheid South Africa still operates under a rights-based development framework, providing for the possibility of planning action to confront socio-environmental injustice (Visser 2001). South Africa has a substantial critical-left scholarly community and activist network to critique sustainable development policy and socio-environmental justice rhetoric, too. Critical academic scholarship in South Africa is still positioned to have political impacts (Swilling and Annecke 2006; McDonald 2002; Beall et al. 2000; Pieterse 2008b).

In one detailed empirical assessment of South Africa's urban justice rubric in practice, geographer Zarina Patel critiques the new South Africa's deliberative planning processes and stakeholder development as exclusive from the outset. She argues that 'policy outcomes do not reflect' the emphases of 'communities and households' they are 'designed to serve' (Patel 2006: 682), largely because the 'typical citizen' is marginalized in deliberative processes (ibid.: 688–9). Dixon and Ramutsindela (2006: 130–31) call for a return to questions of strategies and processes for achieving justice, rather than just seeking and proving injustices exist, using the example of land reform to achieve land rights for the poor. Gustav Visser's (2004) analysis of the inadequacies of redistributive justice without a broader restructuring of society, and Diana Scott and Cathy Oelofse's (2005: 447) deconstruction of Environmental Impact Assessment as still lacking in questions of 'development for whom' and in the inclusion of the poor and marginalized, also come to mind. These authors point to the inherently politicized nature of sustainable development and socio-environmental justice in South Africa, where local power structures override the progressive rhetoric, and they are strong advocates for 'deepening democratic practices' in planning (ibid.: 445; Pieterse 2005).

To make the new participatory map of governance into a relational city, or to have 'practical usefulness in changing the world for the better,' in Soja's phrase, it is, Pieterse (2008a: 162) argues, 'not enough to have democratic systems and a formal commitment to human rights,' but instead 'what is required is vigorous democratic contestation' – this is the 'deepening democratic practices' that Scott and Oelofse intend. The particular arenas of contestation and deepening change with time and geography. There are bound to be fights in any urban society about what it takes to improve the quality of life, or whose quality of life should be improved, or by how much. I include myself among Pieterse's (2008a: 162) group of 'progressives who want to bring more just and inclusive cities into the world,' but justice and inclusivity are rather complicated terms. For the philosopher John Rawls (1971: 136–42), justice emerges for free individuals in the social contract of liberal democracy from abstract deliberation under a veil of ignorance. Rawlsian phraseology and the conceptualization are far from universal and have always seemed to me hard to locate in contemporary Africa, even beyond the Marxist critique of them for leaving questions of production out of the equation of distribution – an argument best exemplified in geography by Harvey's (1973: 96–118) *Social Justice and the City*. Harvey (ibid.: 100) prioritized need, contribution to the common good, and merit among Rawls's benchmarks for assessing possibilities for distributive justice, and attempted to articulate the urban geographies of these themes, but ultimately decried the liberals' 'moral masturbation' over the 'huge dossier on the daily injustices of the populace of the ghetto' (ibid.: 145).

For decades, Harvey's (1996: 401) work on justice has wrapped itself around the powerful argument that 'when encountering a serious problem' such as urban poverty or inequality (whether in terms of distribution or rights), it is 'vital ... not merely to try to solve the problem in itself but to confront and transform the processes that gave rise to the problem in the first place.' Yet Harvey's (ibid.: 401) concerted call for a 'program of radical political action,' even as it may ring in the ears, nevertheless suffers from the universalisms of grand theory that make it as problematic as Rawlsian thought in contemporary urban Africa, particularly given the maldistribution and injustice visited upon urban African peoples in programs of 'radical political action' on the continent for forty years or more, such as Maimire Mennasemay's (2009) example of 'revolutionary' Ethiopia.

Encouragingly, some African studies scholarship has been turning to the possibilities for an alternative theory of justice built around the ideas of Amartya Sen (1993, 1999). As Mennesemay (2009: 13) has noted, 'not much reflection has been devoted' to Sen's ideas as yet in African studies, and the same could be said for much of human geography. There is far too much to Sen's ideas for me to do *them* justice here, but his emphases on 'the expansion of the "capabilities" of people to lead the kind of lives they value' (Sen 1999: 18) and 'the freedom that a person has to lead one kind of life or another' (Nussbaum and Sen 1993: 3) are crucial, particularly because Sen makes these capabilities, freedoms, and rights *relational*. There may be problems in applying Sen's work to African studies because of his emphasis on individuals, but I feel these concerns can be overcome rather readily. Although Sen writes about a 'person,' he is ever cognizant of the social and institutional embeddedness of such persons, and this makes his alternative conceptualization of justice relevant to our questions about urban governance in Africa. 'It would be a mistake,' Sen (1993: 44) argues, to think of a person's 'achievements only in terms of active choice by oneself ... There is a very real sense by which the freedom to live the way one would like is enhanced by public policy that transforms epidemiological and social environments.' Sen (ibid.: 33) moves the question of social – and environmental – justice out of the realm of distribution, out of the lockdown of individual rights, to more ambiguous realms of what a mathematician would see as fuzzy sets. He wants to know 'how people are enabled' by their society 'to imagine, to wonder, to feel emotions such as love and gratitude' (Nussbaum and Sen 1993: 1). His language, here shared with the philosopher Martha Nussbaum, can be vague, and ambiguous, and deliberately so, because these questions about such heady matters are complicated and cannot be reduced by numerology to formulas. At the same time, remembering that Sen is a development economist, he comes to earth to remind us that 'individuals live and operate in a world of institutions. Our opportunities and prospects depend crucially on what institutions exist and how they function' (Sen 1999: 142).

This last point makes Sen's ideas particularly valuable in under-standing justice in alternative governance in African cities. In his analysis of governance in Dar es Salaam, the urban sociologist Brian Dill (2010) picks up on Sen's institutional and relational emphases to connect his work with that of Peter Evans on institutions in development theory. Evans (2002: 55) argues that the democratiza-tion of institutions through 'leadership succession determined by a regular electoral process' is rather 'thin,' where a fully democratic development strategy needs to be 'thick,' in the sense of 'messy and continuous involvement of the citizenry in the setting of economic priorities.' Evans (2004: 33) decries 'institutional monocropping' (e.g. one-size-fits-all institution-building); Dill (2010: 31) sees this sort of institution-building in Dar's gap between 'exogenously derived insti-tutional blueprints' for urban governance and 'the norms and values of recipient cultures.' Mennasemay (2009: 5) develops a similar line of argument, beyond institutions, in the realm of discourse, critiquing what he terms 'concept-stretching,' wherein 'elements constitutive of the original meaning of the concept' (be it democracy, good govern-ance, or the like) are discarded 'to make it cover more cases than the original meaning allows.' He sees this concept-stretching creating a 'theoretical cul-de-sac' in countries like Ethiopia, because when we

stretch the word 'democracy' around such an obviously undemo-
cratic regime as that of Meles Zenawi's Ethiopia, we simply fail to
recognize that 'such regimes are not democratic' (ibid.: 6). Neither
Dill, nor Evans, nor Mennasemay (ibid.: 11) are arguing for 'cultural
relativism'; they simply want our conceptualization, in Mennasemay's
words, 'anchored in the understanding that emerges from one's own
critical reflection on the emancipatory potentials that the past and
present harbor and from one's capacity to exercise one's imagination
to envision a historically rooted alternative future.'

Building on these insights, the goals for those interested in producing work that has practical usefulness in seeking justice in African
cities become a mouthful: *to improve the quality of life for all, while
including more and different people in democratic decision-making
within an overall framework that works toward an expansion of social
and environmental justice through a thick and messy realignment of
state–society relations that enhance people's capabilities for leading
the lives they choose.* The path there will not be universal for African
cities; it will always be contested, and it will always take a different
shape for different cities and different times. But the 'struggles over
space and the right to the city' that emerge on this path can become
a 'powerful source of shared identity, determination and effectiveness
in changing the world for the better' (Soja 2010: 109).

The thickness and messiness of those struggles in the varied
attempts to reimagine governance and service delivery in urban Africa
connect well with Pieterse's notion of the need for expanding and
invigorating democratic contestation, because, as Bob Hendriks (2010:
59) puts it in the Nairobi case: 'participation, citizenship and development is not only about inclusion and voice in projects, programs, and
policies, but also about politics, power and influence.' Politics, power
plays, and influences shape the way projects, programs, and policies
play out, and whether this playing-out improves the quality of life
of the poor or ameliorates the socio-spatial injustices of their lives.
Julie Crespin's (2006) sensitive critique of the failings of 'pro-poor'
development assistance comes to mind here. Real reform of governance, she argues, would require 'poorer groups having the power and
voice to change their relationship with government agencies and other
groups at the local level,' and yet donors in urban Africa, overwhelmingly, funnel money into 'pro-poor' sustainable urban development
via government agencies that the vast majority of the urban poor are
alienated from and marginalized by (ibid.: 434). Crespin (ibid.: 444)

argues that 'poverty cannot be tackled without addressing problems of power relations and the cultural and social interests that sustain unequal access to economic opportunity and social resources.' Poverty, inequality, and injustice are inseparable in African cities, and thus so would be any governance reforms that would proffer solutions to them. Socio-environmental injustice is partly fostered by global processes but ultimately becomes 'bound up with ... the extent to which low-income groups can influence local government policies' (Nunan and Devas 2004: 165). That influence is quite clearly limited in a majority of African cities, but it varies, and it is changing.

The Zanzibar case spelled out in more detail below exemplifies the limited degree of influence that the urban poor majority has in many, if not most, African cities, and the limited engagement thus far with conceptualizations of social and environmental justice to work for a deepening of democratic urban practice. What are local Zanzibaris' ideas of justice, and what does an understanding of them offer back to the broader literature? Zanzibar also offers us an opportunity to examine the salience of neoliberal, materialist, and post-structuralist accounts of governance reform through empirical assessment of governance on the ground in the sphere of urban service delivery.

Zanzibar

With about 425,000 people, Zanzibar is a smaller city than most that I discuss in this book. But in microcosm it illustrates many of the dynamics of governance reform, service delivery, and justice questions that I've presented above. Examples in Zanzibar abound for the transformation of government into governance in a neoliberal ambit. The discourse of good governance, privatization, stakeholder democracy, and sustainable development can be seen wrapped around the city's policy frameworks for the last twenty years. Materialist and post-structuralist critiques are quite applicable, as are the criticisms leveled at such critiques. Given that it is a smaller city, it is potentially easier to identify the systemic drivers of urban development. In doing so, we can see clearly the intense, lively, and occasionally violent local politics of governance, and the ways in which politics, power, and influence diminish the capacity of the urban poor to bring about changes that enhance their capabilities for living lives under improving conditions of their choosing. It is thus a challenging test setting for how we might imagine forms of hybrid governance that can lead to producing just cities.

Although I have placed some vignettes from Zanzibar in Chapter 3, it is useful to begin with some context on the city. Zanzibar as a polity consists of two main islands, Unguja and Pemba, with a combined population of a little over a million people, 40 percent of whom are in and around the city of Zanzibar, on Unguja island (which most outsiders refer to as Zanzibar island). Zanzibar was an Omani sultanate (1690–1890) and a British protectorate (1890–1963) prior to achieving independence in December 1963. Following a January 1964 revolution, its new government united in April of that year with Tanganyika to form the United Republic of Tanzania, in which Zanzibar remains a semi-autonomous partner. Within the union constitution, Zanzibar retains its own presidency and government ministries, and, since 1984, its own House of Representatives. The urban population is about evenly split between Urban District (206,292 in the 2002 census) and West District (184,710 in 2002, but growing more rapidly than the Urban District), which together comprise the Tanzanian government region of Zanzibar Urban-West; each district has its own commissioner and council, with the Urban District's being a municipal council with a mayor.

West District's urbanization has taken place during a transition in Zanzibar's political system and economic development framework more cataclysmic than what has transpired on the Tanzanian mainland. Zanzibar's socialist system remained intact from 1964 through the early 1980s. It has experienced a precipitous opening of its economy to a tourism boom and the reintroduction of multiparty politics over the last quarter-century (Myers 2005, 2008a). This restructuring brought a reform agenda to urban planning, governance, and service delivery, with new development projects, institutions, and legislation. From an avowedly more authoritarian and socialist order than that of the mainland, Zanzibar shifted to a freewheeling capitalist tourist economy overseen by a (nominally) democratically elected government.

Consider the institutional landscape of governance over development as it has changed since the 1984 formation of the House of Representatives. Zanzibar's government reintroduced the Municipal Council (1995), created a Commission for Tourism (1991), a Commission for Lands and Environment (1989–2001), the Zanzibar Investment Promotion Agency (1991), the Zanzibar Sustainable Program (ZSP) for the city (1998–2005) and both the Zanzibar Integrated Lands and Environmental Management (ZILEM) program (1989–96) and the Sustainable Management of Lands and Environment (SMOLE) program (2002–09). All of these institutions received substantial investments of aid and technical support from Western donors intent on a parallel loosening of state control on and proliferation of nongovernmental community-based organizations or civil society institutions (Myers 1996a, 2005). All of them fit within the rubric of neoliberal good governance – the revolutionary government even created a minister for good governance, to whom many of the directors of these programs reported after 2000. None of them succeeded in their finite objectives, nor did they more abstractly lead to the broader re-creation of state–society relations envisioned under neoliberalism.

Instead, each of these programs can be seen at one level as vehicles for either facilitating external capitalist investment or for capital accumulation by local elites, almost all of whom are closely associated with the revolutionary government. Indeed, it has become increasingly difficult to tease out any separation between Zanzibar's political elite and its economic elite: if the family of the recently retired president, Amani Karume (2000–10), is not the wealthiest on the islands, it is surely very near the top. The problem is that no such list would ever exist: despite decades of rhetoric about transparency and openness as a part of the governance reform agenda, Zanzibar's ruling elite remains secretive, distrustful, and elusive. The avenues for private accumulation taken by the last two Zanzibari presidents (Karume and Salmin Amour, who ruled from 1990 to 2000) and those allied with them, are lined with gated mansions, on the way to resort hotels. The disjuncture that has developed between this increasingly ostentatious elite accumulation and the steady decline in basic urban services over the last two decades (not only, as we have seen, in electricity, but also in declining availability and quality of residential water supply, declining solid waste services except for elite or tourist areas, and inadequate legal provision of public land for housing construction) give rise to the clear opportunities for cogent critique from both materialist and post-structuralist perspectives.

Zanzibar reintroduced a multiparty political system in 1992 and multiparty elections in 1995, along with the rest of Tanzania. Political reform in Zanzibar has occurred in fits and starts since then, at best. Even before 1992, infighting within the Revolutionary Party (CCM) had led to bitterly contested single-party polls in 1985 and 1990, for president of Zanzibar and for the House of Representatives. That house passed a significant act for the reform of local government

(1995), with competitive elections for a city council (and a district council for West District), but the practical outcome of that act has been the resurgent power of appointed district and regional commissioners, alongside the reintroduced colonial position of an appointed *sheha* (ward official). These appointed officials' powers have far outstripped those of any elected local councils.

Zanzibar has been beset by political conflict since 1992 (Maliyamkono 2000; Mbwiliza 2000; Mukangara 2000). The defeated candidate in 1985's Zanzibar presidential election within CCM, Seif Shariff Hamad, became the leader of a new opposition party, the Civic United Front (CUF). Sometimes violent and always vituperative conflict between CUF and CCM has endured through four controversial elections (1995, 2000, 2005, and 2010). The Zanzibar Electoral Commission declared CCM the winner of all four contests by narrow margins, but CUF, which regularly wins 80 percent of the vote on Pemba island, refused to recognize the results the first three times, joined by many external observers. Many donors suspended aid from 1996 to 2002. Peace agreements were eventually negotiated in 1999 and 2002, in both cases ending terms of imprisonment without charges for CUF leaders and reducing the general harassment of CUF supporters by CCM government security and party thugs. But in neither case did the agreements hold or were the political reforms agreed to within them ever really implemented. Violence derailed them both. Notably, dozens of CUF supporters were killed in clashes with Tanzanian police in January 2001 in Pemba (Arnold et al. 2002).

A third, sketchy peace agreement appeared in November 2009, leading to a popular referendum in July 2010 through which nearly two-thirds of the Zanzibaris who voted (only about 60 percent of the registered electorate did so) endorsed the idea of a constitutional change to require a government of national unity following the October 2010 elections. The Zanzibar House of Representatives then approved a constitutional amendment to facilitate the formation of this 'government of peas and rice' (*serikali ya mseto* in Kiswahili), wherein the losing presidential candidate would be made the 1st Vice-President of Zanzibar and the losing party would have a set of seats on the President's Revolutionary Council. When the election itself took place, though, despite an extraordinary 89 percent turnout (when turnout on the mainland dipped to 42 percent), the Zanzibar Electoral Commission, in concert with CCM's most powerful elites, still managed to manipulate the results to produce yet another miraculous CCM victory. The former vice-president of Tanzania, Ali Mohamed Shein, was declared the winner of the presidential election with a cleverly crafted 50.1 percent of the vote (to Hamad's 49.1 percent) less than twelve hours after the polls closed, when counting on Tanzania's mainland went on for days. Although CUF's Hamad quickly accepted the results and pleaded for peace to prevail, in fact the new constitution gave his 1st Vice-President post no role or portfolio at all, the president's CCM hand-picked 2nd Vice-President is the de facto chief of all government ministries, and President Shein was free to pick whomever he wished for the cabinet. He did choose six CUF cabinet ministers, mostly for marginal ministries, to work with thirteen CCM ministers and six CCM deputy ministers who seemed at first glance to be tasked with actually running the six ministries given to the CUF. Many CUF supporters have completely lost faith in electoral politics as a mechanism for democracy or justice, expressing outrage in Internet chat rooms and private conversations, while remaining muted in public, at least for the time being.

Given this political context, how is it possible to imagine Zanzibar becoming a relational and just city where the poor majority's lives are getting better, with redistributive justice, enhancement of capabilities, and a restructuring of the conversation between people and government? The path to this sort of future seems quite challenging, but not impossible. Let me retrace relevant points from both materialist and post-structuralist critiques of the neoliberal good governance agenda with which Zanzibar has been working. I use specific examples from the two Finnish land management programs, ZILEM and SMOLE, Zanzibar's Sustainable Cities Program, and a community water project in the interconnected informal settlements of Sebleni, Muungano, and Sogea (collectively, Semuso).

As in Ruiters's (2006) South African case, in Zanzibar roll-out neoliberalism was adapted to fit the rhetoric and policy priorities of a liberation movement. ZILEM evidences this. The establishment of the Commission for Lands and Environment (COLE) in 1989 – with support from Finland and other northern European countries – was a major institutional step toward roll-out neoliberal reform (Myers and Muhajir 1997; Chachage 2000). COLE housed the ZILEM project and led the revision of the legal apparatus for governance over land, writing six major new land laws in five years. These laws did not completely remove the state ownership of land that had been originally declared following the revolution. Still, under 1992's Land

Tenure Act, domestic and foreign private investors and commercial interests became entitled to lands on a long-term leasehold basis. The overall effect of legal and legislative reform was a grafting of neoliberal ideas of individual property and security of land tenure into a socialist system. As a result of COLE and ZILEM's work, right-of-occupancy deeds are now held by foreigners for most of Unguja island's eastern beachfront and for major plots within the city's historic core, Stone Town, as a result of which more than a hundred hotels have been created, generating a major tourist industry from which the government and local elites earn considerable land rents or hotel shares. Within the city and West District, fewer than 5 percent of all residences have proper right-of-occupancy deeds, and almost all of these are in Stone Town, in elite villa zones along the north and south beaches, or in the city's very few formally planned neighborhood units.

The urban poor in Zanzibar have had little say in the conception of what urban service needs should be addressed under neoliberal governance. There remains a dominant atmosphere of policy imple-mentation that leads to the deviation of priorities toward outside interests: both ZILEM and SMOLE were essentially Finnish ideas. Neither project addressed what Zanzibari socio-environmental justice advocates (were there such a civil society movement, akin to that of South Africa, which there isn't) might seek to address. The UN's Zanzibar Sustainable Program emerged from its ostensibly participa-tory, decentralized, and action-oriented stakeholder-democracy city consultancy prioritizing solid waste management. Very few ordinary residents of Zanzibar identify solid waste services as a priority; land and water far outweigh garbage as concerns (Myers 2005, 2008a). The ZSP's one pilot project for solid waste management, in Mkele ward, did operate through a community-based organization for two and a half years, but never with much more than a veneer of popular support; by 2006, the flatbed truck the German embassy had donated to the group was in use hauling rocks and gravel for an informal construction materials supply operation run by the group's former leader. True to the critique of the post-structuralist variety, this proves an example of private, indirect state accumulation: the group leader was a CCM city councilman.

The Semuso water project presents a similar dynamic, albeit with better results. In 2000, the community-based organization (CBO) known as *Umoja wa Mradi wa Maji na Maendeleo* (UMMM, or Unity in the Project for Water and Development) gained funding from the UN Development Program, the Zanzibar Revolutionary Government, and various elites toward a water supply project that would rid the sprawling area of two decades of residential water shortages. Over the five-year life of the project, Semuso gained two boreholes with four pumps, supply lines and standpipes, as well as a water storage tank, more than doubling the percentage of the population with access to clean water. The community group, the Zanzibar government, and the UNDP all made contributions, with UNDP supplying slightly more than half of the project money. UMMM's files document the successes that the CBO had in persistently pushing the people in power to keep the project in mind (Semuso 1997–2006). In the end, for less than US$35,000, Semuso's 17,000 or so residents gained delivery of a crucial urban service through a participatory scheme.

Yet this sort of characterization of the Semuso Water Project is misleading. How did a swampy squatter settlement's CBO garner the attention of Zanzibar and Tanzania's elites and the resources of the UN? The short answer is three letters long: CCM. Tanzania's ruling party counts Semuso as one of its surest urban strongholds, with most residents being either solid CCM mainlanders or southern Ungujans (rural Unguja South Region is CCM's strongest Zanzibar region, but Semuso is the only urban area that is at all comparable). UMMM's secretary was the brother of the powerful Urban District Party Chairman for CCM. The deep involvement of the then deputy minister of the Ministry of Water, Mansour Yussuf Himid, adds to this picture: he was the brother-in-law of then president Karume.

One need not discredit everything about the Semuso Water Project as a result of its neo-patrimonialism. Plenty of poor people, and women-headed households, gained in their capabilities as a result of this water project, reminding us that categorical condemnations of neoliberal good governance need the nuance that comes from empirical study of governance outcomes on the ground. The problem that remains after the empirical nuance lies in the extreme unevenness of governance outcomes across the map of even one small city. The central government all over Tanzania long held tight control over associational life, particularly under *ujamaa* (Tripp 1997). Zanzibar now has dozens of registered NGOs and CBOs, but oppositional voices are rarely heard at 'stakeholder' sessions in the new planning rubric. And government representatives form solid majorities in local working groups for action plans (Halla 2005; Nnkya 2007). Government voices are difficult to disentangle from those of the CCM. Even in Zanzibar, where the CUF has actually held between 34 and 42 percent of elected seats in the House of Representatives and similar proportions of the island delegations to Tanzania's parliament, CCM operates the government more or less just as it did in the single-party era. The dissent that would be open in a genuine stakeholder forum rarely appears, even in stakeholder sessions held in oppositional constituencies. The CBOs that focus on community infrastructure and service delivery are seldom as successful as that of UMMM, when they do not have such high-level and high-power connections (like those of the similarly well-connected 'MONGOs' in Nasong'o's analysis of Nairobi). Dill (2010: 28) calls the neoliberal sorts of CBOs of urban Tanzania a 'poor fit' with 'the norms that have long governed the relationship between the state and society' in Tanzania in terms of how and when (and which) people participate, and a mismatch with the expectations of international donors for CBOs, namely 'the production of public goods that ultimately will benefit a community that extends beyond the membership of the association.'

Zanzibar may be Tanzania's worst-case scenario, where a total reconstruction of local state–society relations is a necessary precondition for socio-environmental justice to be meaningfully discussed, and where a movement for such justice seems as 'impossible' as the legalization of illegally developed land (Kironde 2006: 460). Tanzania's generally 'consensual culture' is part of the reason why the injustices do not transfer into more activism, or even violent action (Kombe and Kreibich 2000); but in urban and peri-urban Zanzibar, that consensual culture is distinctly frayed at the edges.

Considering the Zanzibar case more broadly

So how will positive activism and contestatory political action come in such frayed circumstances? Across Africa, there is great variability in the successful navigation of existing power structures and dynamics, but possibilities for urban poverty reduction through local civil society organizational activism, including on socio-environmental justice issues, seem quite impaired in Zanzibar. One can readily imagine the scenarios by which a post-structuralist could discover Zanzibar's 'floating population' in an invisible, underground necropolis, where order is 'underfunded' in Simone's sense, and the pirates take over – pirates at the top, in the form of elite tycoons and politicians, and pirates underneath, in the form of informal land brokers, garbage collectors, water carriers, unregulated electricians, and other service providers. Many urban Zanzibaris operate with a consciousness of a more imaginative spirit underworld, called Giningi, imagined portals to which are located in a number of locations in and just outside the city, as if they might be doors to citizen non-engagement with the politics above ground. The longstanding moralities of Kinshasa residents (Kinois), whom de Boeck discusses, are different from those deployed in Zanzibar, but one might certainly locate older logics and deeper magic at work in how people get by and obtain services in a city over which the top pirates have surely won control. In some of those older logics of affiliation, we can clearly see Zanzibaris playing the micropolitics of difference versus belonging, where neighbors seem to already have the answer to Ndjio's question of 'who should be allowed to live with us': the answer seems to be 'not *those* people,' i.e. indigenous Unguja islanders seeking to displace the Pemban and mainlander migrants who have overwhelmed West District.

Yet the post-structuralists' dystopia also hides the nuances of governance in the everyday life of urban Zanzibaris. Service delivery in Zanzibar has not been entirely ineffective. In many cases, people disengage – from politics, from centralized planning, and from all of the new governance experiments – and operate quite effectively in a pirate underground. But people in Zanzibar also have close relationships with the agents of the state in surprising and sometimes intimate ways. For example, in the peri-urban informal settlement of Mwera, several development areas exist which consist of any-where from six to twenty square grid house plots with evidence of a planned carriageway in the middle – patches that might be a typical Western suburban street if they received some capital and infrastructure infusion. These plots were surveyed and demarcated by staff from the government survey department in informal con-tracts with landholders, in exchange for the landholders turning over the right to sell a percentage of the plots to the government survey officers. Technically, this violation of policies and procedures is not only illegal but could result in the firing of staff involved. In actuality, landholders, plot holders, and staffers of all different ethnic and political persuasions privately point to this as a good example of how to make new settlements and to make money from doing so (Myers 2010a). Such collaborations are a regular feature of the landscape in West District (Scholz 2008).

When we look at the systemic drivers of urban development in

Zanzibar – at how decision-making works, infrastructure is built, the cityscape shaped, inequality addressed, and economic activity propelled forward – the greatest single finding, much like Nairobi, it seems, is that of a gap, a huge gap, between government, elites, and donors on the one hand, and the masses of the urban poor on the other. All of the new institutions created in the neoliberal era lack embeddedness in Zanzibari communities. The concept-stretching Mennasemay discussed for Ethiopia – 'democracy' stretched to cover an electoral process where the final tabulations are carefully calibrated in advance regardless of the actual votes – has run rampant in Zanzibar. The outline statement of SMOLE in its program preparation phase (Sirve 2003: 5) claimed that the project was 'in harmony with broader frameworks – poverty reduction, the promotion of social equity and the strengthening of democracy, civil society, and good governance. The Zanzibar of today is a far cry from the country fifteen years ago ... Democracy has come to Zanzibar in a pervasive manner.' One could reach such a conclusion only if one shut one's eyes completely to the 'pervasive manner' of the *lack* of democracy in most development matters in Zanzibar from the beginning of the city until now. Community departicipation in the broader array of governance reforms seems to a large degree a response to the donor-funded public sector's complete failure to operate democratically, in contrast with the rhetoric that SMOLE and the government espoused (Andreasen 2001; Mohammed 2001). This phenomenon is present at all institutional levels. Neoliberal reforms have a poor record in transforming land management processes in Zanzibar or building new relationships between people and government. Constructing such a new relationship is going to be rather daunting, considering the negative ways government land and environment officials themselves talk about that relationship, let alone residents of the urban and peri-urban areas whose problems ZILEM, SMOLE and ZSP were meant to address. Multiparty politics has not produced more transparent and consensus-oriented urban governance.

Yet possibilities do exist for the sort of vigorous political contestation Fredericks or Pieterse see as essential to the genuine deepening of democratic decision-making. Below the thin veneer of party politics, with all of its violence and dysfunction, Zanzibari urban culture actually has a thicker layer of social cohesion. The reconstruction of governance in Zanzibar will not happen because the current CUF–CCM peace agreement or the next one after this holds; it demands building from the conversations and dialogue that define day-to-day neighborly interaction. This means finding ways of institutionalizing what is commonly known as the city's 'sisi-kwa-sisi' (us-for-us) system of social interaction.

Sisi-kwa-sisi is the de facto everyday governance framework, reliant on precepts of Sunni Shafi'i Islam (practiced by more than 90 percent of the city population) that encourage consensus-building at the level of the mosque community, the avoidance of harm, and the protection of privacy. Sisi-kwa-sisi, by its very phrasing, is about neighborliness and reciprocity which people seek to deploy in obtaining services. And, above all, sisi-kwa-sisi depends on uwezo, the Swahili term for 'capability,' which is also often translated as 'power.' A genuinely workable reform of governance would rely on consensus-building, harm avoidance, respect for privacy, neighborliness and reciprocal networks to extend the uwezo of every resident. All of these concepts can of course be overly idealized, romanticized, or simplistically deployed, but they all remain manifest in the lifeworlds of even the poorest Zanzibaris I have interviewed – even non-Muslims, or mainlander-origin residents – throughout twenty-two years of fieldwork in the city's informal neighborhoods. This is not a place of 'deep differences' and cultural incompatibilities that derail planning. Externally derived reforms, whether neoliberal or revolutionary socialist ones, will continue to fail unless they can engage the actually existing governance embedded in sisi-kwa-sisi (Myers 2003, 1996a).

Conclusion

Rather than leaving abstract and rarefied conceptualizations of governance or justice to stand alone, in this chapter I have paired the concepts with contexts for the discussion and questions of service delivery (or lack thereof) in African cities. This is in part because I come from a scholarly tradition that wants to seek a path to expanding justice and inclusivity in practical, even activist terms (Soja 2010). That path to the possible city is rocky in much of urban Africa, mostly because of donors, elites, and the holders of state power. The urban places of this chapter – Nairobi, Douala, Dakar, Kinshasa, Zanzibar, and the cities of South Africa – are each distinct spaces for any discussion of reconstructing relationships between ordinary people and the donors, states, and elites responsible for the rocks in the path. Each of the cities can gain from a thickening of an ethos of vigorous democratic practice institutionalized in service provision, in locally understandable ways. This of course may be more feasible in some cities than it may be in others.

Not one of them, regardless of the level of disrepair in which we find their infrastructures, social or physical, or how piratical we might find the governance structures that come into being when order is underfunded, has endured what the city on which I focus in most of Chapter 5, Mogadishu, has faced: two decades without any functioning government at all. Yet even here, one finds creative ways in which the urban is being reimagined. The next chapter marks a shift in tone as well, as I migrate into more literary-cultural realms of African urban studies rather than the policy-oriented debates which have been at the center of these last two chapters. My primary intention in doing so is to point toward more imaginative, creative African alternative visions of cities.

FIVE

Wounded city

Introduction

On 3 October 1993, eighteen US soldiers were killed in gun battles that followed the downing of two Black Hawk helicopters in Mogadishu, Somalia. On 4 October, a video became available to Western journalists, showing Somalis dragging a dead white body down the street by a rope, and abusing another corpse with their rifles. Once these were 'shown repeatedly on American televisions,' the video clips 'fueled public outrage and revulsion' (Hirsch and Oakley 1995: 127; Samatar 1994: 3). From that moment onward, Mogadishu has been represented in the USA as a space outside the norms of social order. For the US public in particular, the *Black Hawk Down* incidents of 1993 and various representations of it (especially in the 2001 film of that title) produced enduring imagery that certifies Mogadishu's otherness. For many Westerners and Americans in particular 'Somalia has gone on record as a nation of intractable savages, and the intervention into its anarchy as a catastrophic global blunder' (Fogarassy 1999: xvii), with Mogadishu as the 'world-capital of things gone to hell' (Bowden 1999: 7). Such imagery was used to justify both the initial US military occupation as a civilizing mission and the eventual withdrawal in March 1994. Media and public representation of US involvement with Somalia since then is refracted through this imaginary lens. A 2009 *New York Times* article (Gettleman 2009: 4) on US military strategy in Somalia fifteen years later was entitled 'The other lessons of Black Hawk Down,' and it began: 'Somalia isn't just a nagging geopolitical headache that won't go away. It is also a cautionary tale.'

The 2000s also brought new, related Somalia and Mogadishu narratives to the fore in the USA. Somali communities in Minnesota, Ohio, or Maine appeared together with Mogadishu on maps of alleged activities of al-Qaeda-linked terrorist cells, as Somalia's seas teemed with the new pirates of the twenty-first century. At the center of it all, *National Geographic*'s Robert Draper (2009: 71) tells us, 'Mogadishu is ground zero for the failed state of Somalia, a place where pirates and terrorists rule.' Draper (ibid.: 77, 80) offers us the 'awful truth' of Mogadishu's 'disfigurement,' where 'violence has a psychic hold on the city.'

I could continue with the dramatic and elegant prose by which the maligning of Mogadishu endures, but my aim in this chapter lies elsewhere, with attempts to envision the wounded city differently. The powerful resonance of the *Black Hawk Down*, terrorism, and piracy narratives and representations of Mogadishu with the contemporary realms of the Somali conflict make Somali attempts to contest them within US or Western media or intelligence spaces exceedingly daunting, especially given Somalia's lack of a stable national government, presence in international media, or national artistic bodies since 1991. Scholars, journalists, and activists within Somalia struggle to publish and distribute internationally basic pamphlet-like texts, while arguing that 'when the plight of the Somali people ... reached the ears of the human family, the nations of the world ... evaded their duty' (Mohammed 1998: xvi). Profound Somali critiques of the US forces in October 1993 for acting 'like tribes who cared little about what happened to other tribes' (Mohammed 1999: 150) or like 'a body without nerves to signal pain to the brain' (Qasim, in ibid.: 150) seldom see the light of day outside of Somali-centered communities.

The Somali novelist Nuruddin Farah (1998: ii) has, however, offered from exile a prominent counter-imaginary for Somalia, and Mogadishu in particular, in his fiction – trying, in his words, 'to keep my country alive by writing about it.' In decades of fictional work in English and largely for a Western audience, Farah (1970, 1976, 1980, 1981, 1983, 1986, 1992, 1998, 2003, 2007a) provides a complex means for Westerners to understand Mogadishu as its people have lived through Somalia's slow implosion. This portrayal of one city over time is inextricably intertwined with Farah's long-running effort to draw attention to the links, literally and figuratively, between Somalia, the Somali diaspora, and the many communities in the world that host Somalis (Farah 2000a). Farah's novel entitled *Links* (2003) is in direct conversation with the *Black Hawk Down* storyline, examining the US military operations from Somali eyes. *Knots* (2007a) is the second novel of Farah's 'Collapse' trilogy, following his two trilogies of novels that chronicled the impacts of Somalia's dictatorship on the cultural life of Somalis, mostly via Mogadishu. Farah called the early novels *Sweet and Sour Milk*, *Sardines*, and *Close Sesame* his 'Variations on the Theme of an African Dictatorship' trilogy, with Mogadishu figuring in all three, and particularly in *Sardines*, set in Mogadishu amid the torment of life in a dictatorship. The 'Blood in the Sun' trilogy of novels, *Maps*, *Gifts*, and *Secrets* expanded the geographical links of rural Somalia, Mogadishu, and the rest of the world through the fantastical and farcical last days of that dictatorship, and this has been followed by the first two 'Collapse' novels (Farah 1986, 1992, 1998, 2003, 2007a).

The core of this chapter analyzes Farah's most recent fiction for its possibilities for African urban theory, by which even the most wounded cities might be constructive of alternative modes of seeing cities. At first glance, this might make the chapter dramatically different from the previous three chapters, and there is, indeed, a methodological shift of a sort. But there are three ways that Farah's writings relate directly to my concerns in Chapters 2–4. First, he is among the most accomplished of African novelists categorized as 'postcolonial' writers because of their efforts to move beyond colonialism in cultural thought. That he does so on the map of Mogadishu makes his work an ideal focus for a book on African cities. Second, Farah's novels are chock-full of informality in the social interactions and built environments depicted. These social interactions, and the production of built environments as he details them in Mogadishu, are rife with the sorts of Afropolitan visions or hidden scripts of citiness I discussed in Chapter 3. Third, Farah's fiction is intensely engaged with questions of urban governance. In fact, Farah belongs with an emerging cadre of postcolonial African novelists creating what John Marx (2008: 597) calls 'failed state fiction' (see also Alidou and Mazrui 2000). This is a genre that seeks to 'shape a counterdiscourse' to that of the social science conception of a failed state (Marx 2008: 599). According to the 'Failed State Index' maintained by the Fund for Peace, Somalia has been a Code Red Failed State since the index began, leading to its portrayal as the world's greatest failed state (Draper 2009). Farah, like other novelists originating in thusly documented failed states, uses his fiction in part to 'present competent management as an aspiration every bit as compelling as the goal of national liberation it displaces' in earlier post-independence African novels (Marx 2008: 597). What Peter Hitchcock (2007: 745) considers Farah's 'wild imaginings' in his novels, from seemingly fanciful or impossibly coincidental global connectivities and unquenchable grandfatherly sex drives to ever-magical children and overtly symbolic animals, offer not just escape from what Hitchcock calls 'brute materiality'; they are also part of domesticating alternatives to the postcolonial reality. It is regularly in the process of remaking a house, reconstructing a family, or rebuilding trust in friendships that Farah situates Mogadishu's rebirth and its process of healing from its wounds. His Mogadishu stories run directly parallel to the '*sisi-kwa-sisi*' ('us-for-us') everyday governance framework for social interaction and the production of urban space discussed in Chapter 4 in the case of Zanzibar, suggesting wider possibilities for such an imaginary in analyzing cities in Africa.

Wounded cities

Let me first set the discussion of Mogadishu and Farah in the context of emerging literature on urban violence on the continent. Africa certainly has its share of wounded cities, urbicide, and near-urbicide. In the north, Algiers is perhaps the most prominent case, given the scars of the long war for independence centered in it in the 1950s and 1960s, the civil war of the 1990s, and the continuing strife of the 2000s, including the 2007 al-Qaeda bombing of UN peacekeeping offices there. The west offers up to the map of wounded cities Monrovia, Freetown, Abidjan, Bissau, Conakry, Ndjamena, and the cities of the Niger Delta, as sites of civil war or guerrilla operations. East and Central Africa count Kinshasa, the cities of eastern Congo, Kigali, Bujumbura, Brazzaville, and Nairobi as cities most wounded by war or political violence. Southern Africa's wounded cities include most cities in Angola and Mozambique, with urban Zimbabwe joining the wounded list as South Africa tries to leave it (Potts 2006: 76–81). Even in leaving that list with the end of apartheid-inspired conflict in 1994, South Africa's cities now endure a continuing wave of crime and violence that runs smack into a 'policing problem' stemming from the sense common across its cities – and those of many countries on the continent – that the police are 'indifferent, inept, inefficient, and corrupt … – or, for the poor, simply absent' (Brereton 2005: 2, 13).

The wounds of colonialism are compounded by those of apartheid in South Africa's urban hierarchy, down to the smallest cities. The small city of Grahamstown (with a population of nearly 130,000), for one vivid example, is fundamentally defined by the spatial gash that separates the elite, white educational center of Grahamstown 'proper' (with about 30,000 people) from the former townships for Indian, coloured, and black residents, with the latter – by far the largest part of the city as a whole – colloquially referred to as Rhini (with around 100,000 people). For Rhini residents, there exists a consciousness of wounds with deep roots that were found, at least in the early 1980s, to be linked with 'an identity of protest, character-ized by a strong sense of oppression and resentment, ... [and] a sense of solidarity' with other South African blacks, Africans, and blacks around the world, through the black consciousness movement in particular (Edwards 1984: iii; Davenport 1980: 50–52; Holleman 1997: 46). Grahamstown, the site of the final arrest of black consciousness movement leader Steve Biko prior to his murder in police custody in 1977, suffered through the brutal oppression of anti-apartheid activists in the Eastern Cape during the last decades of apartheid in particular. Cecil Manona (1988: 1006) researched the 'intense sense of community and reciprocal assistance' that was, he argued, 'rooted in the people's common experience of deprivation' in Rhini. He was at pains to note that the neighborliness and solidarity were not a result of 'any par-ticular humaneness of African social relations but from the fact that every black urban dweller is involved in a complex network of social relations' (ibid.: 104). He contended that Grahamstown/Rhini had developed a 'distinctive urban culture' of its own over many decades (ibid.: 108). We may consider this distinctive culture as Grahamstown's version of the *sisi-kwa-sisi* mode of interaction and everyday govern-ance that I've suggested for Zanzibar in the last chapter, or that Farah's novels suggest. Thus the 'inflammatory rage and sadness' (Meyer 1992: 17) or 'seething frustration' (Nyquist 1983: 16) that helped make Grahamstown's black population extraordinarily creative and try to stand in solidarity had many parallels in South Africa and across the continent, from Mogadishu to Dakar (Simone 2010).

Grahamstown and Rhini combined are a smaller city in 2010 than any I examined in the previous chapters, but one with a longer and bloodier history than most of them. The Colonel John Graham for whom the town was named truly earned his nickname, 'Butcher Graham' (Holleman 1997: 15). One of the first black locations was placed by the Field of Blood where Graham and the British defeated Xhosa forces in 1819. Grahamstown and its environs were then swept up into the major series of Frontier Wars between the British and Xhosa. The most dramatic moment of these came with the horrific cattle killings of the 1850s, as Xhosa followers of the young prophetess Nongqawuse slaughtered livestock to attempt to fulfill visions that she said had come to her, of ancestors arising from the sea to fight the white settlers. Perhaps South Africa's poet laureate Keorapetse Kgositsile (2009: 3) best expressed what generations of systemic violence did to this small cityscape, in his poem about Rhini, 'In the naming':

We now know past any argument
that places can have scars ...
Since the settler
set his odious foot here in 1820
... These hills have not been joyful together.
In Rhini you can go up
or down in any direction
in the lay of the land where
The people have memories as palpable
as anything you can see with your own eye
But in Grahamstown,
those who know say,
any where you go is uphill.

Legacies of violence like that of Grahamstown have been increasingly frequent subjects of interrogation in African urban studies, as they have been in urban studies across Asia and Latin America (Kruijt and Koonings 2009). This relatively recent upsurge in scholarly interest appears to follow actual trends in urban violence, particularly as increasing crime seems to have associations with increasing urban exclusion, inequality, and the uneven governance outcomes discussed in Chapter 4 (Beall 2006; Kruijt 2008); it certainly seems that 'any where you go is uphill' in the battle against violence in many African cities (Schlyter 2006; Pieterse 2005). The less that a city's residents are able to function in an 'us-for-us' relational mode, the more conflictual everyday life appears to become.

There is, however, a 'continuum' to urban violence in Africa that is worth articulating at the outset – in other words, one must not lump all forms of violence together into a notion of all African cities as violent or equally violent in the same ways, as writers prone to the rampant stereotypes and generalizations about the continent are wont to do (Scheper-Hughes and Bourgeois, in Ahluwalia et al. 2007: 1). One must be quite wary of romancing the 'pervasive, almost ritualistic, association of Africa with forms of everyday as well as extreme violence' (ibid.: 1).

At one end of the continuum, it is important to note the degree to which in a great many cities on the continent *non-violence* operates alongside forms of violence (Simone 2007b; Schler 2007). Lynn

Schler (2007: 28) shows, for example, the hidden history of ethnic cooperation and coexistence in the Douala neighborhood of New Bell, discussed in Chapter 4 in decidedly more negative terms in the contemporary era, asking how such 'histories of non-conflict and non-violent cooperation can be reconstructed.' Simone (2007b: 64, 69) traces how what he calls 'sacral spaces' emerged in contemporary Abidjan and Douala, meaning zones that 'permit gatherings of urban actors who are otherwise antagonists or socially distant to transact and collaborate with each other' in an African re-creation of the ancient Greek *agora*, or public space.

On this continuum we then come to a great many other cities in Africa which lack outright war, even of the 'low-intensity' urban warfare that Kruijt and Koonings (2009: 25) associate with expansive incoherent slum development, such as appears to be the case in Douala or Abidjan (despite the above examples of pockets or time bubbles of peace there). Peaceful cities can experience a considerable upsurge of violence, seemingly suddenly. Maiduguri, Nigeria, has a general reputation as a rather quiet and conservative city, but in July 2009 images from five days of street violence there, a clash between an Islamist group and the Nigerian army that left 700 people dead, hurtled around the world (Nossiter 2009). Yet after this explosion, the city quieted down. Colleagues at the University of Maiduguri were flummoxed by the disconnect between the violence and their sense of the city as a moderate, tolerant, and learned modern center, and equally frustrated that as soon as the violence subsided Maiduguri disappeared from the world stage. At least in the media, the city's only utility in the Western imagination of African cities lay in a rare outburst of violence (Karta 2010; Sheriff 2002).

In Chapter 4, I discussed Simone's conception of piracy as a form of governance and its applicability in several African cities, and certainly this is piracy that is not lacking in violence and wounds, longer, slower, and deeper episodes than those of Maiduguri. This sort of piratic violence may take various forms, such as the extensive gang activity often discussed for Johannesburg or Kinshasa. Kinshasa, in Theodore Trefon's (2009: 3) words, is, for instance, 'often portrayed as a forsaken black hole characterized by calamity, chaos, confusion and a bizarre form of social cannibalism where society is its own prey.' Lagos, notoriously, operates on a similar terrain of piracy.

These African mega-cities can be described as ill-governed cities subsisting under shadows of crime and social despair, yet where 'new and remarkable patterns of stability, organization, and quest for well-being have emerged' (ibid.: 3). Maintaining our journey along the continuum of violence, we find a perceptible difference between such wounded cities and cities that endure year after year of open and outright urban civil warfare in them. Jean Omasombo (2005: 96) has written of Kisangani as a 'city at its lowest ebb' in the early 2000s, following its destruction in the civil war that followed the DRC's independence in 1960 and then the 'heavy toll' it paid in 'the protracted war that began in 1998' and which has not really ended yet. Omasombo (ibid.: 99) demonstrates that Kisangani 'stands as the symbol of the collapse of the whole of Congo,' and its residents have little capacity for the 'resourcefulness displayed in other towns' because it is so centrally situated in violent war. Kisangani has parallels across the continent where outright urban warfare incapacitates cities for years on end.

But it is the rubble and live ammunition of Mogadishu which return again and again to prominence, at least in the American theater of imagining what has gone wrong with African cities, emblematic of the societies that build them and then blow them up in war. Through Nuruddin Farah's eyes, we see this city again – never without its fractures, grief, absurdity, or misery, but also never without hope. A Farah novel '*does* something, rather than just means something,' as R. John Williams (2006: 163) would have it, because 'its imaginative interventions into historiography dramatize the potential to shape reality.' Through his re-creation of Mogadishu, Farah breathes life back into Mogadishu. Imaginary cityspaces are no substitute for practical, activist work toward conflict resolution, and Farah quietly devotes a considerable amount of energy to this, outside of the novels (Farah 2007b). But it is also through the anti-nationalist, global connectivity that Farah foregrounds that his novels relink Mogadishu, as a city in a world of cities. Characters from abroad populate all of his novels, with strong ties to Italy (Gorlier 1998), Ireland, North America, India, Arabia and the Gulf, and knowing nods to literature and the arts from the rest of Africa and, indeed, from around the world (Ngaboh-Smart 2000, 2001). Like other African literary 'escapees from the destructive authoritarianisms of postcolonial rule,' Farah is 'caught up in the maelstrom of massive international migrations' (Zeleza 2005: 11). Most obviously in *Maps* and *Gifts*, but more subtly in every novel since, Farah is doing something quite different from 'keeping his country alive by writing about it': he is deterritorializing Somalia as a nationalist project, and reterritorializing it as a place that belongs with the world, with its capital city at the heart of that 'belonging-by-"straddling"' between global connections and local intimacies (Ngaboh-Smart 2001: 97; Yewah 2001; Gikandi 2002; Kazan 2002; Moore 2002).

In *Links* and *Knots*, Farah relies on 'a sense of uncanniness and haunting that stubbornly refuses to forget' the continuities and connectivities in 'contemporary African ... theaters of war,' reminding the readers about Mogadishu's colonial past and its life under dictatorship in the midst of his stories set in the era of 'Collapse,' as his latest trilogy is entitled (Gana and Harting 2008: 5). Mogadishu is one of the most widely represented of these African theaters of war, and certainly the most widely represented *urban* theater of collapse. Let me provide at least a cursory historical context and a short segment on the arc of US involvement in Mogadishu's warfare before turning to analyze Farah's novelistic renditions of this theater.

On Mogadishu

Mogadishu's history stretches back at least to the tenth century (Allen 1993; Jama 1996). Mogadishu had important influences from Arabia and Persia on top of the city's indigenous connections with its immediate hinterland (Jama 1996; Cassanelli 1982). The city endured Arab, Portuguese, and British imperial incursions, before becoming the capital of Italian Somaliland in 1908 (Alpers 1983; Marchal 2006). Like colonial cities across Africa, under the Italians, Mogadishu experienced pass laws and segregation that warped and retarded its growth. Its postcolonial population began to expand dramatically only after the 1969 military coup that brought General Mohamed Siad Barre to power as Somalia's president. During the early 1970s, this rapidly expanding city was – while not exactly the thriving 'spectacular city' (Draper 2009: 77) of the Western imagination's collapse narrative – the bustling and clan-diverse cosmopolitan center of Somalia (Farah 1981; Hartley 2003: 185; Korn 2006: 60–104; Makinda 1993: 17). By the latter part of that decade and through the 1980s, 'profound changes in the social fabric of the capital city' with substantial in-migration from rural areas, growing inequalities, and increasing deprivation began to implode in 'small urban conflicts' built upon clan polarization, the proliferation of Cold War weaponry, and the heavily militarized paranoia of Barre's regime (Marchal 2006: 211; Farah 2000a). Mogadishu's growth rate 'accelerated dramatically' in the 1980s, and 'water, sanitation, and health services and housing stock could not keep up' (Wisner 1994: 29). Barre's regime reacted to growing protests within the city by calling out troops to open fire on demonstrators, but the unrest continued until Barre had become, by 1990, little beyond 'the mayor of Mogadishu' (Lyons and Samatar 1995: 21). Then, in January 1991, even his control over that space collapsed, and he fled the city for exile.

From the full onset of Somalia's civil war in 1990 until today, Mogadishu has had no single functioning government authority managing its economy or society. Mogadishu's territorial space has, indeed, been the center (albeit not the only center) of Somalia's civil war for most of these twenty years (Gutale 2008). From the 1980s onward, Mogadishu has survived in part as a recipient city for migrant remittances. The degree and tenor of outright violence in the city have ebbed and flowed since the collapse of Barre's regime, with highly unregulated economic development here and there (Eno 2005). Private telecommunications or computer firms, private universities, luxury high-security hotels, a thriving import-export trade sector, massive informal land, real estate, and construction industries, and lucrative money services firms and private security services make Mogadishu for some a prime example of an 'economy without state' (Little 2003). Through their 'creative institutional and behavioral responses,' Somalis maintained 'a level of economic welfare comparable to' neighboring states for many years (ibid.: xv). Mogadishu University, for example, ran distance-education courses on social science methods and on the world economy in partnership with my home institution, the University of Kansas, through the second half of the 2000s despite increasing security risks. New and constructive nongovernmental organizations and community-based organizations, many led by Somali women, 'mushroomed' in the post-government era, too (Bryden and Steiner 1998: 59).

Yet innovations and relations that have perpetuated conditions for survival in rural Somalia mean less in Mogadishu and other Somali cities now, as rural–urban ties dissipate and resentments, general social inequalities, and masses of the internally displaced concentrate in urban settings (Little 2003: 45–64; La Sage and Majid 2004: 382–4). Even just a few years into the post-Barre civil war, archeologists and preservationists estimated that more than half of the historic quarter of the city had been leveled (Jama 1996; Samatar 1994). Most urban services are not systematically provided, or at least not by a governance network that is threaded through a government. The Ethiopian army's US-backed expulsion of the Islamic Courts Union from Mogadishu at the end of 2006 ultimately made matters worse, as Mogadishu seesawed back and forth between Ethiopian/US-backed Transitional National Government control, resurgent Islamists (now under the banner of al-Shabab, among other groups), and various clan forces through the next three years, crumbling further, block by block (Human Rights Watch 2007). The blocks had certainly begun to crumble by the time the US military arrived in the early 1990s to 'restore hope,' but the 'hope' the soldiers brought to the city only accelerated the crumbling. Because Farah's alternative visions of Mogadishu in *Links* and *Knots* come out of a response to that operation, it is useful to review it briefly here.

Black Hawk Down

The US military's direct involvement in Somalia's civil war, for the time being, can be said to have peaked in the period from December 1992 through March 1994, putting aside more recent assistance to the Ethiopian invasion, drone aircraft attacks, counter-terrorism kill-teams, or counter-attacks on pirates at sea. The early-1990s involvement focused on humanitarian relief, but by summer 1993 US forces were drawn into the war for Mogadishu. Both before and after this direct engagement, the USA was and has continued to be indirectly fundamental to Mogadishu's conflicts. Throughout the steady deterioration of Somalia in the 1980s, the US funneled substantial military and technical assistance to the Barre regime as a Cold War counterweight to Soviet aid to Ethiopia (Hirsch and Oakley 1995: 7; Casper 2001: 141–2; Rawson 1994; Hashi 1996; Makinda 1993: 56–7). After the withdrawal of US forces in 1994, the US government remained in contact with and acted as a financial and strategic support for a number of individuals and organizations within the city and the country, including human rights organizations and clan-based militia.

But it is during the 1992–94 action, initially named Operation Restore Hope, that the US military's representation – and by extension the prevailing popular and media representation – of Mogadishu had its genesis. One construction of perceived space of Somalia, from their perspective, was certainly that of a theater for a US colonial mission. The commander of US Army forces in Somalia for much of the campaign, Lieutenant General Thomas Montgomery (2003: 19), justified the intervention, in his Foreword to the *After Action Report*

(Center of Military History 2003), as 'a new kind of mission' into a 'failed nation-state.' The early part of that mission centered on providing food and relief supplies in rural southern Somalia. But, in the words of Brigadier General John Brown (2003: iii), 'greeted initially by Somalis happy to be saved from starvation, US troops were slowly drawn into inter-clan power struggles and ill-defined "nation-building" missions.'

Chief among the 'power struggles' was that which took shape largely in and around Mogadishu, between forces loyal to Ali Mahdi Mohamed in the environs of the northern third of the city and those loyal to Mohamed Farah Aideed, concentrated in the southern half of the city. Aideed became the focus of US military concerns (Center of Military History 2003: 102). In June 1993, his militia killed or wounded eighty Pakistani soldiers serving as UN peacekeepers, during simultaneous attacks. US admiral Jonathan Howe, chief of the UN operation in Somalia, put out wanted posters for Aideed, dead or alive, and US/UN forces began directly attacking Aideed's forces. Day after day, violations of the UN peacekeeping mission occurred. Pertinently, a 12 July assault on an alleged Aideed-allied clan meeting resulted in the massacre of more than fifty Somalis, mostly women, children, and the elderly – after which angry Somalis attacked and killed four foreign journalists attempting to cover the assault's aftermath (Hartley 2003: 275–83). Escalating violence both by and against the Americans and other UN forces throughout the next month prompted the late-August deployment of a unit of US Army Rangers, but even these elite forces, as Hartley (ibid.: 294) put it, 'grew so frustrated by failure that they resorted to acts of childish nastiness,' such as games trying to blow roofs off residences with helicopter air currents. Some accounts document far worse acts, including civilian killings, torture, and sexual assault (Afrah 1994: 86; Mohammed 1998; Razack 2004: 71–3).

The worst violence occurred on the night of 3 October, and into the following morning. Largely because of the book and film *Black Hawk Down*, the basic outline of these events is well known. Perhaps the appropriate way to recount them here is in the official language of the US forces' *After Action Report*'s chronology of events (Center of Military History 2003: 156, capital letters in original):

TASK FORCE RANGER CONDUCTS RAID VIC OLYMPIC HOTEL IN MOGADISHU. 18 US SOLDIERS KIA WITH 84 WIA; 1 MALAYSIAN

SOLDIER KIA, 10 WIA; 2 PAKISTANI SOLDIERS WIA; AND 300+
SOMALIS KILLED, 700+ WOUNDED (ACCORDING TO SNA REPORTS)
AND 22 DETAINEES CAPTURED.

The fact that 'foreign forces killed or wounded more than a thousand Somalis during the battle,' the majority of whom were civilians
(Hartley 2003: 295), is almost parenthetical here, justified by the end
of the sentence above: the twenty-two detainees captured in the initial
raid before the helicopters went down. However, in contrast to the
precise figures for 'coalition' casualties (killed in action, or KIA, and
wounded in action, WIA), the numbers for Somalis are listed vaguely,
as '300+,' or '700+,' and no characterization of who these people
were ever appears. Other US military accounts place the blame for
the Somali casualties on Aideed's forces and their 'erratic mortar
fire' (Casper 2001: 73).

From that night's disaster onward, UN forces 'would hardly leave
Mogadishu' despite the fact that the food security issues that had
brought them to Somalia were largely rural in character (Sahnoun
1994: 37). To secure that UN presence, the UN and the USA expanded
around their base at the national airport and created an expansive
base farther to the northwest within the city. Once the images of
American bodies being dragged through the streets appeared on US
television on 4 October, it took then US president Bill Clinton less
than seventy-two hours to go before the nation and declare that US
forces would be withdrawn by March of the following year. General
Brown (2003: iii) called the whole operation 'costly' and 'shocking.'
After the *Black Hawk Down* battle, Mogadishu became a byword
for justifying non-intervention, and warnings about 'crossing the
Mogadishu line' – taking sides in a peacekeeping operation – blos-
somed around the world (Clarke 1997: 3). UN–US relations soured
considerably with the sense of 'betrayal' the UN felt after the US
unilateral withdrawal from Somalia (Howe 1997: 177). The US failure
to respond to the Rwanda genocide is regularly referred back to the
Black Hawk Down experience (Clarke and Herbst 1995).

Brown (2003: iii) closed his introduction to the *After Action Report*
by noting that this was an 'extraordinarily important US operation'
because 'these disturbing events of a decade ago have taken on increasing meaning after the horrific attacks of September 11, 2001.'
The movie made from Mark Bowden's book, *Black Hawk Down*,
was 'all but finished by September 11' of 2001, and released in the

holiday movie season of 2001/02 to US audiences ready to make the connections to the plane attacks in New York (Bowden 2002: xv). Despite a script pared back to a strict focus on American-centered combat on the night of 3 October, the filmmakers, producers, and distributors of it missed no opportunity to promote the movie as a patriotic rendering of America's broader fight against terrorism, even if that meant blanketing the potential audience with 'a fog of half-truths' (Kaus 2002; Fryer 2002; Nolan 2002; Bowden 2002).

At the same time, though, thoughtful military analysts began to see the 3/4 October 1993 fiasco as emblematic of the US Army's 'victory disease,' where 'an arrogant belief in the superiority of US forces coupled with a complacent underestimation of the opponent' caused the failure of the mission (Karcher 2004: 34). It appears that the actions of US forces in Mogadishu provided a preview of the wars in Iraq and Afghanistan, albeit without broad appreciation of the 'victory disease.' *Black Hawk Down* became a training film for these wars, and the book of that name 'required reading for some courses at West Point' (Gettleman 2009: 4). Since it was in this imagery that Mogadishu became, in Bowden's (1999: 7) words from *Black Hawk Down*, the 'world capital of things-gone-completely-to-hell ... ravaged by some fatal urban disease,' it is a quintessential example of the generalizing logic of the 'Africa talk' that I discuss in the introduction as a discursive field to be deconstructed in this book (Ferguson 2006: 2). It also provided Nuruddin Farah with a story of global significance to respond to in his engagements with Mogadishu.

Nuruddin Farah's representational space

For many Somalis – those forced into exile by the Barre regime or the aftermath of its collapse, or those forced to live in Mogadishu since 1991 – there is in contemporary times a 'dual sorrow,' over the 'indignities' of daily life and the 'deep shame of a fallen people' (Samatar 2002: 217). Somalis, in common conceptualizations of their plight, are either forced to be 'scruffy refugees' or to 'exist in the foul debris' of the city the refugees left behind (ibid.: 217–18). They must deal with the dual tendency of outsider understanding of their predicament – in essence, that the West was crazy to intervene but that the failure of that intervention was the fault of the Somalis themselves (Stevenson 1995). And they must confront conceived spaces of the Mogadishu known to those outsiders, the 'world capital of things-gone-completely-to-hell' of *Black Hawk Down*.

Farah does not shy away from criticisms of Somalis, nor does he prettify Mogadishu in his work. Perhaps this is part of what makes Farah's work controversial among Somalis (Samatar 2000), especially since he has admitted that 'any talk of Somalia brings me sad associations' (Farah 2000a: 7). Farah is often praised for his female-centered writing: Kwame Anthony Appiah (Farah 2004) called Farah 'a feminist novelist in a part of the world where that's almost unknown among male writers.' Yet that can produce a backlash, for instance when Farah wrote of his countrymen who have become European asylum seekers by complaining that 'Somali men tend to work as little as possible,' often subsisting 'on the incomes of their female counterparts' (Farah 2000b: 12). He despaired that 'Somalis do not place themselves, as individuals, *in the geography of the collective collapse*, but outside of it' (Farah 2000a: 187–8, emphasis added). He himself is very much like the refugees he interviewed for his book, *Yesterday, Tomorrow: Voices from the Somali Diaspora* (2000a: 37), who 'kept Mogadiscio afloat in their memories of it' (Farah, here as elsewhere, strangely prefers the Italianized spelling of the city's name). He claims to have 'dwelt in the dubious details of a territory I often refer to as the country of my imagination' (ibid.: 48) during his decades of exile, and he once made the bold claim of seeking to 'engrave the name of Somalia on the skin of the world' (Vivan 1998: 790). But that country is a city-state in his novels; he does his engraving on the skin of Mogadishu, 'the world of the city and of civic culture' (Alden and Tremaine 1999: 44). Farah's novels are essentially or ultimately Mogadishu stories (*Links* and *Knots*, as well as *Sardines, Close Sesame, Gifts* and *A Naked Needle*, with *Secrets* split between the city and a nearby farm, and the stories in *Maps, Sweet and Sour Milk*, and *From a Crooked Rib* moving to Mogadishu midway through), and in each case Farah most decisively places individual Somalis, increasingly empathetically, at the very center of the 'geography of the collective collapse.' The city is the map of the story. In *Links* in particular, Farah (2004) has said that he tried 'to view the city as the principal character, and the people living in it or visiting it become secondary characters.' Territory, space, and place in and around the city are principal characters in the narratives of all these books – each one set at a particularly defining moment – and at the same time each book has a central character tied to the worldwide diaspora.

Farah was born in Baidoa in 1945 and grew up some three hundred miles from Mogadishu in the Ogaden, developing strong connections to his father's commercial farm ten miles out of town, a site for memories put to use in *Secrets* (Farah 1998, 2000b, 2009). His family moved to Mogadishu when he was seventeen, and he resided there for eight of the next dozen years (he earned his BA in India from 1966 to 1970), beginning his writing career while working as a clerk and then as a lecturer at the national university (Farah 2009; Wright 2004). Fluent in Amharic and Arabic, he chose to write in English for a number of reasons – his first typewriter was an American-made Royal, Somali had no written script until a government commission that Farah worked with established it in 1972, and he felt he 'received' his 'intellectual makeup' in English (Farah 2000b, 2006, 2009). He left Somalia in 1974 to study for his masters degree, intending to return, but the publication of his second novel, *A Naked Needle*, led to his enforced exile from his homeland and the dictatorship of Siad Barre, an exile that lasted twenty-two years.

Farah is an outlandish and unique writer, and his games with narrative, narration, plot (some novels, such as *Sardines*, don't really have one) and prose itself sometimes make interpreting meanings in his ten novels hard work. Derek Wright (1998: 733) critiqued Farah's 'habit of overloading and super-charging his writing, of clouding meaning with the sheer fertility of allusion and suggestiveness.' Said Samatar (2000: 140) complained that *Secrets* was full of 'the weirdest of sentence-constructions since Adam babbled his first halting syllables in the Garden of Eden.' But the geographical dimensions of his stories are more easily accessible, and representations of the city and its environs especially so, down to the intricate details of streets, homes, and gardens (Ngaboh-Smart 2001). These geographical dimensions, and indeed the narrative structure and prose, of both *Links* and *Knots* are clear, plain, and unembroidered in a manner unlike his previous novels (Ngaboh-Smart 2004). 'Some of us think of the cities we know very well and where we've lived as intimate friends,' a character says at the beginning of *Links* (2003: 6), and Mogadishu is clearly an intimate friend for Farah despite his long periods of exile. In each of his urban novels, but most obviously in his last two, Farah constructs in the city a 'loc[us] of passion, of action, of lived situations' (Soja 1996) that assertively counters a notion of Mogadishu as dead or of Somalis as sacrificial others.

In *Links*, the main character's feet have just 'touched the ground in Mogadiscio' in the second line, after his landing at a 'desolate airstrip' (Farah 2003: 3). As readers we immediately experience the banal, everyday shock of the place along with this character, a Somali-American named Jeebleh, as he finds this intimate friend, his city, suddenly strange and frightening:

> Jeebleh observed that after retrieving their baggage, the passengers congregated around the entrance to a lean-to shed ... A minute later, he worked out that the shack was 'Immigration,' when he saw some of the passengers handing over their passports ... If the lean-to was the place to have his passport stamped, who, then, were the men inside, since they had no uniforms? What authority did they represent, given that Somalia had no central government ...? Jeebleh couldn't imagine how anyone could survive and prosper in the conditions of Mogadiscio. (Ibid.: 4)

Jeebleh is disoriented from the start, as he tries to 'adapt to the new situation' (ibid.: 5), surrounded by suspicious people and murderous teenagers, in a city brutally divided between Strongman North (Ali Mahdi Mohamed) and Strongman South (Aideed). The novel works toward its resolution in a place Farah terms The Refuge, a physical and imaginary space stuck between the territories of the Strongmen. Farah's vision of The Refuge is a small compound, but one that represents in magical terms the imagined or longed-for Mogadishu of his (and Jeebleh's) youth: 'orderly, clean, peaceable, a city with integrity and a life of its own, a lovely metropolis with beaches, cafes, restaurants, late-night movies. It may have been poor but ... no one was in a hurry to plunder or destroy what they couldn't have' (ibid.: 35). Farah is never blind to problematic aspects of Somali society or history, though, and so he tells us that by 1993 Mogadishu had become a 'city vandalized, taken over by rogues' (ibid.: 35).

Two crucial aspects of Farah's representation of the city distinguish it from the prevailing representations in the US military, Western media or movies. The first is the nature of the US presence in the story, beginning to end. Jeebleh is partly an American character, since he is a New York resident, married to an American, carrying an American passport. The US forces' departure is noted on the first page; the last page finds Jeebleh en route to New York. The whole book is a conversation about the *links* between Somalia and the USA, Mogadishu and New York, and between *Black Hawk Down* and 11 September 2001.

Jeebleh is ostensibly back in town to pay his respects at his mother's grave. But Farah allows Jeebleh to disguise from himself the hidden dimensions of his reasons for returning to Somalia, and to wander blindly through the city's fiercely contested sides (between Strongman North and Strongman South) until he is, like the US forces before him, quite clearly drawn into the internecine conflict that is destroying it. Like Task Force Ranger, he leaves the city after a painful and traumatic series of events that shape the plot of *Links*, but with many of his questions still unresolved.

Farah frames the narrative with quotations from Dante's *Inferno* at the opening of every section of the novel, as Dante was often on his mind while writing the novel (Farah 2006). Jeebleh becomes irretrievably enmeshed in the affairs of his people immediately around him in the Inferno of post-1991 Mogadishu, a place where 'fraud ... eats away at every conscience' (Dante, in Farah 2003: 243). Farah (ibid.: 243) uses Dante's raging anger to ask, 'Who, even with untrammeled words and many attempts at telling, even could recount in full the blood and wounds that I now saw?' The Mogadishu that Jeebleh had refused to claim as home becomes his once again through his recognition of his own culpability in the disastrous American misadventure in the city. There is no Beatrice to pull him out of himself alive, but Jeebleh learns to think through his own Inferno together with his old mates, as they discuss the *Black Hawk Down* battle.

His Somali and Irish graduate school roommates from long-ago days in Rome, Bile and Seamus, are running an orphanage and health clinic in The Refuge. Seamus says the Americans 'came to show the world they could make peace-on-demand in Somalia, in the same dramatic fashion as they had made war-on-demand in the Gulf' (ibid.: 261). Farah's Somali characters are actually more nuanced and generous in their understanding. We eventually see the *Black Hawk Down* story through the eyes of a Somali mother whose small child miraculously survived being swept up into the blades of a helicopter as it crashed in Mogadishu that day, and the words of a fighter, Dajaal, who helped hunt down the US soldiers in the streets.

As he walks with Jeebleh to visit the injured girl and her mother, Dajaal talks about the battle, admitting

> my heart went out to the young Marines and Rangers ... I imagined
> them wondering what they were doing in Africa, away from their
> loved ones, asking themselves why some skinny Somalis in sarongs
> were taking potshots at them ... As fighters, there was a major flaw

in their character, however. They thought less of us, and that was ultimately the cause of their downfall. (Ibid.: 267)

Like European colonialists before them, the Americans in Somalia could not systematically see the humanity in the people whose land they occupied. Individual exceptions to this can certainly be found, but the frame as a whole, the system, 'thought less of' *them*.

The second key distinguishing feature of Farah's representation, though, is the obvious empathy he expresses for those in the misery of the actual space of Mogadishu, even for those Somalis who are part of inflicting misery on others. Through Jeebleh and through his conversations with Somalis of all persuasions in the novel, a sense of Mogadishu as lived space is unmistakable, and the possibilities of spaces of resistance provide the novel with its sustaining rays of hope. This is geographically expressed in the imaginary Refuge at the heart of the city, much as his Eden-like gardens in the Mogadishu his main character dreams up in *Maps* provided a dream of escape from dictatorship (Ngaboh-Smart 2001: 90). The Refuge, though, is a lived space in Lefebvrean terms, real and imagined at the same time. We see this from the moment we arrive, inauspiciously, at its entrance: 'The gate slumped on its hinges, creaking forward, its bottom edge almost touching the ground, its paint flaking off' (Farah 2003: 154), but 'peace reigned here,' in one of the very few 'oases of comfort in a land of sorrow' (ibid.: 155). Bile had created The Refuge out of the ruins of a Catholic home for abandoned children that had, before that, been an Italian colonist's villa. There's no mistaking the (postcolonial discursive) point: Mogadishu's people inherited a colonial ruin, but that doesn't inevitably mean the rest of the city needs to be the hellhole it has become. Bile steadily took on children abandoned in the fighting until The Refuge became a village of its own, 'eating together daily from the same *mayida* [bowl],' according to Bile (ibid.: 157), 'in the belief that we create a camaraderie and we'll all trust one another.' Bile seems to recognize that such idealism might appear as 'hogwash,' but says their 'experiment bears it out,' since people 'who look one another in the eye as they eat together are bound closely to one another' (ibid.: 158). Thus the scale of the lived space comes down to the dinner table. People create places looking each other in the eye over a common plate, not by looking down on them through night vision goggles and calling them 'moon crickets,' as the US Rangers had (Casper 2001: 78). The parallels with de Boeck and Plissart's (2004: 244) discussion of what they term 'the (im)possibilities of the possible' in Kinshasa are uncanny here. Like Farah, de Boeck and Plissart (ibid.: 249) do not 'deny the ruptures and fragmentations' at work in 'reshaping the landscapes of kinship' in the wounded city; but these intimate domestic relations and social units, reconstructed and reinvented, are 'the most important remaining' entities through which 'to explore and redefine anew the rhythms of reciprocity, commensality, conjugality and gender relations in the urban context.'

Knots is set a few years later, and it is in part a continuation of the storyline of *Links*, of the struggles over 'reshaping the landscapes of kinship' in Mogadishu. The main character this time is a woman, Cambara, returning to Mogadishu from her shattered life in Toronto, rather than New York, to recover her family home from the grip of the murderous warlord who seized it in the early 2000s, a plot element that overlaps with events in Farah's (2009) own life. She is, like Jeebleh in *Links*, grieving over a profound loss – this time, of her child, who drowned in her ex-husband's Canadian swimming pool. As is common in Farah's three trilogies (see Alden and Tremaine 1998), characters from another novel (here, *Links*) reappear: Bile, Dajaal, and Seamus, facing down demons of madness (Bile), political Islam and fundamentalism (Dajaal), and sheer pain (Seamus). Jeebleh is an absent presence in the book. Somehow, his insertion into the life of The Refuge had brought it down, and Bile most of all has suffered for this. Farah tricks the reader in Bile's first appearance in *Knots*, as a 'ramrod-straight man' who comes by chance with Dajaal to assist Cambara, who has just kick-boxed two would-be attackers on one of her ill-advised walks in the violent streets (Farah 2007a: 167). She is immediately wary of 'surrendering to Bile's magic charm: a handsome man with a distinctively remote gaze' (ibid.: 168).

The next time readers meet Bile, though, Dajaal has taken Cambara to the flat the two men share. She walks into the flat to find Bile 'lying on his side, dissipated, with no more energy to expend' (ibid.: 313). He has soiled himself, and he is talking nonsense, overcome by madness. Seamus later explains to her that his friend has lost 'his emotional fix' and replaced it with 'sadness' from childhood trauma, and on days when he does not take his self-prescribed mix of anti-depressants, 'the well of his bottomless sorrow' from years in detention and years watching the civil war and state collapse take his Mogadishu away, he seems to have a 'death wish' (ibid.: 328).

Seamus recounts to Cambara the rise and fall of The Refuge, 'our own paradise in a country that had gone to hell' (ibid.: 329). It simply wasn't enough, this small clinic and orphanage astride the abyss. As in *Links*, Seamus is again in *Knots* the voice explaining the larger canvas of failure:

> there was – there is – need for more universal commitments; no do-gooders can do as much as it will take to reconstruct the country's infrastructure, reorient the people of this nation so they might find their proper bearing ... Boring rhetoric, boring politics, yes, but the truth is that the political class has failed this country. (Ibid.: 329)

However pained and jaundiced Seamus has become as a character, though, Farah is still not willing to give up on his country or his city. The wounds are as deep as Bile's well of bottomless sorrow. But in *Knots*, it is a quiet, shadowy network of women peace activists who are taking little steps to keep the city alive, combating its many wells of sorrow with home-schooling collaboration, food distribution, medical care, and, through Cambara, creative arts. Cambara writes and stages a puppet play in the property she reacquires with Dajaal's military assistance. Where *Links* is playing off of the smoke from Dante's *Inferno*, *Knots* concludes with a play on a very different Italian work, *Pinocchio*, with plot elements from works by Ama Ata Aidoo and James Kwegyir Aggrey. The dreamlike and *almost* too-good-to-be-true ending comes with the staging of the play to a gathered audience of the women's network and the volunteers who put the makeshift theater together: 'It is characteristic of every one of Cambara's new friends that each contributes his or her fair share in the hope of making a difference in her life here in this city' (ibid.: 400).

Yet Farah is never one for simple happy endings, and we know there cannot be one, even in the fanciful puppet play. Cambara becomes distraught as the play opens, since 'she has woven nearly every thread of her private, professional and public life into the yarn that is about to be presented,' such that she 'loses touch with everything that matters' and 'sneaks away' to hide (ibid.: 417). When she comes back in, she becomes bizarrely overjoyed at the sight of a woman named Maimouna, a friendly acquaintance, seating herself in the front row, so much so that 'several members of the audience' let it be known that she is 'disturbing their enjoyment, creating a racket and moving about as though she is mad' (ibid.: 418). Although ultimately the play is judged a success, and her mother, Arda, newly arrived to see the only performance of the play, gets to meet her daughter's new love, Bile, the novel ends up in the air, as Arda talks privately with Bile, but 'no one gets to hear what the two have said to each other' (ibid.: 419).

This ambivalent ending is about as positive a twist as Farah can muster. As is the case with the other nine novels, 'there is no final commitment to any single point of view' in *Knots* (Wright 2004: 18). The reader knows that Cambara can continue to reside in the family house in Mogadishu, with Bile, but she would be confronted with his madness and the harrowing details of everyday life in the series of security bubbles that manage to survive the carnage around them. Or perhaps Arda is discussing how to arrange for her daughter and Bile to depart from Mogadishu back to Toronto, in which case we know that Dajaal and Seamus would be trapped alone in the wounded city, potentially along with the boy, SilkHair, that Cambara has attempted to rehabilitate from child-soldier life. This is still the imaginative lived space, but the only refuges left are found in exile or in theater.

The fictional narrative of *Knots* parallels that which Farah (2009) provided in a non-fiction essay about his own family house in Mogadishu. He recounted his attempt to locate this house in the war-ravaged neighborhood nicknamed Bermuda for its triangulated devastation as a trip into 'a zone of total grief. I had never seen so much devastation in my life. What I saw called to mind wartime images of humans with their eye sockets emptied, their noses removed, heads bashed in until they were featureless and couldn't be recognized as humans anymore. The houses of Bermuda looked like no houses at all' (ibid.: 14). His family's place was, he discovered, destroyed beyond recognition: 'I dared not step inside, lest I should feel sadder than I already felt, having seen so much devastation all around' (ibid.: 14). Bermuda's actual warlord at the time offered to help get the house rebuilt for a mere US$2,000, and to then rent it out, sending Farah the rent money anywhere he wished to have it sent. 'I said I would think it over,' Farah (ibid.: 14) recalled.

The difference between Farah's non-fiction experience and the similar plot device in *Knots* is instructive. It seems to me to be a decisive example of what John Marx (2008) meant about novelists writing 'failed state fiction' in a conscious effort to affect a 'counter-discourse.'

Farah's counter-discourse is about 'identity in relationship to others' where 'the family is the framework in which this struggle' over identity 'is carried on,' as a metaphor for the larger Somali society (Alden and Tremaine 1998: 759). For Farah, 'the patriarchal family is the micro-cosmic model and school of dictatorship' (Sugnet 1998: 740). In *Links* and even more so in *Knots*, as in *Sardines*, *Maps*, *Secrets*, or *Sweet and Sour Milk*, the dictatorial family is blown apart, but then reconstructed in a different form. In *Links*, the reconstructed family is a refuge for the city's children and other victims. In *Knots*, we literally see the family house reconstructed, stripped of its patriarchal warlord. Remaking Mogadishu, and remaking all of Somalia's wounded cities, requires, for Farah, both the reconstruction of social and familial relationships (literally and figuratively removing 'the gun' from Somalia; Farah 2004) and the physical reconstitution of domestic and municipal spaces as places of refuge and hope.

Conclusion

Representations of space have consequences. Mogadishu is a vital place, a city with 2 million people and a thousand years of connectivity with the wider world. But as a result of the events of October 1993, of imaginary depictions of those events, and now of piracy and terrorism, to most Americans and many Westerners Mogadishu is conceived as exceptional. Its people are represented as residing outside the boundaries of a normal social order that the West's elite controls, or thinks it controls. It is exceptional, too, because this business of residing outside the boundaries gives rise to justifications of exceptional behavior by US and US-allied military forces against Somalis.

Through consideration of Farah's re-creation of Mogadishu as a lived space, and of The Refuge as a 'new form of urban life,' though, we see how the author seeks to breathe life back into Mogadishu. In Farah's vision, Mogadishu is no longer the 'world capital-of-things-gone-completely-to-hell' whose people get what's coming to them. It is a place where people can reconstruct Somalia without living in denial over all that has transpired. It is a place that can genuinely 'restore hope.' The Ethiopian army, the US Army, the warlords, and the Islamists cannot penetrate The Refuge of *Links* or the puppet show of *Knots*. Such imaginary third spaces are no substitute for activist work toward conflict resolution. Equally, however, there can be no real rebirth for Mogadishu without imagination.

Henri Lefebvre's spatial triad (1991) provides a framework by which we might comprehend how these contesting representations intersect. As 'the proliferation of links and networks, by directly

connecting up very diverse places ... tends to render the state redun-
dant' and 'innumerable groups' seek 'to invent new forms,' Lefebvre
(ibid.: 378–9, 400) reminds us that perceived, conceived, and lived
spatiality still 'meet at the crossroads.' Although 'an architecture of
pleasure and joy, of community in the use of the gifts of the earth,
has yet to be invented' (ibid.: 379), these liberated, lived spaces, like
Farah's Refuge in the midst of Mogadishu, provide vital counter-
spaces to the perceived and conceived spaces of the dominant elites.
Even from the most wounded cities of Africa, creative voices emerge
with alternative visions that challenge prevalent conceptualizations
of African urbanism.

SIX

Cosmopolitan cities

Introduction

> Our imaginations have lived so long with the ... deadening images
> of power drawn on the ground ... Can we begin to shift our experi-
> ences and our visions to capture the world of always-moving spaces?
> What do the spaces of dynamism and change look like? (Robinson
> 1998: D5)

In an essay on exile, Nuruddin Farah wrote that 'one of the pleas-
ures of living away from home is that you become the master of your
destiny, you avoid the constraints and limitations of your past and, if
need be, create an alternative life for yourself' (Farah, in Zeleza 2005:
13). In this chapter, I seek to extend from this thought, looking at
the cosmopolitanism characteristic of the increasingly stretched-out
geographies of African cities, through the eyes, words, and images
of its 'straddling' artists, writers, and exiles, among other voices and
sources of alternative visions.

Nuruddin Farah is hardly the only Somali creating 'an alternative
life for himself' (or herself) these days. More than a million Somalis
now reside in various forms of exile abroad. By 2008, the Somali
population of the US Minneapolis-St Paul metropolitan area in Minnesota alone neared 100,000, and Somali rivaled Spanish for status as
the second language of the Twin Cities. Accurate numbers for Somali
migrants living in the USA are elusive. Officially, 30,260 Somalis were
documented as admitted immigrants to the USA between 1991 and
2003, and immigration numbers were minuscule prior to 1991. The
US Census Bureau's 2003 estimate of Somali-born residents counted
35,760 Somalis living in the entire country at that point. Yet there is
no denying that the local Somali population in 'Mogadishu on the
Mississippi,' as the Minnesota conurbation is known, is far above that
2003 estimate for the USA as a whole. More than 45,000 Somalis live
in Columbus, Ohio, and communities in the thousands can be found
in every major US city (including some 25,000 in San Diego, 5,000 in
Kansas City, 2,000 in Lewiston, Maine, more than 1,000 in Wichita,

and, for a few years, 2,000 in tiny Emporia, Kansas, who migrated there for employment in a meat-packing plant, which subsequently closed, leading to the community's onward migration to Iowa and elsewhere). Clearly the national government's figures are inaccurate, but few on-the-ground observers miss the range of significant impacts Somalis have had in the various communities of concentration socioculturally, politically, and economically. Similar stories exist for Somali migration to Europe.

What do these particular 'spaces of dynamism and change look like,' as signposts of globalization? The first nods to notoriety tend to drift toward the usual misunderstandings of Africans and Muslims in the USA (and similarly in Europe), inflamed by the post-11 September 2001 political climate. Somali taxi drivers' rejection of passengers traveling with alcohol at Minneapolis airport, Somali youths linked to terrorism disappearing from Minneapolis only to re-emerge in combat in Mogadishu, or Somali gangs troubling the Twin Cities' schools – the theme changes, but not the basic flavor. And similar stories appear from Lewiston, Columbus, Kansas City, and Emporia. Yet other storylines steadily grow in relation to these Somali nodes in the USA, too. In 2009, *Newsweek* wrote of Somalis in Maine as the 'refugees who saved Lewiston' (Ellison 2009). The first Muslim elected to Congress in US history, Keith Ellison, credited his successful campaign to the votes of naturalized Somali-American citizens in the Twin Cities. Minneapolis Somalis have become highly organized, not simply for election campaigns, but for social services, education, and even urban agricultural extension services. Somali social service organizations are active and engaged across potentially divisive Somali communities, and in relationships with other immigrant, refugee and hometown associations in city after city in the USA. In Chapter 5, I noted the Kansas African Studies Center's formal connection and online collaborative courses with Mogadishu University (MU) – this was born out of a fruitful and productive relationship with both the Somali Foundation in Kansas City and with Somalis in the Columbus community.

The biggest successes of Somali diaspora communities in US Midwest cities, arguably, are, like Mogadishu University, made manifest back in Somalia. Remittances are the 'lifeline' for basic survival for many Somalis in Somalia, and business surveys in Mogadishu – including one conducted by MU students trained in the MU–Kansas linked course on social survey methods – have shown that 80 percent of the startup capital for small and medium-size companies comes from abroad (Saltmarsh 2009: A13; Hansen 2007). The UNDP estimates that Somalis living in exile send at least a billion US dollars to Somalia a year, nearly 20 percent of the country's estimated GDP; a large share of this money comes from Mogadishu-on-the-Mississippi (Marchal 2006; Roble and Rutledge 2008).

Across the continent of Africa, with increasing frequency, collaborative and creative energies of different cities reach across borders and oceans into 'always-moving spaces' like Mogadishu-on-the-Mississippi. Although Robinson was writing directly about apartheid South African cities in the piece from which the quotation that begins this chapter comes, it is a passage that can open out onto a more continent-wide multiplicity of attempts to shift experiences and visions in imagining cities amid globalization, from Johannesburg detective stories to Nollywood videos from Lagos, from diasporic narrations of Nigeria to Senegalese nostalgia for home as seen from Italy (Nuttall 2008: 215; Barrot 2008; Benga 2005; Kehinde 2007; Carter 2010). As we have seen in the last four chapters, the globalizing and stretching of citiness bring urban Africa into ever firmer links, whether postcolonial, informal, unruly, or wounded, with other cities around the world. This final chapter explores the generative and imaginative cultures of contemporary urban Africa and their cosmopolitan and globally interconnected character, as my attempt to suggest what the 'spaces of dynamism and change look like' for African urbanism. A turn toward critical analysis of African urban cultures *in situ* and through wider connections with processes of globalization is abundantly evident in African urban studies in general, in broad urban histories, focused anthropological analyses of events and relations in small urban spaces, experimental fiction, religious studies, or analyses of migration (Falola 2005; Coquery-Vidrovitch 2005b; Livermon 2008; Weiss 2005; Stoller 2005; Abdoul 2005; Saleh 2009; Yeboah 2008c). This chapter is partly my foray into making some broader sense of this turn, with an emphasis on the arts and the African urban experiences of diaspora and transnationality.

Globalization and cosmopolitanism

African cities are not typically considered in urban studies analyses of globalization and the parallel development of 'world cities' or 'global cities' research (Friedmann 1986; Sassen 1991). If they do appear, it is typically as marginal, third- or fourth-tier cities in a world cities hierarchy, or 'black holes' in the hierarchy (Castells 1997; Short 2004). In what Bill Freund (2007: 171) calls the 'scary stories of the Afropessimists,' globalization leads to even further marginalization and deprivation for African urban dwellers, stuck in the 'global ghetto' of neoliberal capitalism (Smith 1997; Davis 2005). To be sure, in economic terms, the magnitude of African urban 'uplinking' with other major cities is much smaller than that of cities that are not 'off the map' of global cities (Kruijt and Koonings 2009: 16; Robinson 2002a). But both globalization's supporters and naysayers 'vastly oversimplify complex states of affairs' for African cities (Malaquais 2006: 33). Globalization in broader terms – including its political, sociocultural and environmental dimensions alongside the economic ones – has actually profoundly impacted African cities in diverse and complicated ways.

These impacts should not be seen as uniformly positive or negative. As Ferguson (2006: 26) put it, Africa is 'an awkward case for globalization's polemical boosters and detractors.'

Africa's 'inconvenience' for the grand theorists on either side lies in part with the general lack of 'convergence' one sees across the continent, in the oft-theorized sense of collapsing space-time, which is highly uneven between and within most African cities (ibid.: 27; Malaquais 2006: 32–3). In cultural, economic, or political terms, globalization's flows are 'disjunctive' (Appadurai 1996) in Africa – Ferguson (2006: 38) asks us to think of 'hops' rather than flows, where 'useful Africa' (a place where resources or profits may be extracted) has hops that land in it and 'useless Africa' (a place lacking resources or interest from investors) does not. But I believe it is even more variegated than this fairly simplified bifurcation or disjuncture.

Grant (2009: 9–11) identifies three interrelated 'globalizing movements' in his study of Accra that may be usefully extended to analysis of other cities. Globalizing processes are occurring, in Grant's terms, from 'above,' from 'below' and 'in between.' Globalization from above is a movement led by the liberalization policies we have seen in Chapters 3 and 4 that privilege 'the role of external actors and foreign capital in the local economy.' More than anything else, this sort of globalization exacerbates and expands existing inequalities spatially and socially in African cities, but its impacts may not be entirely negative in all cities, depending on local policy responses (Rodrigues 2009: 39–41; Freund 2007: 192–3). Globalization from above in the form of wealthy sponsors for local artists, for example, has been critical to African cities becoming, in Malaquais's (2006: 33) terms, 'staging areas for remarkable cultural innovation ... in the international art world.' Globalization from below, as the discussion of Grant's research in Accra in Chapter 3 showed, can result in non-governmental civil society linkages across and between 'slum dwellers' that may empower heavily marginalized urban communities; Roland Marchal's (2006: 221) work on Mogadishu offers further demonstration of this in the effectiveness of residents in 'forging new links with the outside world' through innovations in the communications and money transfer sectors.

Grant's third movement is my main, though not exclusive, interest in the chapter. This in-between globalization 'has been facilitated by the fluidity of international migration and travel back and forth,' as new networks are forged across boundaries (Grant 2009: 10). Grant's in-between globalization example hinges on return migrants, as 'missing and unknown agents' who can pursue transnational networking – 'their lives revolve around linking different places and practices.' These agents, of course, have been around a long time, but their exchanges have picked up in intensity as they have become more regular. Migrants and transnationals in diasporic communities 'now remain much more closely connected with the places they come from' – the two groups, return migrants and diasporic communities, after all, can be interchangeable (Chabal 2009: 148). If we think back to Chapter 1's discussion of the term cosmopolitan, Appiah's (2006: xiv) recovery of the ancient sense of its meaning is of value here: a 'cosmopolitan' would be a 'citizen of the cosmos' who belonged both to a 'particular city' and to the 'world.' Cosmopolitanism can also be at work in globalization from above and below, but it is most approachable as a phenomenon of the 'in-between' variety. This is especially so if we think about the potential implications for deepening democratic practices in Africa's cities (as discussed in Chapter 4) or symbolic, potentially transformative representations of urban politics (such as Farah's Mogadishu from Chapter 5): Africa's in-between, cosmopolitan globalizers may (or may not) be ideally situated for transforming wider images of cities and may (or may not) be valued for the resources at their disposal being put to use in democratization in those cities.

Cosmopolitanism, much like my other theme-words in this book, is a very complicated term with ever-shifting definitional values (Nava 2007). Soja (2000: 229–32) used the term 'cosmopolis' as one of his six discourses of the postmetropolitan order, borrowing from a number of scholars who had also used this term, such as Stephen Toulmin, Engin Isin, and Leonie Sandercock. Sandercock deployed 'cosmopolis' as a term meant to convey the 'challenge of building a new multicultural city' (Harrison et al. 2008: 113). Soja's discussion of her work suggests, as Appiah's idea of cosmopolitanism does, a helpful means of seeing both the very deep histories of interplay between cities and globalization, and the ways in which contemporary globalization is not simply a negative force but also a 'source of new opportunities and challenges' (Soja 2000: 231). Mica Nava (2007: 3) adds to this the notion of seeing cosmopolitanism as – in Raymond Williams's phrase – a 'structure of feeling,' or 'an empathetic and inclusive set of identifications' people belonging to or identifying with a particular city have with one another and with worldly ideas. Still, the utility of cosmopolitanism for creating the sort of relational and just city Pieterse (2008a) envisioned may be problematic. Cosmopolitans may have less at stake in the city as a place. As Simone (2001a: 46) has noted, 'erstwhile connections between physical and social spaces are progressively disjoined, as identity formation, belonging and social allegiance are less rooted in specific localities than spread across multiple territories, sectors and nations.' Part of my goal in this chapter is to examine in more detail what circumstances favor cosmopolitanism's development as an agent for deepening democratic practices, and what circumstances do not.

There are many cities in Africa that can and should be conceived of as cosmopolitan – and indeed some of these have been for many centuries (Nuttall and Mbembe 2008: 16; Simone 2004: 10–13; McDonald 2008; Gensheimer 2004). One of the deepest discussions of cosmopolitanism in Africa belongs to Zanzibar, where 'intense global interconnectivity' was a defining feature of city life from the eighteenth century CE onward – indeed, the Swahili coast exists as a culture region because of this interconnectivity from the first century BCE, picking up in intensity in the medieval period (Prestholdt 2008: 89; Gensheimer 2004; Sheriff 1987). Cosmopolitans were there at the beginnings of Swahili coastal urbanism, and they became central to its core ideas with the rise of Islam (Larsen 2009). Contemporary globalization has done nothing but further the worldliness of their connections, and even when boxed in by a colonial or socialist order it produces new opportunities along with challenges (Bang 2008; Gurnah 1996). Hence my excavation of cosmopolitan cities in Africa in this chapter centers on the worldly geographies of Zanzibar and Zanzibaris, though not exclusively.

Zanzibar's example also provides us with a very valuable window onto the meanings of *diaspora* and *transnationality* as two other key concepts in contemporary scholarly discussions of how to think of cosmopolitanism for urban Africa in connection with a globalizing urban world. Sheffer (1986: 3) defined diaspora as referring to a minority ethnic group 'of migrant origins residing and acting in host countries but maintaining strong sentimental and material links with their countries of origin.' Africanist geographers are increasingly interested in links of diasporic communities back into the politics and development programs of countries of origin, or around the world (Mercer et al. 2008). As Lie (1995: 304) put it, 'it is no longer assumed that emigrants make a sharp break from their homelands.' Migration patterns have become much more varied and the 'broad topography of interconnections' (Simone 2004: 119) for African communities has expanded and diversified (Carter 2010). New African diaspora communities are expected wellsprings of great hopes for development. The UK's Department for International Development (DfID), for one, 'sees in recent African diasporas the opportunity for the African continent to benefit from globalization ... [and] reverse the deleterious effects of the "brain drain"' (Koser 2003: 10; Mercer et al. 2008). It is uncertain how significant a force for African development diasporic communities can be, though. There are great differences 'both between and within' African diasporas, with some evidencing the hope that DfID and others have placed in them and others undermined by internal fractures, illegality, exclusivity, or elitism (Koser 2003: 10; Dosi et al. 2007). Zanzibar's fractious diaspora is a model example for these points.

Transnationality can be defined as the status of people who are 'at least bi-lingual, move easily between different cultures, frequently maintain homes in two countries, and pursue economic, political, and cultural interests that require simultaneous presence in both' (Portes 1997: 16; Willis et al. 2004). Transnationality is still going on when only some of these restrictive conditions exist. Gupta and Ferguson (1992: 9) see transnationality as a kind of 'bifocal' experience – where migrants think both locally and globally, with varying degrees of success. Zanzibari transnationalism is again quite illustrative.

One common conception of geographies of transnational and diasporic communities is a rhizomatic one – a 'chaotic network of several interconnected nodes' (Fortier 2005: 183). In these geographies, 'belonging may involve both attachment and movement' (ibid.: 184). Hamilton (2007: 2) considers these themes 'connections' and 'mobility,' as part of the 'geosocial circulatoriness' of African diasporas. Gilroy's (1995: 26; 1993) arguably more poetic way of meshing the 'roots and routes' comes in the form of his notion of the 'changing same' in African diasporas. Essentially, Gilroy suggests that both what and where a people have been is inseparable from their present state, and likewise from what they are becoming. The 'changing same' idea is appealing, but it is a notion that depends on forging collective memory, and in practice this can be difficult to separate out from the homogenizing power dynamics of nationalism, or class (Mitchell 2005; Dosi et al. 2007). There is a tendency to argue or to assume from this view 'that the diasporan subject has replaced the anti-hegemonic heroism of the earlier working class and subaltern subjects' (Manger and Assal 2006: 17). Instead, we need to start the analysis from the recognition of 'dynamism, heterogeneity, [and] variation' in diaspora communities (ibid.: 7). To begin with, appropriately enough for this book, we often assume diasporic African communities to be urban communities in the West, linking to urban communities in Africa – but this is not always remotely accurate (Mercer et al. 2008). There are actually many Zanzibari diasporas, let alone many African diasporas, and the political projects of forging some coherent univocality that might foster further development of a relational city back home are fraught with potential biases toward elitism, nationalism, or ethnocentrism. In the chapter sections that follow, I examine Zanzibari cosmopolitanism through different narratives – on Zanzibaris in exile, including Zanzibar's former Sultan, its most well-known novelist, and more ordinary folk; and transnational experiences and impacts in peri-urban informal settlements in Zanzibar itself. I then expand from Zanzibar to consider other dimensions of African urban cosmopolitanization elsewhere – the growth of arts festivals, and the expanding realm of transnational and diasporic 'African' arts. These later examples and emphases in the chapter are tied, first and foremost, to my effort to suggest that I am not studying some sort of Zanzibari exceptionalism: the phenomena discussed in the section below could easily be articulated for a great many African cities in their complex cosmopolitan relationships with an urban world.

Zanzibar's diasporas

In January 1964, the British press created a media flurry around the entourage of the Sultan of Zanzibar, newly arrived in exile after his regime was overthrown in the revolution on the 12th of that month. At first, more than thirty family members and twenty-five servants were housed in a decidedly upmarket Westminster hotel at a cost to the Commonwealth Relations Office of more than £1,500 pounds over five days. The British government moved the seemingly bedraggled royal house to 'a cheaper hotel in South Kensington' (hardly a downmarket area of London) and carted the servants off to a Salvation Army hostel (*Observer*, 26 January 1964: 1). As the Sultan's relatives 'moved from the Edwardian splendour of chambers near Buckingham Palace to more functional quarters' in an only slightly less posh neighborhood, they apparently 'trailed sadly across London with a minimum of luggage and what possessions they had, mostly packed in plastic bags' (*Sunday Times*, 26 January 1964: 1). Eighteen months later, the *Observer* found Zanzibar's last Sultan, Jamshid bin Abdullah, in the 'modest semi-detached' house in Southsea where he has long remained, living off the £100,000 the government had given him to 'play with' and a 'modest' annual top-up, wanting 'to go where the weather is warmer and the income tax lower' (*Observer*, 4 July 1965: 1). Most of his servants had wandered off into factory jobs or the dockyards, others disappearing into any number of London neighborhoods.

In January 1999, Kombo Mbarouk Hassan took a bus from Kennedy Airport into Manhattan to catch a train for Washington. Kombo had arrived from Zanzibar alone, with limited English, a shy personality, and a tourist visa obtained with a slight bit of fraud, on a plane ticket his brother was able to buy for him only by selling the dearly obtained family car. Kombo had a Zanzibari friend in Seattle who said he had a job on a fishing boat plying the waters from there to Alaska. Since Kombo had not only grown up in a fishing settlement on Zanzibar but had a degree in fisheries management and experience as a professional researcher, his friend guaranteed him a job if he arrived on time. Unfortunately, when Kombo asked Amtrak for a ticket to Washington, he ended up in the District of Columbia. Immediately recognizing that Union Station was nowhere near the ocean he was looking for, Kombo sought out the ticket office to demand a refund and a new ticket to Seattle. He was, at first, refused. He had virtually no more money to his name and spent the night in the station, before an understanding agent took great pity on him and let him board the first of a series of trains that took him to the Pacific Northwest over the next several days. When he finally reached Seattle, there was no fishing boat, and no job. Eighteen months later, after several bouts with homelessness, Kombo worked two jobs in two different nursing homes and traveled the bus system of the Puget Sound, largely alone, occasionally scraping money together to wire home to his wife and to both of their parents. By 2010, Kombo had changed his name to take on a Somali identity and managed to bring his wife to Seattle from Zanzibar. They have subsequently had three children, but Kombo will spend his entire life repaying the hospital where his first son's birth created catastrophic danger to his wife's health, putting them more than US$100,000 in debt. He can also never anticipate going home again.

Both the Sultan and Kombo are residents of Zanzibar's global diaspora, but they exemplify the very different times and circumstances that have created it. Zanzibar's indigenous people have a 2,000-year history of connectivity with the entire Indian Ocean rim and the Congo basin, with diasporic communities settled in places from Durban and Kigali to Dubai and Mumbai. But contemporary Zanzibar's diaspora is more sizable, far-flung and interconnected. It has been created largely out of two different cataclysmic events and processes over the last half-century. First, both the 1964 revolution and the police state that ruled the islands for the next decade caused many Zanzibaris, particularly former elites or those of Asian (here meaning Yemeni, Omani, Iranian, Pakistani, Indian, or mixed Asian) descent, to flee the islands (Petterson 2002). Most of these émigrés settled in the Gulf states or – like the Sultan – in the UK, with a scattering in Scandinavia, Canada, and the USA. Second, the reintroduction of multiparty politics in 1995 led to a resurfacing of political conflict, manifested in multiple riots over the past fifteen years, and this has created a second set of émigrés, this time comprised much more of Zanzibaris of all classes and origins, including fisherfolk like Kombo. Comparatively larger numbers of Zanzibaris have settled in the USA and Canada since 1995, in contrast with the earlier burst of exiles.

Exiled Zanzibaris of both strata live a generally less well-financed version of the 'new cosmopolitanism' that Appiah (2006: 32) sees among African diasporic communities more generally, people with 'many intimate connections with places far away' who, with Salman Rushdie (in ibid.: 52), celebrate 'hybridity, impurity, intermingling,

[or] the transformation that comes of new and unexpected combinations of human beings.' Their strategies of transnationality can produce a form of what Appiah terms a healthy 'contamination' of cultures. Transnational spaces are always in motion and collision. Yet, like diaspora, the concept also implies a less positive contamination, 'a kind of passage, yet a passage that encompasses the possibility of never arriving. Of drifting endless on the betwixt and between of the world's boundaries ... of being "other" among the established' (Carter 2003: xiv).

Indeed, May Joseph (1999: 3) argues that East African Asians, including Zanzibaris of Arab/Asian ethnic origin, have ended up in a 'disaffected space of inauthentic citizenship' and are forced to form 'nomadic identities' out of the 'trauma of dispossession and displacement.' There is a growing sense for them of what she terms an 'ambivalent cosmopolitanism' in their 'global citizenship' (ibid.: 8). I stretch her idea farther, to include Zanzibaris of any ethnic background in either era as those for whom diaspora can potentially be a highly ambivalent experience of disaffection. Zanzibar, with the revolution, a socialist dictatorship, and then four disputed or fraudulent elections since 1995 tied in with a long-simmering regional conflict between its islanders, has for some of its citizens become 'unlivable,' as one Zanzibari resident of the USA put it to me in 2005. The USA, Canada, and the UK, though, as places of refuge, have also proved less than welcoming to both generations.

Coming to these countries is, for most Zanzibaris, at best an ambiguous adventure: most struggle to make ends meet, work in jobs below their educational level, contend almost daily with immigration technicalities or racism, and often deeply regret their decision to be in the West. Almost all live in cities, typically the largest cities in the USA, without understanding of or access to US social services or social welfare networks, when they are coming from a much smaller city where an us-for-us informal governance regime does much to provide mechanisms for the survival of poverty and oppression.

Questions surrounding who the Zanzibaris are and where they came from are deeply problematic. Although the questions originate in a very distant past, it is a past dredged up daily in Zanzibar, articulated with the rise of mass tourism as the mainstay of the city's, and the islands', economy, and the consequent commodification of history. It is a past reconstructed regularly across the diaspora as well, across many forms of media and in everyday conversation. Hence any answer to the question of how to define a Zanzibari diaspora has to start with the creation of some idea of where this idea of Zanzibar came from and the tortuous path that the idea has followed over the last 2,000 years. I don't have space for that much deep history in this book, but just suggest that the identity questions Zanzibaris experience in the twenty-first-century diaspora have very deep roots stretching back well past the contemporary city of Zanzibar's foundation in the 1690s.

That contemporary city grew in relation to the rise of Omani power. The Omani sultanate supplanted Zanzibar's indigenous rulers and, more immediately, the Portuguese (who ruled Unguja – Zanzibar – island from 1501 to 1690), and established their capital at what became Zanzibar town in the last decade of the seventeenth century. This modest outpost collected tariffs and customs duties for the Omani empire, and its merchant class steadily expanded its investments in long-distance trading for slaves, ivory, and spices, principally cloves. The era of 'clove mania' in Zanzibar, from the 1810s on, and the movement of the Omani Sultan Seyyid Said to Zanzibar permanently from Oman in the early nineteenth century, sparked the city's great expansion and the intense intermingling in it of Arabian, South Asian, Iranian, and African influences and peoples (Sheriff 1987). The British had established their dominance among European interests in the sultanate well before declaring it a protectorate in 1890. The British colonial regime saw Zanzibar city in racial categories expressed directly in spatial terms. Zanzibaris came to use those categories to their own ends. The decade Zanzibaris call the Time of Politics (1954–64) that came at the end of colonialism, in particular, was a time of politics orchestrated explicitly around race and racial geography in the city. Some of the same divides of the Time of Politics have been reproduced and re-engineered for the ongoing Second Time of Politics in the city (since the 1992 reintroduction of multiparty politics).

The long arc of social history leaves Zanzibar with a fractured homeland and a fractured diaspora. Every homeland and every diaspora has its complications. But the Zanzibari one is particularly politicized in its complications. There is a Zanzibar that belongs to the United Republic of Tanzania, and a Zanzibar that belongs to history as many different things. Distinctly Pemba, Tumbatu, Hadimu/Makunduchi, African, Shirazi, Omani, Yemeni, Tanganyikan, and even Kenyan visions of Zanzibar exist, each of them further fractured by class or gender. Zanzibar is claimed by pan-Africanists and African nationalists and communist revolutionaries and Arab nationalists and Islamists and Pembanists and human rights activists and hip-hop artists (*Zenji flava* for Zanzibar city, *Bongo flava* for Dar es Salaam). What unites Zanzibar, what is held in common as Zanzibar, or who belongs to *what* Zanzibar, and who gets to decide which Zanzibar is which? The Zanzibari novelist Abdulrazak Gurnah (1996) speaks through his narrator in the novel *Admiring Silence* to best express this postcolonial cosmopolitan muddle:

> We liked to think of ourselves as a moderate and mild people. Arab African Indian Comorian: we lived alongside each other, quarreled and sometimes intermarried. Civilized, that's what we were. We liked to be described like that, and we described ourselves like that. In reality, we were nowhere near *we*, but us in our separate yards, locked in our historical ghettos, self-forgiving and seething with intolerances, with racisms, and with resentments.

Gurnah's observation is crucial to the questions of what cosmopolitan globalization and contemporary diasporic connections mean for the potential of a city like Zanzibar to become a more relational and just city. If 'we are nowhere near we', how can the sort of 'us-for-us' governance system that I discussed in Chapter 4, or which Farah gives life to in his Mogadishu novels of Chapter 5, work for all of the 'us'? One of the ramifications of the creation of a cosmopolis is its extrinsic diversity. But the Zanzibar example shows that just as a city's diasporic reach may begin to expand into a vast array of cities and towns of the globe, back within the city itself the ties across community lines may be frayed. These tensions then may play out abroad.

Like his friend Nuruddin Farah, Gurnah lives in exile from his homeland, but seems to live in its imaginary departure lounge, a diasporic space of bifocal experience. Though Gurnah and Farah are somewhat older than the 'new generation of African writers' upon whom Brenda Cooper (2008) focuses in her recent study, they share with these others – for instance Moses Isegawa and Chimamanda Ngozi Adichie – a straddling between a homeland and a diasporic existence, with migration and mobility as central themes. Zanzibar city finds its way into all seven of Gurnah's novels, even those that are set mostly in Europe (Gurnah 1987, 1988, 1990, 1994, 1996, 2001a, 2005). Like Farah, Gurnah (2004: 26) writes in English, because, even while recognizing the historical depth and contemporary vibrancy of written works in KiSwahili, the limited reach of such works, and the fortitude it takes to get them published, are serious impediments (but make no mistake: the few Zanzibari Swahili novels of these last two decades are equally cosmopolitan works of fiction – see Khamis 2009 for a review). Born in Zanzibar in 1948 and raised there, he left at eighteen to study in the UK, fleeing what he has described as 'a time of hardship and anxiety, of state terror and calculated humiliations' in the first years after the revolution (Gurnah 2004: 26).

That revolution – both memories of it and reverberations of its aftermath into the decades beyond it, in Zanzibar and around the world, even when from a distance – is central to five of Gurnah's novels, *Memory of Departure* (1987), *Pilgrims Way* (1988), *Admiring Silence* (1996), *By the Sea* (2001a) and *Desertion* (2005). These last two are more complicated tales with deeper and more intricate histories and geographies in them. *By the Sea* – along with *Paradise* (1994), the historical novel set largely on the East African mainland – is widely considered his finest work; in narrative terms, it is his tightest novel, while *Desertion* is his most fragmented.

There is both a cosmopolitan connectivity at the heart of Gurnah's depictions of Zanzibar city and a haunting sense of abandonment – or, following the title of the most recent novel, we might simply call it *desertion*. Gurnah (2004: 26) began to write in his early twenties out of this very sense of abandonment, and his memories of 'a life left behind, of people casually and thoughtlessly abandoned, a place and a way of being lost to me forever.' Gurnah is guilty of some desertion in this novel, since he starts, and then deserts, several different narratives in the book. Part I of the novel revolves around a dazed and disillusioned British geographer, Martin Pearce, who wanders out of the desert of northeastern Kenya in the opening days of the colonial era and collapses into a Swahili family that he becomes a part of, then abandons. Pearce is nursed to health by a shopkeeper, Hassanali, and his sister, Rehana. Rehana had herself been abandoned by her first love, from India, and she and Pearce secretively become lovers, but almost from the moment Gurnah suggests this possibility, he sows doubt in the reader's mind about whether it would really have been possible. Part I ends with 'An Interruption,' a short chapter where the contemporary narrator's voice takes over, admitting about Pearce and Rehana that 'I don't know how it would ever have happened. The unlikeliness of it defeats me' (Gurnah 2005: 110). He presents readers with a variety of possible ways this unlikely love affair might have transpired, closing the interruption with an acknowledgment that 'there is, as you can see, an I in this story, but it is not a story about me … It is about how one story contains many and how they belong not to us but are part of the random currents of our time, and about how stories capture us and entangle us for all time' (ibid.: 120). This is a beautiful statement of the strengths of cosmopolitan global urbanity in narrative form – of routes and roots – and it is, perhaps appropriately enough, an 'interruption' in the midst of the fragments of storylines.

Part II hops from the Swahili coast of Kenya to Zanzibar in the 1950s and early 1960s, and a seemingly disconnected second storyline 'entangles' us. Gurnah details the adolescent awakenings and educational dreams of two brothers in the city, Amin and Rashid. The illicit love affair of Amin with an older woman, Jamila, is at the center of this section of the novel, ending with the 'inevitable' discovery of their furtive and scandalous romance. By Part III, Rashid has gone to university in the UK, rueful about leaving Amin and the family behind just before the revolution, just after Amin's catastrophic affair with Jamila has been exposed and Jamila has disappeared. Rashid struggles to deal with his alienation from London and from events in Zanzibar at the same time.

Then Amin's notebooks appear, as a second 'interruption' in the novel's flow, and we learn that Jamila was the daughter of the love child from the romance between Pearce and Rehana of Part I, as we learn Amin's view on the miseries that Zanzibar city endured after the revolution. The novel ends with a chapter entitled 'A Continuation,' where Rashid meets and befriends the English granddaughter of Pearce. When this woman suggests that Rashid join her in a search for her cousin, Jamila, he is ambivalent: 'I don't know … Everything is scattered, dispersed to the farthest corners of the world' (ibid.: 261).

All of the scattering and dispersal of the narratives themselves, which Gurnah (ibid.: 261) has Rashid describe as one 'abandoned memoir' after another, add up to key statements about abandonment and desertion. The colonialists were the first deserters, in Gurnah's construction, and his first cosmopolitan step is to tie the British desertion of Zanzibar to the rest of postcolonial Africa. The British deserted their empire's people and the grand missions and ambitions they claimed to have for them in Africa. In the end they would 'break camp and dash off home, leaving behind them a series of paper-thin treaties that they felt no obligation to honour'; in *Desertion*, decolonization was 'a mad scramble out of Africa' (ibid.: 150). Not long after that scrambling out, the Zanzibar Gurnah himself knew as a young man was changed for ever by the revolution. Then the revolutionaries deserted their ideals, too, and the intellectuals that fled it deserted the cause of its true liberation.

And yet, Gurnah insists in drawing us to the recognition that all of these desertions fail, because none can make a complete break, there are too many links. In *Desertion*, Pearce leaves a child behind with Rehana, and his grandchildren on either end of the encounter eventually come almost to be connected. There may be an incompleteness to every story, Gurnah is suggesting, but colonizer and colonized, revolutionary and collaborator, are inseparable in their displacements, disorientations, ambivalences, and regrets.

In *Desertion*, colonialism's poisons sink into many aspects of the imaginative capacity of cities like Zanzibar. In much of Africa, European colonial rule set up the intertwining of the stories of citiness, whether by accident or design, and colonialism's desertions set in motion the urban-based linkages by which our world is so intimately defined today. The Us and Them of the colonial urban world – if indeed such categories were ever clearly definable – are side by side, part of one another in ways that grow more dramatic and intensive every day in cities (Gurnah 2004).

The second theme in Gurnah's work is indeed the links that tie Zanzibar's most intimate stories with the rest of the world (even if *Links* is, of course, Nuruddin Farah's novel). *By the Sea* is just such an intimate – and intricate – story. It starts with the experiences of its first main character, Saleh Omar, a middle-aged Zanzibari seeking political asylum in Britain, and the reader is meant to empathize with his plight as he encounters the institutional racism and callous disregard of the immigration system at Heathrow Airport while recalling the bitter circumstances that led him to become a refugee. Yet by the narrative's end, for many scholars and reviewers of the novel, Saleh Omar has become a less sympathetic character, as he confesses his life story to the book's other Zanzibari character, Latif Mahmud, and listens to Latif recite his. Latif is a former refugee, now well established in London, having fled a bleak educational scholarship program in the former East Germany. Latif gained that scholarship out of his family's affiliation with the Revolutionary Party (CCM), while Saleh fled Tanzania after more than a decade in detention as an alleged counter-revolutionary. Although the immigration agent who introduces them believes them to be strangers who might gain from one another's company as fellow Zanzibaris, it turns out that Latif and Saleh have each gone through life seeing the other as the cause of his family's ruination.

By the Sea works as a story on its own, but it also is meant to serve as an allegory of Zanzibar's cultural-political crisis, its ambivalent place in the world, and its intricate links as a city, within and without Africa. As in all of his novels, Gurnah is equally unforgiving toward inter- and intra-family 'cruelties' in the pre-colonial, colonial, revolutionary, post-revolutionary, and diasporic Zanzibari context (Gurnah, cited in Deckard 2010: 119). It is for some readers an impossibly simplistic allegory, its critique of nationalism and socialism rendered as a petty family squabble, 'an inadequate response to the material phenomena of globalization,' and an ambivalent, elitist postcolonial copout (ibid.: 126). Fair enough: as Sharae Deckard points out in an endnote in her recent book, it is the ironically entitled *Paradise* which is the only Gurnah novel for sale at Zanzibar's only internationally oriented bookstore, and its US$16 sticker price puts it well out of the realm of affordability for Zanzibari readers, few of whom would have the English skills to parse its literary-theoretical narrative gymnastics. Yet if the bookstore were oriented toward a Zanzibari readership, and the book were more reasonably priced, *By the Sea* would reach and touch a great many readers in the city, because Latif and Saleh's difficult and intertwined stories relate directly to realities in Zanzibar's diaspora, to Zanzibari experiences of transnationality, and to its ambivalent status as a political unit. *By the Sea* is fundamentally a book about diasporic identity and transnationality. According to literary theorist Sissy Helff's (2009: 67) reading of the book, in this narrative 'a complex and heterogeneous picture emerges which challenges common stereotypical images of "the African refugee."' Her argument is that Gurnah successfully renders the complexities and nuances by which African migrants to Europe are both excluded and included – within both host communities and diaspora communities. Although it is set in East Germany and London, many of the experiences both Latif and Saleh endure in attempting to re-establish their lives in exile resonate with my own findings in research on Zanzibar's far-flung diaspora. Unlike Nuruddin Farah, though, Gurnah does not leave the reader with a productive sense of how one might reimagine Zanzibar itself, or how the roots and routes of exile might lead back to a relational or just city. There is no 'Refuge' in his imagined Zanzibar.

Let me use one of Kombo's friends in Seattle, whom I shall call

Khatib, to illustrate what happens to the exile who lacks a 'refuge' at either end. Khatib is a refugee from Zanzibar in the 2000s, a young CUF activist, originally from Pemba, who lived as a squatter in Stone Town. He was dragged off to prison in Zanzibar when a CUF rally turned violent in the face of a brutal police crackdown. He was a victim of male rape in prison, denied food on several days, denied toilet privileges or water for bathing. Having been held for months without charge, he was released without trial. With the help of extended family members he made his way to Seattle – his journey much like Kombo's, albeit without the mistaken train ride. After months of failing to find adequate work, Khatib decided to try his luck with immigration law and seek political asylum. The odds were against him from the start since he had not declared his intention to seek asylum upon arrival in the USA and his visa was out of date by the time he did. He had a credible and verifiable fear of persecution based on the documented abuse he had suffered. The judge, though, dismissed his case because, he said, Khatib had proved his well-founded fear of persecution for *Zanzibar*, but not for Tanzania, the entity that had issued him a passport, and therefore he was deemed not in danger once deported to the mainland of that republic. So Khatib was, in effect, now not a Zanzibari, but instead a Tanzanian, when he had a most plausible case for belonging to a diaspora caused by forced dispersal. He was deported back to Dar es Salaam, where he now resides, renting a room in an informal settlement.

If the diaspora is to be the engine for creating a democratized, relational, and just city of Zanzibar, it is a challenging task to imagine how, given its fractious and ill-defined nature. It is even a diaspora that can prove hard to find, at least on paper. The Zanzibari diaspora is hidden in census or immigration figures, since all Zanzibaris are 'swallowed' by Tanzania (Abdulla 1976). Zanzibaris anecdotally appear to comprise a far higher proportion of Tanzania's fairly insignificant documented totals in the USA than the territory's 3 percent share of Tanzania's population would warrant, for example. Since there are several hundred people who identify themselves with the Zanzibari community in the DC area, several hundred more in New York, Chicago, and Los Angeles, and at least a hundred in Seattle, if we total those hundreds with the hundreds more scattered from Tampa to Memphis to Houston to Dallas to Wichita to San Francisco and back to Columbus and Boston, we can come close to half of the official list of Tanzanians admitted since 1991, without even trying.

A great many Zanzibaris navigate in an 'out of status' undocumented universe throughout the USA. Hence organizing this diaspora, or these diasporas, into entities that might foster the development of a relational and just city at home in Zanzibar is quite daunting – to say nothing of the absence of relationality or socio-environmental justice in the inner cities of so many US urban areas where Zanzibaris end up.

Like most African immigrants to the USA since 1990, a considerable majority of Zanzibaris in the USA – including undocumented migrants – are highly educated and well-trained people seeking to establish themselves in a new land. This leads them toward attempts to increase their participation in local US-based Zanzibari cultural institutions, but also to deeper commitments to Zanzibari family members around the globe, especially though not exclusively in Zanzibar. There are the ordinary and everyday connections that mobile phones enable between people and parents or grandparents, brothers, sisters, children, or spouses, be they in Tanzania or Denmark. But it often goes farther than this, to the level of formal organizations like Zanama, the Zanzibar-American Association.

Zanama was formed in 2003, with headquarters in Philadelphia but with six of its twelve original board members, and three out of twenty-two board members in 2010, resident in Wichita, Kansas. Zanama is ostensibly a community organization for Zanzibaris in the USA. It has a set of practical objectives, including assisting Zanzibaris with housing, employment, healthcare, immigration, and legal issues. It is also sponsors local social and cultural events. For instance, although it did not host the embassy officials, Zanama did make its members aware of the presence of Tanzanian embassy officials in Wichita in June 2005 to assist people applying for the new Tanzanian passports that were then required. It played a valuable role in gathering medicines to send home during a cholera outbreak around the time of its creation in 2003.

Like many new diasporic hometown associations in the USA with links to countries of origin, Zanama looks homeward, but with a twist. Its leaders seek to provide a forum for supporting their vision of democratization. Zanama wants to foster 'the rule of just law, enlightened and mature political leadership and democratic governance in Zanzibar that guarantees the participation of the public in the process of government' while working to 'inculcate in Zanzibaris born abroad the rich history and ethos of the people in their land of ancestry' (zanamadc.tripod.com). Hence it was no surprise to find that many Zanama people were very suspicious of the entire program for providing Tanzanians with new passports, seeing it as a way the Union government sought to *map them out*, to literally locate them. Reading the announcement about Zanama's foundation in 2003, in the government-run daily newspaper in Zanzibar, and talking about the article with my friends there, it was clear to me that there was equal suspicion in the Zanzibar government about what Zanama was, why it was formed, who was behind it, and what links they must have had to CUF, given the political tenor of the mission statement. Zanama members' reasoning regarding the passports may not be flawed: the revolutionary government of Zanzibar, at least, for its part, seemed to want to know who its enemies were and where they resided. Regardless of these suspicions at both ends, Zanama remains an organization of the transnational diaspora that explicitly seeks a relational and just city at home in its mandate.

I am interested in both sides of the hyphen in the Zanzibar-American Association. On one side we find the hybrid, ambivalent disjunctures that have brought Zanzibaris to the USA in this phase of cultural globalization, through 'stretched out geographies of flows and connections' (Power 2003: 122). Carter (1997: 3) has written that 'the economic, social, and political problems of "over there" – that is, some imagined space beyond the West – is now "over here", a part of the very rhythm of life in Western democracies.' We see this in the streets of our cities in the USA in the 2000s, as we see it in the streets of Paris, Copenhagen, or London. On the other hand, we find transnationality and diasporic connectivity to the USA, even to Kansas, in peri-urban informal settlements in Zanzibar.

In the same research program that led Ali Hasan Ali and me to dis-cover people living in a chicken coop in Uholanzi (see Chapter 3), we also came to a reasonably nice home in the peri-urban neighborhood of Mwera, where Ali suggested that a retired teacher, whom I shall call Salma, would be able to give us a valuable interview. Indeed, this woman had great knowledge of Mwera's development and thoughtful analyses of informality in the peri-urban zones of the city. It turned out that the primary reason her house and plot looked a little nicer than many of her neighbors had to do with money sent home to her from her son in America. 'I think he is somewhere in the middle of the country, a place called, maybe, Kansas?' Salma said. Unbeknown to either of us before the interview began, I had been playing soccer with her son in Lawrence, Kansas, for seven years.

Beyond the happenstance of that Lawrence-in-Zanzibar moment, across the belt of neighborhoods that surround Zanzibar Urban District in peri-urban West District, from Bububu and Kijichi in the far north to Chukwani and Kiembe-Samaki in the south, and dominated by the stretch colloquially referred to as the Gaza Strip in the middle, cosmopolitanism, diaspora, and transnationality are made manifest in multiple forms. We can see at least three versions of what the built environment of a 'trans-territorial city' may look like (Simone 2010: 175). These correspond roughly with the varieties of globalization to which Grant (2009) refers in Accra. The 'globalization-from-above' sort of neighborhood appears in the gated compounds of elite Zanzibaris whose other residences are in Copenhagen, Frankfurt, Muscat, Sharjah, Los Angeles, or Milton Keynes, and the international schools that proliferated in their midst. Alongside are a handful of foreign-owned luxury beach hotels, which combine with the gated compounds to increasingly close off the beachfront from the ordinary residents of the peri-urban zone. Taken in combination with the luxury hotels and guest houses scattered throughout the renovated streets of Stone Town, and the general decline of most of the rest of the city's neighborhoods, the growing inequality most researchers associate with globalization-from-above can be said to be amply in evidence in Zanzibar. We also find globalization-from-below neighborhoods in abundance. Toponymy alone gives us a hint: Gaza, Baghdad, Uholanzi (Holland), Hawaii. The residents give their neighborhoods names that connect them with other stories. Sometimes this is a sardonic statement on current conditions (as in 'this neighborhood is like Baghdad, it looks like a war zone'). At other times it is an insistent wish to belong to the world, to remind visitors and residents that this place looks like Hawaii, or wherever. Some of these neighborhoods are thus able to link up with donors – the Daraja Bovu area of Uholanzi has been exceedingly successful in obtaining aid for its community groups, and, appropriately enough, aid from Holland. In-between globalization is arguably the most common but least conspicuous manifestation of globalization, in the homes like that which Salma's Kansas son has built for her, where the struggling and straddling transnational migrants like Kombo invest their hard-earned savings in a small patch of home. Surveys in different neighborhoods in different years show that the majority of 'improved' homes with increased permanence are those with some remittances sent home or other connections abroad (Muhajir 1993; Azzan 2006; Myers 2010a).

Thus, just as Zanzibar has many diasporas, these many diasporas have quite varied manifestations in Zanzibar itself.

All of these manifestations come together in the city during the two weeks of the Zanzibar International Film Festival (ZIFF) each June or July. Globalization-from-above made the festival possible, with the strong influences of local elites and expatriate investors matching the heavy presence of well-to-do outsiders and the art-house films of the Indian Ocean rim. Globalization-from-below insistently makes its presence known in the heart of the festival, the Forodhani Garden, a public square at the beachfront in Stone Town, where people of all income levels gather and mingle. And in-between globalization gradually has made the ZIFF its own, as transnational migrants return home at festival time. This complex and multilayered experience of the movements and interconnections of cosmopolitan Zanzibar leads me to my next chapter segment, on the phenomenon of festivalization across the continent.

The festivalization of African cities

Despite my emphasis on Zanzibar, the ideas for this chapter segment actually began to emerge at the 2009 South African National Arts Festival in Grahamstown, when a local street theater troupe, Ubom, performed Daniel Buckland's play *Float*, in a co-production with Barefeet, a street theater troupe from Lusaka. The play illustrated the confluence of sensibilities on the manipulation and misuse of power between elites and local chiefs in the building of a dam that would flood a mythical village for hydroelectric development. This is a story all too familiar in outline form in either country. What is less familiar, at least to most outsiders to urban Africa, is the notion of street theater groups from cities in two different countries collaborating together.

Grahamstown has hosted the National Arts Festival for nearly thirty years. As such, it is, like Zanzibar, a staggeringly cosmopolitan place for such a small city, at least for one fortnight every year. Yet even more than a half century ago, after an exhaustive study of the ecological structure of Grahamstown, sociologist Hilstan Watts (1957: 171) concluded that the city was 'not as isolated or as much a backwater as might at first be supposed.' Somehow Grahamstown's imaginative, always-moving cosmopolitan spaces continue to contribute to the richness of everyday life there. For a variety of reasons, at the end of apartheid the local activist Helen Holleman (1997: 59) was able to point to 'a willingness to learn to live together and to weld the disparate parts of our community into one that shares a common identity.' A little more than a decade later, sociologist Valerie Møller's survey on 'Living in Rhini' (2008: 40–44) found a substantial amount of improvement in the quality of life from 1999 to 2007 in the city's former townships discussed in Chapter 5 – despite persistent problems with poverty and crime, Rhini has greater residential stability, more permanent and higher-quality housing, smaller households, improved standards of living, and improved urban service provision.

Such improvements may help people to learn to live together and to share a common identity. In a different way, so may the vigorous and contested municipal politics Grahamstown experienced in 2009 (Butana 2009; Buckland 2009). It is the National Arts Festival, though, which stands the best chance of ever providing Grahamstown's 'sides' with tools for living together, or with a shared identity. It has a long way to go, but if the 2009 iteration of the festival can be taken as evidence, then there are signs of a relational city with fluid, hybrid governance in the formative stages. For the first time, formal festival events actually took place in Rhini, and Rhini's artists, musicians, poets, sculptors, hawkers, and performers dominated much of the festival space on the Grahamstown side, with tens of thousands of visitors from around the world in attendance. Egazini Cultural Center in Rhini, for example, hosted an extraordinary photography exhibit from five Rhini women artists documenting their everyday lives (Koegelenberg 2009). Nombulelo Hall in Rhini hosted the play *Ingcwaba Lendoda Lise Cankwe Ndlela* (The grave of the man is next to the road) and other events (Mophophe 2009), while Xhosa, Zulu, and Tswana musical, literary, and theatrical events – in addition to the play *Float*, and a poetry reading by Keorapetse Kgositsile (see Chapter 5) – took place in the hallowed venues on the elite side of town. Outside of the formal festival program, in the heart of the old white downtown, Xhosa youth drumming and dancing troupes performed for coins, but with joy, energy, and discipline lacking in some of the main program events. Festival organizers' attempts to separate out the formal 'Village Green' market stalls area from the historically informal 'Fiddlers Market' stalls by moving the former onto the Rhodes University campus and leaving the latter back in the low-lying grounds where the Village Green had been in previous years failed miserably, and the Fiddlers Market hawkers took it upon themselves to take over Church Square at the heart of town as a response. The municipality and festival organizers relented, and the informal hawkers recovered the losses they had been building up in the first site (Moreland and Richards 2009).

It is in these infrapolitics and the 'always-moving spaces' (quite literally in this case) associated with them that I see Grahamstown reinventing itself as a relational city, hybridizing its worlds of governance. That it does so most cogently for a fortnight a year in the context of playing host to the world as the holder of the mantle for a 'national' arts festival points to recognition that cosmopolitanism and a positive generativeness can most assuredly go together in African cities, large or small.

International arts festivals, whether focused on music, film, theater, dance, sculpture, photography, or painting, or all of the above, are crucial sites of the worlding of African cities (Simone 2001a). St Louis, Senegal, has hosted a major festival, arguably Africa's most significant international jazz festival, occurring every April, building on the tremendous melding of Senegalese and Cuban jazz styles for which the city has gained renown since the 1930s. Like Grahamstown, St Louis has also built itself into an international tourist destination with a combination of a festival and a dedication to highlighting its bloody history – in this case, as a UNESCO World Heritage site. Ouagadougou, Burkina Faso, has ridden a similar globalizing wave via FESPACO, the Pan-African Film and Television Festival of Ouagadougou, which has grown since its 1969 founding into Africa's largest and most globally significant film festival. Essaouira, Morocco, has hosted the Gnaoua (Gnawa) and World Music Festival, meshing ecstatic Sufi spiritual performance with an increasingly wide array of world music forms and attracting an ever-increasing international audience (Kapchan 2008). Not to be outdone, Zanzibar now holds both ZIFF (also called the Festival of the Dhow Countries), which is slowly coming to rival FESPACO in size and reach, and an international music festival, *Sauti za Busara*. Similar globally marketed international arts festivals occur in Cape Town, Essakane and Segou, Mali, Casablanca, Rabat, Carthage, Harare, and elsewhere. It would be easy to dismiss many of these as copycats, thin or shallow expressions of deep local cultures, globalization from above masquerading as a championing of the 'others' below, disorganized messes, or borderline successes financially. But taken as a whole, the festivalization of African cities, even for a few days a year in each case, marks the profoundly cosmopolitan, globalized, imaginative, generative, and dynamic character of the continent's 'always-moving spaces.'

Mapping and picturing African cities from America

In this final chapter section, I point to some other examples of diasporic imaginations in art and photography that build new ways of representing African urban geographies beyond the festivalization discussed above (Roble and Rutledge 2008; de Boeck and Plissart 2004; Kashi and Watts 2008). Visual artists – photographers, painters, and sculptors alike – are directly re-envisioning urban Africa. The Somali Documentary Project (SDP) of the Somali-American photographer Abdi Roble (Roble and Rutledge 2008), for one great example, grew out of Columbus, where he worked as a freelance photographer for several newspapers. Columbus's Somali population grew from the two families he found there in the early 1990s to 45,000 by 2008. Together with the anthropologist Doug Rutledge (ibid.: viii), Roble formed the SDP 'to record the history of the Somali Diaspora through photography and writing, to educate hosting communities, and to bring international attention to the plight of the Somali people.' In their book on the project, *The Somali Diaspora: A Journey Away*, they trace migrations via a refugee camp in Dadaab, Kenya, to Somali communities in San Diego, Lewiston, Minneapolis, and Columbus. Roble's black-and-white photographs capture brilliantly the everyday lived spaces of Somalis in America, always-moving spaces of dynamism and change: a husband and wife adjusting to a comfortable kitchen in an Anaheim duplex, the same man sprawled on the floorboards of an empty new apartment in Portland, Maine, watching his children look out the window, teenage boys swimming in a Columbus pool, Somali women voting in Minneapolis in the November 2006 election (wherein Keith Ellison won his seat in Congress) or joining a picket line with fellow members of the Service Employees International Union, and Eid ul-Fitr celebrations in the Mall of America. Rutledge's captions and short essays demonstrate keen sensitivity and solidarity with Roble's photographic subjects, a solidarity they acknowledge as hard won in some cases. They end with a vision of hope, in words and pictures, recognizing that Somali mobility has shifted from transhumant pastoralism to the following of 'economic and cultural opportunities across the globe ... Somali grace and hospitality are a worldwide phenomenon now,' Rutledge (ibid.: 183) writes, 'and people in the rest of the world have only to learn to appreciate this gift.'

Another major African photographer, Zwelethu Mthethwa, has an increasingly geographically stretched biography, spanning South

Africa, Europe, and the United States – having studied in Rochester, New York, with galleries in Italy, the USA, and South Africa representing him (Peffer 2009: 263). Mthethwa's first innovation, odd as it may seem, was to engage in color photography in portraits of residents of Crossroads in Cape Town. He told Bongiwe Dhlomo in a 1999 interview that the 'choice of photographing in black and white by most photographers gives an acute political angle of desertion and emptiness' (Mthethwa, in ibid.: 264). In an interview four years later, he told Sean O'Toole: 'colour is just so beautiful. When you see beauty you think less of poverty. You think of design and composition.' As John Peffer (ibid.: 265) writes, Mthethwa's images 'evoke human environments that make do against great odds, they are clearly the products of a self-made aesthetic, and they give evidence of a kind of lived-in-ness. These are homes, made beautiful, however humbly.' What perhaps saves the photographs from a fairly easy critique of their aestheticization of urban poverty and consumerism, as Peffer (ibid.: 267) sees it, is 'his stated intention to act as both collaborator and artistic director … to create community through the collective act of depiction,' where all of the 'photographs are consciously posed after a careful negotiation between both sitter and artist.'

Outside of the realm of photography, the Ethiopian-American artist Julie Mehretu has developed a very geographical body of work that visualizes alternative modes of seeing cities. In her words, as she began to work with forms of painting that layered information in spatial arrays, she 'began thinking about them as aerial views of cities, as maps of imagined cities and narratives … One cluster of marks was battling another cluster, to make a particular pattern with a certain social characteristic' (Mehretu, in Abrams 2006: 248). Her own biography flows from alternative cartographies of belonging – her father is the Ethiopian-born urban geographer Assefa Mehretu, and although she was born in Ethiopia as well, she was raised in East Lansing and Detroit, Michigan, and lives in New York. 'There's not really one particular dynamic that has informed my identity as an Ethiopian-American, no single place or experience that defines who I am. One's identity is constructed partly from your parents and the context you come from, but also very separately from that. It's informed by all these elements, but it's something else altogether' (Mehretu, in ibid.: 249). The cities imagined in her canvases are not immediately apparent as belonging to Africa – indeed, some paintings are explicitly about New York, or about the 'Black City.' But the scale (her paintings are usually huge, and they take months and several assistants to create), depth (as many as seven layers are visible), and both narrative and visual complexity of Mehretu's paintings speak to the challenges inherent in mapping alternative visions of African cities. Janet Abrams (ibid.: 249) argues that the paintings are 'ultimately about the relationship between the individual and the larger (social) arrangement of which each of us is a part. Her work lures you toward it, but then – like a map – refuses you admission: it's only a drawing, not a real place.' Her works encapsulate the tension between an ordered frame of citiness and the ever-expanding, hard-to-encompass ongoing processes and dynamics of African urbanism (Allen et al. 2007; de Zegher et al. 2007; Dillon et al. 2010).

Several works by Mehretu and Mthethwa were included in *Africa Remix*, the sprawling 2004–06 exhibition that became the 'largest exhibition of contemporary African art ever seen in Europe' (Malbert 2005: 9). *Africa Remix* included the work of more than eighty artists from all across the continent. The cosmopolitan character of the vast majority of these artists is evident first and foremost in the frequency of slashes and hyphens in the gallery label lines where their places of residence appeared in the exhibit. The exhibition's book has a list of contributors that is piled high with: 'Nigerian; born in Oxford, UK; lives in Berlin' or 'Born in Luanda, Angola; lives and works in Brussels and Luanda,' and many more (Njami 2005: 217–23). Yet it is in the art itself that the citizen of a place meets with the citizen of the cosmos. The exhibition book and the exhibit space were divided into three segments, entitled *Identity & History*, *Body & Soul*, and *City & Land*; obviously the last of these is the most pertinent for my interests, and this was where both Mehretu and Mthethwa's work was placed, along with that of more than thirty other artists.

Three among these stand out for their profound alternative urban visions: Bodys Isek Kingelez of Kinshasa, Moshekwa Langa of Johannesburg/Amsterdam, and Allan de Souza of Nairobi/Los Angeles. Kingelez's most striking piece, *Projet pour le Kinshasa du troisième millénaire*, is a multimedia model imaginarium for the DRC's megalopolis in the future, the 'Third Millennium.' Langa's four *Collapsing Guides* are reimagined city maps, with black plastic trash bags serving as the base, multiple colors of masking tape as the streets, and a collage of cutout advertisements and photographs from African and European newspapers as the buildings. De Souza, like Kingelez, has constructed models of urban landscapes, in this case set against photographic skies or with various optical effects, most stunningly in *A blurring of the world, a refocusing seconds, minutes, hours, days, maybe years later, with everything put together differently, in ways he doesn't understand.* This photograph of a diorama, constructed in 2001, has as its centerpiece the image of a burning skyscraper in evident reference to the World Trade Center attack of 11 September, but with parts of the cityscape referencing Mombasa, Nairobi, Los Angeles, Johannesburg, and elsewhere. In all three cases, what most distinguishes these works is that they are all built, literally, using garbage, used electronic parts, dead batteries, plastic bags, and bits of tape and glue. They are all examples of making beauty out of junk.

The idea of making beauty out of junk is also graphically depicted in the cityscape of Douala, Cameroon, as Simone (2004) shows in his chapter on the city in *For the City Yet to Come.* The sculpture known as *La Nouvelle Liberté*, created out of the patronage of the urban art center, Doual'art, by Cameroonian artist Joseph Francis Sumegné, was installed in a major traffic circle in the city's Deido area in 1996. It depicts a giant human, 'holding up a sphere, and lifting one leg' as if in a state of joy (ibid.: 113–14). Despite the controversies that swirled around the sculpture faster than the traffic at the potholed roundabout, and despite its still-incomplete form, Simone argued for several key lessons from this alternative vision. For many Douala residents, *La Nouvelle Liberté* affirmed their notion that 'recycled and secondhand materials can indeed make up a good life' (ibid.: 114). It certainly 'got people to talk about the city in ways that were probably unprecedented,' and they repeatedly spoke to him of how they 'cherished' the sculpture as a means for reminding the city 'to recognize its own resourcefulness' (ibid.: 117). Remembering Basile Ndjio's (2006a) vision of Douala as a necropolis from Chapter 4, of course, we may note that some of that resourcefulness emerges in desecrating cemeteries, trafficking in dead bodies, operating institutions of brutal popular justice, robbing the victims of a plane crash, and other shocking ways. But then we can also think of Dominique Malaquais's (2006) vision of Douala: a city in constant circulation, such that it is in what she calls (following Dear and Leclerc 2003) a 'postborder' urban state. So many residents 'are in dialogue with multiple otherwheres half a world away' that 'movement, in a sense, becomes place,' lashed with 'incessant, overlapping flows' (Malaquais 2006: 46). The challenge for cities of beauty-out-of-junk cityscapes, she suggests, is to 'harness' all of the knowledge embedded in 'processes of moving, thinking, and planning movement' into a 'productive, tangible re-thinking of the city' (ibid.: 47).

Conclusion

By its endpoint, this chapter has roamed across Africa and the world, much more so than the other chapters. From Zanzibar, but also from Grahamstown to the UK to Seattle to Wichita to Minneapolis to Mogadishu to Douala and to other elsewheres, this has been a journey following and exploring the stretched and straddling geographies of urban Africa in the early twenty-first century. Whether in movements, festivals, exhibitions, novels, community organizations, or works of art, the point has been to see the character and qualities of cosmopolitanism as manifested in these various forms, events, or processes. In some cases, the rhizomatic, transnational, or translocal manifestations make beauty out of junk, in an Africa remix that articulates possibilities for productive and tangible re-visions of citiness, or of African urban geographies. In other examples, indeed in most I have offered here, we have seen the limitations of networks or of 'straddling' visions. In Carter's evocative phrase, one can sense the 'possibility of never arriving' in many – but not all – of these cosmopolitan journeys toward Soja's idea of 'practical usefulness in changing the world for the better.' Many of the possibilities are a bit like Mehretu's cityscapes, luring us toward them yet refusing admission.

It is evident that the 'always-moving spaces' of African cosmopolitan urbanism are fragile and transitory. The 'spaces of dynamism and change' that Robinson sought still contend with the 'images of power drawn on the ground.' For every new connection, one can usually find a corresponding abandonment. Yet the roots and routes of the 'changing same,' when merged with deeper, more contestatory applied urban politics, might lead to connective scar tissue healing over the gap between cosmopolitan consciousness and an effective relational city, in the dimension of 'symbolic politics' that Pieterse (2008a) noted among his elements of relationality. In the book's conclusion, I suggest an agenda for research and action toward a multi-dimensional range of relational ways to achieve better city futures in Africa, beyond these symbolic means. In any case, the empathetic and inclusive identification with one another and the world that encapsulates the best intentions of straddling cosmopolitanism can be a part of these better futures.

Conclusion

Cities in Africa belong to the world. Models of world cities and global cities either disregard the continent's cities or push them to peripheral margins. Intellectual thought and planning practice in urban studies more broadly often do much the same. Certainly, the region has been among the least urbanized parts of the earth, but that has been steadily changing. To be sure, few of Africa's cities are among the world's largest or most economically powerful, but the interconnections of African cities with those of the rest of the world make it necessary to link the discussions and academic literatures far more than has been the case. Too often, still, a kind of tokenism prevails, or an alarmist African exceptionalism, when African urbanism does enter the broader literature.

As I've tried to show in this book, the ever-expanding African urban studies bookshelf has much to say to both urban studies and African studies. The first thing is that, despite my book's title, it may be preposterous to speak about 'African cities' – it is certainly wrong to do so as if there is one type, or one theme. I have tried in this book to engage with the diversity and range of urban practice in Africa, including imaginative, literary, and artistic practices. That established for me the task of combing the new urban studies writing on Africa for a manageable set of themes, mixing that broader reading with my own research, in discussing a diversity of cities to underscore the plurality of citiness on the continent.

Second, the Africa fable that lumps cities together typically collectivizes a crisis narrative, even in progressive accounts. There are surely elements of a crisis in many cities, but the 'Africa talk' misses quite a lot that is either not in crisis in African cities or is far more complex and nuanced than a lot of outside observers allow. As Chapters 2, 3, and 4 showed, there are quite different manifestations of postcoloniality, informality, and new regimes of governance across the continent by which Africans are negotiating and navigating these crisis points, with significant variation in the effectiveness of this negotiation and navigation.

Without being blind to socio-economic or political problems in

Africa's cities, I have set out to resist an overarching crisis narrative, in the interests of maintaining a concern with both theory and practice. 'Critical theory,' Soja (2010: 69) writes, 'is primarily concerned with usefulness in praxis, especially with regard to achieving freedom from oppression and domination.' This reminder, among insights I have chosen to take from Soja here and there in the book, sets me the task of balancing those two key words of my book's subtitle (*theory* and *practice*) on a notion of the third key word there (*visions*): visions not beholden to a strict ideological line, whether neoliberal, materialist-Marxist, or post-structuralist.

Even the five themes that I have attempted to excavate here barely scratch the surface of the expanding research output of African urban studies; they inevitably reflect my own sense of how to categorize a broad intellectual terrain. Some of my themes are more appropriate to certain cities than others (e.g. we could or should never claim all African cities as 'wounded'), and others take distinctly different forms in each example (as in Chapter 3's delineation of how 'informal settlements' are understood in Cape Town, Accra, and Dar es Salaam). Another scholar might emerge from extensive reading of this vast literature and delineate rather different themes, or discuss the ones I've raised from a different angle entirely, or draw a quite different map of the literature. Invisibility, for instance, is a trope that numerous African urban studies scholars have put to good use in recent works (Simone 2004; de Boeck and Plissart 2004; Carter 2010). Others would create a more hands-on critique of economic development, electoral politics, gender issues, biophysical hazards, or environmental health than I have produced, or would place more emphasis on North African or francophone West African cities. There is just no way to encompass all of urban studies for all of Africa.

The threads connecting each of my chapters together relate to the broadest questions I asked in my introduction. Are African cities exhibiting patterns and processes that are new and distinct from those in other cities of the world? And, if we work to build on the experiences, theories, and practices emerging in urban Africa, is this local knowledge usable in alternative planning practice, or replicable in other cities – whether in Africa or elsewhere? Overall, this book has highlighted the importance of fostering the sorts of 'zones of exchange' Harrison (2006a) argued for, to support the emergence of forms of 'hybrid governance' (à la Trefon 2009) that bring informal, indigenous, or Afropolitan ideas into dialogue – however contentious this dialogue might be – with Western-derived ideas about formal, modern urbanism.

Pieterse (2008a) suggests that we model these zones of exchange in terms of a 'relational city.' His five avenues of relationality are not intended as the only arenas of the contestations that comprise such cities, but they are a good start. He argues for examination of representative politics, stakeholder forums, campaigns of direct action, alternative projects of grassroots development, and symbolic politics. I have shown examples, successful and unsuccessful, of some of this relationality at work in different ways in different African cities, from participatory solid waste management in Lusaka to reframing of the new Tanzanian capital at Dodoma, from re-engineering governance in Nairobi to reimagining a literary lived space in Mogadishu, from Zanzibari migrants unmoored in Seattle to a Somali Eid ul-Fitr in the Mall of America.

In Chapter 1, I asked what happens if we start the discussion about understanding what is going on in cities of the world from a city like Lusaka. There have indeed been some 'profound material changes' in the last thirty years in Lusaka, as in most African cities, some of which parallel those of Los Angeles or other Western cities. But my task has not been to compare and contrast. I aimed to begin thinking about these themes from a different place. My version of 'taking Lusaka apart' suggested the themes that I then explored in the ensuing chapters: legacies of colonialism and their contestation in African cityscapes; informality; the transformation of governance; violence, insecurity, and dislocation (which I put together as a sense of woundedness); and cosmopolitanism.

In Chapter 2's discussion of postcolonialism, I made a conscious choice to tack close to colonialism's material legacies and the applied attempts to transcend them in the postcolonial era, enabling me to focus on actually existing postcolonialism rather than the more abstract theoretical discourse that often dominates postcolonial studies. The answer I offered to Mbembe's question of whether we have really moved beyond colonialism is mixed. Colonialism's legacies in terms of imbalanced urban primacy, weak urban hierarchy development, retarded functionality, segregation, or inequality surely remain in the postcolonial era, even in cities built essentially after colonialism as a means of contesting those legacies. Yet both colonial and postcolonial elite-driven efforts to reorder African urban spatiality failed in their intentions in most cases, and the urban poor majorities endured in the cracks in the system. The ingenuity of these poor majorities needn't be blindly championed, yet in some cases the ways and means of producing urban space they've developed and maintained may challenge and confront even the most repressive state orders in potentially liberative ways.

In Chapters 3 and 4, I explored the ramifications of that last sentence above – that the poor majorities of Africa's cities produce space in ingenious ways under oppressive conditions – through debates about informality and governance. Those debates are complex, in some ways irresolvable, and yet of immediate importance to improving the quality of life for the urban poor majority. They are also intertwined. Any rethinking of how informality and formality can work together – the sort of hybrid or mutual acceptance I discussed – requires a realignment of governance. The deepening of democracy, not in rhetorical, concept-stretching or electoral terms but in terms of contestation, enhancement of capabilities, and genuine decentralization of decision-making, rests on a renegotiation of state–society relationships that inevitably depends on coming to grips with informality. The routes to a relational city are myriad and sundry and unpredictable, but unlikely to be found in the conditions of donor dependency and severe injustice that predominate in many African cities.

The unevenness of governance and justice outcomes across African cities, or even within one African city, appears to result from the clash of the dance steps of neoliberal reform with the politics, power, and influences that shape participation, or that map out rights to the city. Neoliberal policies are often involved in exacerbating that unevenness, further splicing cities already divided by colonial legacies and global capital flows. Yet I am wary of the 'radical political action' espoused by neoliberalism's fiercest materialist critics, and I am worried about the hyperbole and anecdote that often take the place of data in arguments developed via post-structuralist thinking. It is my sense that we need much more concrete analysis of governance on the ground. At times that analysis will take us into the examination of movement, mobility, circulations, and fluidity, which are key themes of post-structuralist analysis. But there are tangible questions begging answers in many cities about the shape and character of the drivers of urban development and about how, exactly, low-income groups can influence urban decision-making. Some cities are farther along the path out of citizen non-engagement, or out of stymied movements for collective action, and we need to know how their positive routes might be replicated and brought to other cities. Doing so requires evidence and recognition of the great diversity of politics and governance regimes across cities.

Therefore, the directions of future research in urban Africa ought to accommodate a comprehensive, rigorous, manageable, and comparable approach to data gathering. The African Centre for Cities, in partnership with the Cities Alliance and local branches of Slum/ Shack Dwellers International, has ambitions for creating mechanisms for establishing and sustaining just such urban data sources across the continent. They may or may not succeed, but the effort is long overdue, and the development of collaborations in that project between state and city planning units, community organizations, and international donors and activists, across and between different African cities, might provide a spark for more relational city formation.

Reconceptualizing states' relationships with people in African cities based around clear knowledge from grounded comparative research will be fundamental to re-envisioning urbanism on the continent. But in my last two chapters, I've tried, in different ways, to show that alternative visions of theory and practice needn't come only from traditional sites of urban activism – planners, politicians, bankers, engineers, or community groups. For one of Africa's most deeply troubled cities, Mogadishu, a literary voice, Nuruddin Farah, provided us with a refuge, a counter-discourse that avoids what one of his novel's characters called the 'hogwash' of nativism, reconnects the city to the world, contests the failed state and both the Islamist, nationalist, and US military intervention in it, and shows a way to rehumanize urban dynamics. If 'crossing the Mogadishu line' could mean coming over to the place where Farah resides – in the international departure lounge of the imagination where the 'gun' has left the equation – rather than its conventional translation as choosing sides in peacekeeping such that one can never come back to the neutral side, what could that sort of literary imagination do for urban studies in the world, let alone Africa? In the always-moving spaces of our young century, alongside of the imagery that portrays not just Mogadishu but all of urban Africa as the world capital of things gone to hell, the literary voices and artistic visions found in both straddling and stranded artists are astoundingly full of lived possibilities.

This book is an experiment, and an invitation toward an opening of discussion. Appropriately enough, my last full chapter traced a set of threads of stretched and straddling geographies of how diasporas and transnationality play into contemporary urban African dynamics. There are a number of ways to question the viability of transitory and fragile communities, connections, and organizations. Literary renditions of productive links between cities rest side by side with narratives of abandonment.

After exploring the more artistic or imaginary dimensions of cosmopolitanism, though, let me come back around to architecture and urban planning to draw the discussion directly into the practice of producing concrete alternative visions of African cities. Harrison (2006a) wants us to examine what 'practices' have come to the fore as the poor majority in African cities have 'found ways to live' with the conditions they are in, and he asks whether these can be put to use in creating alternative visions for African cities. There are certainly practices by which the residents of places like Sodom and Gomorrah, Crossroads, or Rangi Tatu have found ways to live with their conditions, but I find it hard to see these as replicable models for a broader vision of equitable and just cities as a whole. Chiefly this is because so often such practices are basically survival mechanisms or stopgap measures on a very small scale. Likewise, many of the inspiring networks or activist programs I discussed in Chapter 2 have possibilities for engaging in the creation of more livable cities for poor majorities gaining in their capabilities to live lives they choose, but the success stories will be uniquely situated in contexts where the drivers of urban development genuinely engage in deeper, contestatory politics together.

This brings me to the ultimate challenge of my book: is there any potential for 'African' urban studies to be part of this alternative visioning of a deeper democracy that might lead to imaginative, relational, and just city-spaces? One way to foster that potential could emerge through developing responses to Western urban studies. For example, we might look back to Soja's six discourses of the post-metropolis and respond from Africa. In doing so, we would articulate the following claims. There would be less emphasis on post-fordist industrialization as a driver of urban geographies, though this may not always be so for African cities. Cosmopolis looks a bit different than he might have imagined when we take the idea to African cities: Simone's (2010) 'trans-territorial cities' are full of both connections and abandonments. The growth of outer cities that Soja identified would mean something quite different in most African contexts, where suburbs of deep poverty and exclusion are interspersed with gated communities. We might see a fractal city; there is increased fragmentation, polarity, and segmentation, but across Africa this has quite diverse manifestations. The fortified character of urban space Soja identified with the post-metropolis might be somewhat recognizable in South Africa but not so much elsewhere – in fact, it is increasing *insecurity* one finds as a more notable outcome lately in African cities. Finally, for Soja's notion of the restructuring of the urban imaginary, we might see in African cities increased festivalization of urban space and a reclamation of indigeneity in architecture.

But for such an approach to *not* end up unnoticed in urban studies writ large, or for it to avoid being seen as an attempt at what might be called special pleading on behalf of Africa, it is crucial to put African cities at the center from the outset, to start from there, unapologetically. Such a resituating of the discussion might lead to global rethinking of housing, land, industrial development, labor, governance, historical legacies, hierarchies, forms, functions, primacy, cultural production, migration, and demographics: in essence, all the stuff of urban geography. One outcome of this is simply to force us to see the complexities, or the multiplexities, of urbanism, *from* Africa.

Africa is not all one thing, and no one country or city can be used as the example to stand in for all the rest – especially not South Africa or its major cities, but also not extreme and exoticized megacities. Johannesburg probably shares as many themes of urban theory and practice with New York as it does with Dar es Salaam; Grahamstown reminds me in some very tangible ways of the small American college city I live in, at the same time that it has other concerns in common with New Bell in Douala. Each city in Africa is itself multifaceted and comparable with both other cities on the continent and with cities around the world. Mere comparability should not mask the reality that neoliberalism is not the same across Africa's cities, nor is informalization, governance reform, impacts of violence, or cosmopolitanism. While there are bleak stops on any tour of urban Africa, like New Bell, not all is negative by any means. There are possibilities for deepening democratic practices in quite a few cities. Blanket approaches, whether of cheerleading or critique, such as those on neoliberalism, fall apart on closer scrutiny.

African studies is definitely done with its rural bias, if it ever really had one. But as a field it too should be careful to attend to the historicity and geographical particularities of cities. Part of my rationale for the sometimes rather different approaches I've taken in the six prior chapters is that African urban studies itself has such different approaches within it as a field. Scholars from economics, planning, history, sociology, anthropology, geography, and the humanities enter into discussions of African cities from different angles.

Strangely, political science seems only an occasional presence in African urban studies, when it ought to be a central field in our analyses, because these are such fascinating years for urban politics in Africa. Surely cities in many parts of the world could gain from more 'vibrant politics' and 'vigorous democratic contestation' (Pieterse 2008a: 162–3), but this seems to be a time for concerted efforts to bring these into being on the continent. Pieterse speaks to an African studies audience in focusing on his agenda items for building such politics: urban governance that opens up decision-making to that vibrant politics, revising technological standards, or building and landscape design, rethinking production systems, and tackling inequality.

Despite huge variation, each city on the continent negotiates with some similar hauntings and conundrums. There is great diversity and range to the negotiating, but it still makes a lot of sense to work to further develop an 'African' urban studies. There may be a different path for each city, and no one single agenda, but each city is navigating through its historical and geographical narratives of what others see and mark out as 'Africa.' The goals, as I see it, for African urban studies, are about negotiating and navigating more relational and just cities, deepening the democratization of urban practice, and turning urban studies as a whole toward the deeper examination of those African urban narratives. Urban dwellers in Africa often develop their own forms and norms. Whether we say these emerge from 'subaltern reason' or not, clearly the moment has emerged for building on possibilities for dialogue and conversation across the divide between these forms and norms and those of urban planners and practitioners from elsewhere. There is a transformation of consciousness implicit in the carrying out of such conversations, undergirded by a desire for it to have practical consequences that make the lives of the urban poor better, richer, fuller, and more just.

Bibliography

Abani, C. (2009) 'Stories of struggle, stories of hope: art, politics and human rights', Hall Center for the Humanities Lecture, University of Kansas, Lawrence, 17 November.

Abdoul, M. (2005) 'Urban development and urban informalities: Pikine, Senegal', in A. Simone and A. Abouhani (eds), *Urban Africa: Changing Contours of Survival in the City*, London: Zed Books, pp. 235–60.

Abdulai, R. (2007) 'The operation of urban traditional landholding institutions in sub-Saharan Africa: a Ghana study', Unpublished PhD thesis, University of Wolverhampton.

Abdulai, R., I. Ndegugri, P. Olomolaiye and D. Proverbs (2007) 'Land registration and security of land tenure: case studies of Kumasi, Tamale, Bolgatanga and Wa in Ghana', *International Development Planning Review*, 29(4): 475–502.

Abdulla, M. S. (1976) 'Ufafanuzi wa "Shamba"' [An explanation of 'Shamba'], in A. Haji, S. Muhammed, A. Hamad and M. Omar (eds), *Uandishi wa Tanzania, Kitabu cha Kwanza – Insha* [Tanzanian Writing, Book One – Essays], Nairobi: East African Literature Bureau.

Abrahamsen, R. (2000) *Disciplining Democracy: Development Discourse and Good Governance in Africa*, London: Zed Books.

Abrams, J. (2006) 'Epic vessels', in J. Abrams and P. Hall (eds), *Else/Where: Mapping New Cartographies of Networks and Territories*, Minneapolis: University of Minnesota Press, pp. 248–53.

Abumere, S. (1998) 'Abuja: planning and development of the new Federal Capital Territory', in O. Areola and S. Okafor (eds), *50 Years of Geography in Nigeria: The Ibadan Story*, Ibadan: Ibadan University Press, pp. 387–410.

Adama, O. (2007) *Governing from Above: Solid Waste Management in Nigeria's New Capital City of Abuja*, Stockholm: Stockholm University Press.

Afrah, M. (1994) *The Somalia Tragedy*, Mombasa: Mohamed Printers.

Agyeman J., R. Bullard and B. Evans (2003) 'Joined up thinking: bringing together sustainability, environmental justice, and equity', in J. Agyeman, R. Bullard and B. Evans (eds), *Development in an Unequal World*, Cambridge, MA: MIT Press, pp. 2–16.

Ahluwalia, P., L. Bethlehem and R. Ginio (eds) (2007) *Violence and Non-Violence in Africa*, New York: Routledge.

Ahmed, A. (1995) *The Invention of Somalia*, Lawrenceville, NJ: Red Sea Press.

Alden, P. and L. Tremaine (1998) 'Reinventing family in the second trilogy of Nuruddin Farah',

World Literature Today, 72(4): 759–66.

— (1999) *Nuruddin Farah,* New York: Twayne Publishers.

Alexander, L. (1983) 'European planning ideology in Tanzania', *Habitat International,* 7(1/2): 17–36.

Ali, A. (2007) Personal communication between author and Ali Hasan Ali, 14 July, Zanzibar.

Alidou, O. and A. M. Mazrui (2000) 'Secrets: Farah's *Things Fall Apart*', *Research in African Literatures,* 31(1): 122–8.

Allen, J. (1993) *Swahili Origins,* Athens: Ohio University Press.

Allen, S., G. Beal, J. Mehretu, R. Hart and K. Katchka (2007) *Julie Mehretu: City Sitings,* Detroit, MI: Detroit Institute of Arts.

Alou, M. (2009) 'Public goods and the management of collective infrastructure: the case of the drinking water supply systems in the Maradi region of Niger', in G. Blundo and P.-Y. Le Meur (eds), *The Governance of Daily Life in Africa: Ethnographic Explorations of Public and Collective Services,* Leiden: Brill, pp. 317–39.

Alpers, E. (1983) 'Muqdishu in the nineteenth century: a regional perspective', *Journal of African History,* 24(2): 441–59.

AlSayyad, N. (2004) 'Urban informality as a "new" way of life', in A. Roy and N. AlSayyad (eds), *Urban Informality: Transnational Perspectives from the Middle East, Latin America, and South Asia,* Lanham, MD: Lexington Books, pp. 7–30.

AlSayyad, N. and A. Roy (2004) 'Prologue/dialogue: urban informality: crossing borders', in A. Roy and N. AlSayyad (eds),

Urban Informality: Transnational Perspectives from the Middle East, Latin America, and South Asia, Lanham, MD: Lexington Books, pp. 1–6.

Alston, L., T. Eggertsson and D. North (1996) *Empirical Studies in Institutional Change,* Cambridge: Cambridge University Press.

Alston, L., G. Libecap and B. Mueller (1999) *Titles, Conflict and Land Use: The Development of Property Rights on the Brazilian Frontier,* Ann Arbor: University of Michigan Press.

Andreasen, J. (2001) 'The legacy of mobilisation from above: participation in a Zanzibar neighborhood', in A. Tostensen, I. Tvedten and M. Vaa (eds), *Associational Life in African Cities: Popular Responses to the Urban Crisis,* Uppsala: Nordic Africa Institute, pp. 263–81.

Appadurai, A. (1996) *Modernity at Large: Cultural Dimensions of Globalization,* Minneapolis: University of Minnesota Press.

Appiah, K. (2006) *Cosmopolitanism: Ethics in a World of Strangers,* New York: Norton.

Armstrong, A. (1987) 'Master plans for Dar es Salaam, Tanzania', *Habitat International,* 11(2): 133–46.

Arnold, N., B. McKim and B. Rawlence (2002) *The Bullets Were Raining: The 2001 Attack on Peaceful Demonstrators in Zanzibar,* New York: Human Rights Watch.

Arthur, J. (2000) *Invisible Sojourners: African Immigrant Diaspora in the United States,* Westport, CT: Praeger.

Askew, K. (2006) 'Musical reflections

on Tanzanian postsocialisms', *Africa: Journal of the International Africa Institute*, 76(1): 15–43.

Awasom, F. (2001) 'Autochthony and citizenship in postcolonial Africa: a critical perspective on Cameroon', Paper presented to the African Studies Seminar, University of Leiden, Leiden.

Ayeni, B. (1998) 'Urban geography', in O. Areola and S. Okafor (eds), *50 Years of Geography in Nigeria: The Ibadan Story*, Ibadan: Ibadan University Press, pp. 75–97.

Azzan, R. (2006) Author interview with Rashid Azzan, Department of Lands, Revolutionary Government of Zanzibar, 19 July.

Ballard, R., A. Habib, I. Valodia and E. Zuern (eds) (2006) *Voices of Protest: Social Movements in Post-Apartheid South Africa*, Scottsville: University of KwaZulu-Natal Press.

Balzerek, H. (2001) 'Applicability of IKONOS satellite scenes: monitoring, classification and evaluation of urbanisation processes in Africa: case study of Gombe/Nigeria', Proceedings of the International Symposium on Urban Remote Sensing, Regensburg, Germany.

— (2003) 'Achievements and problems in the evolution of urban centres in the Nigerian savannah: case study of Gombe', Proceedings of the International Conference on Environmental and Cultural Dynamics in the West African Savanna, Maiduguri, Nigeria.

Banda, N. (2002) Author's personal communication with Kalikiliki (Lusaka) resident Naomi Banda, 17 December.

Bang, A. (2008) 'Cosmopolitanism colonised? Three cases from Zanzibar 1890–1920', in E. Simpson and K. Kresse (eds), *Struggling with History: Islam and Cosmopolitanism in the Western Indian Ocean*, New York: Columbia University Press, pp. 167–88.

Barrot, P. (ed.) (2008) *Nollywood: The Video Phenomenon in Nigeria*, Oxford: James Currey.

Bates, R. (2008) *When Things Fell Apart: State Failure in Late-Century Africa*, Cambridge: Cambridge University Press.

Beall, J. (2006) 'Cities, terrorism, and development', *Journal of International Development*, 18(1): 105–20.

Beall J., O. Crankshaw and S. Parnell (2000) 'Victims, villains and fixers: the urban environment and Johannesburg's poor', *Journal of Southern African Studies*, 26(4): 833–55.

Beall, J., B. Guha-Khasnobis and R. Kanbur (2010) 'Introduction: African development in an urban world: beyond the tipping point', *Urban Forum*, 21: 197–204.

Becker, C., A. Hamer and A. Morrison (1994) *Beyond Urban Bias in Africa: Urbanization in an Era of Structural Adjustment*, Portsmouth, NH: Heinemann.

Bekker, S. and A. Leilde (eds) (2006) *Reflections on Identity in Four African Cities*, Johannesburg: African Minds.

Benga, N. (2005) 'Meanings and challenges of modern urban music in Senegal', in T. Falola and S. Salm (eds), *Urbanization and African Cultures*, Durham, NC: Carolina Academic Press, pp. 155–65.

Berman, B. (1984) 'Structure and process in the bureaucratic states of colonial Africa', *Development and Change*, 15(1): 23–41.

Best, A. (1970) 'Gaborone: problems and prospects of a new capital', *Geographical Review*, 60(1): 1–14.

Bissell, W. (2007) 'Casting a long shadow: colonial categories, cultural identities, and cosmopolitan spaces in globalizing Africa', in F. Demissie (ed.), *Postcolonial African Cities: Imperial Legacies and Postcolonial Predicaments*, New York: Routledge, pp. 25–41.

Blundo, G. and P.-Y. Le Meur (2009) 'Introduction: an anthropology of everyday governance: collective service delivery and subject-making', in G. Blundo and P.-Y. Le Meur (eds), *The Governance of Daily Life in Africa: Ethnographic Explorations of Public and Collective Services*, Leiden: Brill, pp. 1–37.

Blunt, A. and C. McEwan (2002) *Postcolonial Geographies*, London: Continuum.

Bond, P. (2000a) *Elite Transition: From Apartheid to Neoliberalism in South Africa*, London: Pluto.

— (2000b) 'Economic growth, ecological modernization or environmental justice? Conflicting discourses in post-apartheid South Africa', *Capitalism Nature Society*, 11(1): 33–61.

— (2002) *Unsustainable South Africa: Environment, Development, and Social Protest*, London: Merlin Press.

Bowden, M. (1999) *Black Hawk Down: A Story of Modern War*, New York: Atlantic Monthly Press.

— (2002) 'Foreword', in *Black Hawk Down: The Shooting Script*, New York: Newmarket Press, pp. vii–xv.

Brennan, J. (2002) 'Nation, race, and urbanization in Dar es Salaam, Tanzania, 1916–1976', Unpublished PhD thesis, Northwestern University.

Brennan, J. and A. Burton (2007) 'The emerging metropolis: a history of Dar es Salaam, circa 1862–2000', in J. Brennan, A. Burton and Y. Lawi (eds), *Dar es Salaam: Histories from an Emerging Metropolis*, Dar es Salaam: Mkuki na Nyota Publishing, pp. 13–75.

Brenner, N. and N. Theodore (2002) 'Cities and the geographies of "actually existing neoliberalism"', *Antipode*, 34(3): 349–79.

Brereton, C. (2005) 'Mapping Grahamstown's security governance network: prospects and problems for democratic policing', Unpublished MA thesis, Rhodes University.

Briggs, J. and I. Yeboah (2001) 'Structural adjustment and the contemporary sub-Saharan African city', *Area*, 33(1): 18–26.

Brown, A. and M. Lyons (2010) 'Seen but not heard: urban voice and citizenship for street traders', in I. Lindell (ed.), *Africa's Informal Workers: Collective Agency, Alliances, and Transnational Organizing*, Uppsala: Nordic Africa Institute, pp. 33–45.

Brown, J. (2003) 'Introduction', in *The United States Forces, Somalia After Action Report and Historical Overview, The United States Army in Somalia, 1992–1994*, Washington, DC: United States Army Center of Military History, p. iii.

Brown, T. (2005) 'Contestation,

confusion, and corruption: market-based land reform in Zambia', in S. Evers, M. Spierenburg and H. Wels (eds), *Competing Jurisdictions: Settling Land Claims in Africa*, Leiden: Brill, pp. 79–102.

Bryceson, D. (2006) 'Fragile cities: fundamentals of urban life in East and Southern Africa', in D. Bryceson and D. Potts (eds), *African Urban Economies: Viability, Vitality or Vitiation?*, New York: Palgrave Macmillan, pp. 3–38.

Bryceson, D. and D. Potts (eds) (2006) *African Urban Economies: Viability, Vitality or Vitiation?*, New York: Palgrave Macmillan.

Bryden, M. and M. Steiner (1998) *Somalia between Peace and War: Somali Women on the Edge of the 21st Century*, Nairobi: UNIFEM.

Buckland, R. (2009) 'Who, but Politicians, Would Have Wanted to Win the June Election?', *Makana Moon* (Grahamstown), 6 July, p. 3.

Burgel, G., G. Burgel and M. Dezes (1987) 'An interview with Henri Lefebvre', *Environment and Planning D: Society and Space*, 5(1): 27–38.

Burton, A. (2005) *African Underclass: Urbanization, Crime and Colonial Order in Dar es Salaam*, Oxford: James Currey.

Butana, K. (2009) 'New mayor to focus council on service delivery', *Grocott's Mail* (Grahamstown), 21 July, p. 5.

Byerley, A. (2005) *Becoming Jinja: The Production of Space and Making of Place in an African Industrial Town*, Stockholm: Stockholm University Press.

Byrne, J., C. Martinez and L. Glover (2002) 'A brief on environmental justice', in J. Byrne, C. Martinez and L. Glover (eds), *Environmental Justice: Discourses in International Political Economy*, Brunswick, NJ: Transaction Publishers, pp. 3–17.

Cameron, R. (2006) 'Local government boundary reorganization', in U. Pillay, R. Tomlinson and J. du Toit (eds), *Democracy and Delivery: Urban Policy in South Africa*, Cape Town: HSRC Press, pp. 76–106.

Capital Development Authority (1976) *National Capital Master Plan: Dodoma, Tanzania*, Toronto: Project Planning Associates.

Caplan, P. (2004) 'Introduction', in P. Caplan and F. Topan (eds), *Swahili Modernities: Culture, Politics, and Identity on the East Coast of Africa*, Trenton, NJ: Africa World Press, pp. 1–18.

Carter, D. (1997) *States of Grace: Senegalese in Italy and the New European Immigration*, Minneapolis: University of Minnesota Press.

— (2003) 'Preface', in K. Koser (ed.), *New African Diasporas*, London: Routledge, pp. ix–xix.

— (2010) *Navigating the African Diaspora: The Anthropology of Invisibility*, Minneapolis: University of Minnesota Press.

Casper, L. (2001) *Falcon Brigade: Combat and Command in Somalia and Haiti*, Boulder, CO: Lynne Rienner.

Cassanelli, L. (1982) *The Shaping of Somali Society: Reconstructing the History of a Pastoral People, 1600–1900*, Philadelphia: University of Pennsylvania Press.

Castells, M. (1997) *The Power of Identity*, Oxford: Blackwell.

CCDC (Capital City Development Corporation) (1972) *Lilongwe: New Capital City*, Lilongwe: CCDC.

Celik, Z. (1997) *Urban Forms and Colonial Confrontations: Algiers under French Rule*, Berkeley: University of California Press.

Center of Military History (2003) *The United States Forces, Somalia After Action Report and Historical Overview, The United States Army in Somalia, 1992–1994*, Washington, DC: United States Army Center of Military History.

Chabal, P. (2009) *Africa: The Politics of Suffering and Smiling*, London: Zed Books.

Chachage, C. (2000) *Environment, Aid and Politics in Zanzibar*, Dar es Salaam: University of Dar es Salaam Press.

Chamley, S. (2006) 'Malawi: urban explosion is choking capital city to death', *New African*, February, pp. 48–9.

Cheatle, M. (1986) 'Water supply, sewerage, and drainage', in G. Williams (ed.), *Lusaka and Its Environs*, Lusaka: Zambia Geographical Association, pp. 250–58.

Cherry, J. (2000) 'Kwazekele: the politics of transition in South Africa: an Eastern Cape case study', Unpublished PhD thesis, Rhodes University.

Chirambo, R. (2008) 'Banda's monuments and the narrativization of Malawi's history in the post-Banda era', *Journal of Social Development in Africa*, 23(1): 139–60.

Christopher, A. J. (1994) 'Urbanization and national capitals in Africa', in J. Tarver (ed.), *Urbanization in Africa: A Handbook*, Westport, CT: Greenwood Press, pp. 408–22.

Clarke, W. (1997) 'Failed visions and uncertain mandates in Somalia', in W. Clarke and J. Herbst (eds), *Learning from Somalia: The Lessons of Armed Humanitarian Intervention*, Boulder, CO: Westview Press, pp. 3–19.

Clarke, W. and J. Herbst (1995) *Somalia and the Future of Humanitarian Intervention*, Princeton, NJ: Center of International Studies.

Coetzee, J. (2003) *Life on the Margin: Listening to the Squatters*, Grahamstown: Rhodes University.

Cohen, A. (1969) *Custom and Politics in Urban Africa: A Study of Hausa Migrants in Yoruba Towns*, Berkeley: University of California Press.

Collins, J. (1977) 'Lusaka: urban planning in a British Colony', in G. Cherry (ed.), *Shaping an Urban World*, New York: St Martin's Press, pp. 227–41.

— (1986) 'Lusaka: the historical development of a planned capital, 1931–1970', in G. Williams (ed.), *Lusaka and Its Environs*, Lusaka: Zambia Geographical Association, pp. 95–137.

Connell, J. (1972) 'Lilongwe: another new capital for Africa', *East African Geographical Review*, 10(1): 90.

Cooper, B. (2008) *A New Generation of African Writers: Migration, Material Culture and Language*, Rochester, NY: Boydell & Brewer.

Cooper, F. (1983) *Struggle for the City: Migrant Labor, Capital, and the State in Urban Africa*, Beverly Hills, CA: Sage.

Coquery-Vidrovitch, C. (2005a) *The History of African Cities South of the Sahara from the Origins to Colonization*, Princeton, NJ: Markus Weiner.

— (2005b) 'Urban cultures: relevance and context', in T. Falola and S. Salm (eds), *Urbanization and African Cultures*, Durham, NC: Carolina Academic Press, pp. 17–22.

Cosgrove, D. (2008) *Geography and Vision: Seeing, Imagining and Representing the World*, London: I. B. Tauris.

Crankshaw, O. and S. Parnell (1998) 'Interpreting the 1994 African township landscape', in H. Judin and I. Vladislavic (eds), *Blank_: Architecture, Apartheid and After*, Rotterdam: NAi Publishers, pp. 439–44.

Crespin, J. (2006) 'Aiding local action: the constraints faced by donor agencies in supporting effective, pro-poor initiatives on the ground', *Environment and Urbanization*, 18(4): 433–49.

Cull, P. (2009) 'Water infrastructure may see parts of East Cape declared disaster areas', *The Herald* (Port Elizabeth), 22 July, p. 4.

Dahiya, B. and C. Pugh (2000) 'The localization of Agenda 21 and the Sustainable Cities Programme', in C. Pugh (ed.), *Sustainable Cities in Developing Countries*, London: Earthscan, pp. 152–84.

Daily Dispatch (2009) 'Service delivery protests turn violent', 22 July, p. 3.

Daley, P. (2007) *Gender and Genocide in Burundi: The Search for Spaces of Peace in the Great Lakes Region*, Oxford: James Currey.

Darkoh, M. (1994) *Tanzania's Growth Centre Policy and Industrial Development*, Frankfurt: Peter Lang.

Davenport, T. (1980) *Black Grahamstown: The Agony of a Community*, Johannesburg: South Africa Institute of Race Relations.

Davidson, J. (1985) 'An assessment of hawking activities in Fingo village', Unpublished MA thesis, Rhodes University.

Davies, A. (2008) *The Geographies of Garbage Governance: Interventions, Interactions and Outcomes*, Aldershot: Ashgate.

Davis, M. (2005) *Planet of Slums*, London: Verso.

De Boeck, F. (2010) 'Spectral Kinshasa: building the city through an architecture of words', Paper presented to the Workshop on 'Beyond dysfunctionality: pro-social writing on African cities', Nordic Africa Institute, Uppsala, 21 October.

De Boeck, F. and M.-F. Plissart (2004) *Kinshasa: Tales of the Invisible City*, Tervuren: Royal Museum for Central Africa.

De Soto, H. (2000) *The Mystery of Capital: Why Capitalism Triumphs in the West and Fails Everywhere Else*, New York: Basic Books.

De Zegher, C., J. Mehretu and T. Golden (2007) *Julie Mehretu: Drawings*, Rizzoli International Publications.

Dear, M. and G. Leclerc (2003) 'The postborder condition: art and urbanism in Bajalta California', in M. Dear and G. Leclerc (eds), *Postborder City: Cultural Spaces of Bajalta California*, New York: Routledge, pp. 1–30.

Debbane, A. and R. Keil (2004)

'Multiple disconnections: environmental justice and urban water in Canada and South Africa', *Space and Polity*, 8(2): 209–25.

Deckard, S. (2010) *Paradise Discourse, Imperialism, and Globalization: Exploiting Eden*, New York: Routledge.

Demissie, F. (2007a) 'Imperial legacies and postcolonial predicaments: an introduction', in F. Demissie (ed.), *Postcolonial African Cities: Imperial Legacies and Postcolonial Predicaments*, New York: Routledge, pp. 1–10.

— (2007b) 'Visual fragments of Kinshasa', in F. Demissie (ed.), *Postcolonial African Cities: Imperial Legacies and Postcolonial Predicaments*, New York: Routledge, pp. 131–42.

Deutsch, J.-G., P. Probst and H. Schmidt (eds) (2002) *African Modernities: Entangled Meanings in Current Debate*, Oxford: James Currey.

Dierwechter, Y. (2002) 'Lefebvre's modernities: informality, planning and space in Cape Town', in A. Thornley and Y. Rydin (eds), *Planning in a Global Era*, Aldershot: Ashgate, pp. 189–209.

Dill, B. (2010) 'Community-based organizations (CBOs) and norms of participation in Tanzania: working against the grain', *African Studies Review*, 53(2): 23–48.

Dillon, B., J. Mehretu and J. Young (2010) *Julie Mehretu: Gray Area*, New York: Solomon Guggenheim Museum.

Diouf, M. (2008) '(Re)imagining an African city: performing culture, arts and citizenship in Dakar (Senegal), 1980–2000', in G. Prakash and K. Kruse (eds), *The Spaces of the Modern City: Imaginaries, Politics, and Everyday Life*, Princeton, NJ: Princeton University Press, pp. 346–72.

Dirlik, A. (2001) 'Place-based imagination: globalism and the politics of place', in R. Prazniak and A. Dirlik (eds), *Places and Politics in an Age of Globalization*, Lanham, MD: Rowman & Littlefield, pp. 15–51.

Dixon, J. and M. Ramutsindela (2006) 'Urban resettlement and environmental justice in Cape Town', *Cities*, 23(1): 129–39.

Djokotoe, E. (2004) 'Prostitutes' play hits stage', *Zambian Post*, 11 July, p. 15.

Dosi, M., L. Rushubirwa and G. Myers (2007) 'Tanzanians in the land of Oz: diaspora and transnationality in Wichita, Kansas', *Social and Cultural Geography*, 8(5): 657–71.

Drakakis-Smith, D. (2000) *Third World Cities*, 2nd edn, London: Routledge.

Draper, R. (2009) 'Shattered Somalia: can the world's number one failed state reverse its course?', *National Geographic*, 216(3): 70–99.

Driver, F. and D. Gilbert (1999) 'Imperial cities: overlapping territories, intertwined histories', in F. Driver and D. Gilbert (eds), *Imperial Cities: Landscape, Display and Identity*, Manchester: Manchester University Press, pp. 1–17.

Edwards, D. (1984) *Black Identity in Grahamstown and Ciskei: A Psychological Investigation*, Grahamstown: Rhodes University.

Egbo, G. (2010) 'Debate review: Lagos … mega city or crisis

city?', *ArchiAfrika Newsletter*, September, pp. 4–6.

Elleh, N. (1997) *African Architecture: Evolution and Transformation*, New York: McGraw-Hill.

— (2001) *Abuja: The Single Most Ambitious Urban Design Project of the 20th Century*, Weimar: VDG.

— (2002) *Architecture and Power in Africa*, New York: Praeger.

Ellison, J. (2009) 'The refugees who saved Lewiston', *Newsweek*, 17 January.

Englund, H. (2001) 'The politics of multiple identities: the making of a Home Villagers' Association in Lilongwe, Malawi', in A. Tostensen, I. Tvedten and M. Vaa (eds), *Associational Life in African Cities: Popular Responses to the Urban Crisis*, Uppsala: Nordic Africa Institute, pp. 90–106.

— (2002) 'The village in the city, the city in the village: migrants in Lilongwe', *Journal of Southern African Studies*, 28(1): 13–54.

Eno, O. (2005) 'Somalia's City of the Jackals: politics, economy, and society in Mogadishu, 1991–2003', in S. Salm and T. Falola (eds), *African Urban Spaces in Historical Perspective*, Rochester, NY: University of Rochester Press, pp. 365–79.

Enwezor, O. (2003) 'Terminal modernity: Rem Koolhaas's discourse on entropy', in *What Is OMA: Considering Rem Koolhaas and the Office for Metropolitan Architecture*, Rotterdam: NAi Publishers, pp. 103–19.

Epstein, A. L. (1958) *Politics in an Urban African Community*, Manchester: Manchester University Press.

Evans, P. (2002) 'Collective capabilities, culture and Amartya Sen's *Development as Freedom*', *Studies in Comparative International Development*, 37(2): 54–60.

— (2004) 'Development as institutional change: the pitfalls of monocropping and the potentials of deliberation', *Studies in Comparative International Development*, 38(4): 30–52.

Falola, T. (2005) 'Urban cultures: the setting and the situational', in T. Falola and S. Salm (eds), *Urbanization and African Cultures*, Durham, NC: Carolina Academic Press, pp. 3–16.

Falola, T. and S. Salm (eds) (2004) *Globalization and Urbanization in Africa*, Trenton, NJ: Africa World Press.

— (eds) (2005) *Urbanization and African Cultures*, Durham, NC: Carolina Academic Press.

Farah, N. (1970) *From a Crooked Rib*, London: Heinemann.

— (1976) *A Naked Needle*, London: Heinemann.

— (1980) *Sweet and Sour Milk*, London: Heinemann.

— (1981) *Sardines*, Saint Paul, MN: Graywolf Press.

— (1983) *Close Sesame*, Saint Paul, MN: Graywolf Press.

— (1986) *Maps*, New York: Penguin.

— (1992) *Gifts*, New York: Penguin.

— (1998) *Secrets*, New York: Penguin.

— (2000a) *Yesterday, Tomorrow: Voices from the Somali Diaspora*, London: Cassell.

— (2000b) 'Citizens of sorrow', *Transition*, 91(2): 10–20.

— (2003) *Links*, New York: Penguin.

— (2004) 'Interview with Nuruddin Farah by Kwame Anthony Appiah', *Bomb*, 87: 54–9.

— (2006) Personal communication between Nuruddin Farah and the author during 'A conversation with Nuruddin Farah', Hall Center for the Humanities, University of Kansas, 13 September.

— (2007a) *Knots*, New York: Riverhead (Penguin) Books.

— (2007b) 'My life as a diplomat', *New York Times*, 26 May.

— (2009) 'The family house', *Transition*, 99: 6–16.

Farrier, D. (2008) 'Terms of hospitality: Abdulrazak Gurnah's *By the Sea*', *Journal of Commonwealth Literature*, 43: 121–39.

Ferguson, J. (1999) *Expectations of Modernity: Myths and Meanings of Urban Life in the Zambian Copperbelt*, Berkeley: University of California Press.

— (2006) *Global Shadows: Africa in the Neoliberal World Order*, Durham, NC: Duke University Press.

— (2007) 'Formalities of poverty: thinking about social assistance in neoliberal South Africa', *African Studies Review*, 50(2): 71–86.

— (2008) 'Global disconnect: abjection and the aftermath of modernism', in P. Geschiere, B. Meyer and P. Pels (eds), *Readings in Modernity in Africa*, Bloomington: Indiana University Press, pp. 8–16.

Florin, B. (2005) 'Urban policies in Cairo: from speeches on new cities to the adjustment practices of ordinary city dwellers', in A. M. Simone and A. Abouhani (eds), *Urban Africa: Changing Contours of Survival in the City*, Dakar: Codesria, pp. 29–67.

Fogarassy, H. (1999) *Mission Improbable: The World Community on a UN Compound in Somalia*, Lanham, MD: Lexington Books.

Fortier, A.-M. (2005) 'Diaspora', in D. Atkinson, P. Jackson, D. Sibley and N. Washbourne (eds), *Cultural Geography: A Critical Dictionary of Key Concepts*, London: I. B. Tauris, pp. 182–7.

Fraser, A. and M. Larmer (eds) (2010) *Boom and Bust on the Zambian Copperbelt*, London: Palgrave Macmillan.

Fredericks, R. (2009) 'Doing the dirty work: the cultural politics of garbage collection in Dakar, Senegal', Unpublished PhD thesis, University of California, Berkeley.

Freund, B. (2007) *The African City*, Cambridge: Cambridge University Press.

Friedmann, J. (1986) 'The World City Hypothesis', *Development and Change*, 17: 69–83.

Fryer, J. (2002) 'Jingoism jibe over *Black Hawk Down*', *BBC News Online*, 21 January.

Fu, A. and M. Murray (2007) 'Cinema and the edgy city: Johannesburg, carjacking, and the postmetropolis', in F. Demissie (ed.), *Postcolonial African Cities: Imperial Legacies and Postcolonial Predicaments*, London: Routledge, pp. 121–30.

Gana, H. (2009) 'Interview with Libyan artist Hadia Gana, by Rachel Stella Jenkins', *Archi-Afrika Newsletter*, May, pp. 3–5.

Gana, N. and H. Harting (2008) 'Introduction: narrative violence: Africa and the Middle East', *Comparative Studies of South Asia, Africa and the Middle East*, 28(1): 1–10.

Gana, N. and H. Heike (2008) 'Introduction: narrative violence: Africa and the Middle East',

Comparative Studies of South Asia, Africa and the Middle East, 28(1): 1–10.

Gaonkar, D. (ed.) (2001) *Alternative Modernities*, Durham, NC: Duke University Press.

Gathanju, D. (2009) 'Nairobi redraws its planning strategy', *Planning* (American Planning Association), July, pp. 28–31.

Geiger, S. (1997) *TANU Women: Gender and Culture in the Making of Tanganyikan Nationalism, 1955–1965*, Portsmouth, NH: Heinemann.

Gensheimer, T. (2004) 'Globalization and the medieval Swahili city', in T. Falola and S. Salm (eds), *Globalization and Urbanization in Africa*, Trenton, NJ: Africa World Press, pp. 171–85.

Geschiere, P., B. Meyer and P. Pels (2008) 'Introduction', in P. Geschiere, B. Meyer and P. Pels (eds), *Readings in Modernity in Africa*, Bloomington: Indiana University Press, pp. 1–7.

Gettleman, J. (2009) 'The other lessons of Black Hawk Down', *New York Times*, 18 October, p. A4.

Ghanadan, R. (2009) 'Connected geographies and struggles over access: electricity commercialization in Tanzania', in D. McDonald (ed.), *Electric Capitalism: Recolonising Africa on the Power Grid*, London: Earthscan, pp. 400–436.

Gikandi, S. (2002) 'The politics and poetics of national formation: recent African Writing and *Maps*', in D. Wright (ed.), *Emerging Perspectives on Nuruddin Farah*, Trenton, NJ: Africa World Press, pp. 449–68.

Gilbert, A. (2002) 'On the mystery of capital and the myths of Hernando de Soto: what difference does legal title make?', *International Development Planning Review*, 24(1): 1–19.

Gilroy, P. (1993) *The Black Atlantic: Modernity and Double Consciousness*, London: Verso.

— (1995) 'Roots and routes: black identity as an outernational project', in H. Harris, H. Blue and E. Griffith (eds), *Racial and Ethnic Identity: Psychological Development and Creative Expression*, London: Routledge, pp. 15–30.

Goodwin, S. (2006) *Africa's Legacies of Urbanization: The Unfolding Saga of a Continent*, Lanham, MD: Lexington Books.

Gorlier, C. (1998) 'Nuruddin Farah's Italian domain', *World Literature Today*, 72(4): 781–5.

Gough, K. (2008) '"Moving around": the social and spatial mobility of youth in Lusaka', *Geografiska Annaler B: Human Geography*, 90(3): 243–55.

Gough, K. and P. Yankson (1997) 'Continuity and change in peri-urban Accra', Copenhagen: Danish Council for Development Research.

— (2000) 'Land markets in African cities: the case of peri-urban Accra, Ghana', *Urban Studies*, 37: 2485–500.

Grant, R. (2006) 'Out of place? Global citizens in local spaces: a study of the informal settlements in the Korle Lagoon environs in Accra, Ghana', *Urban Forum*, 17(1): 1–24.

— (2009) *Globalizing City: The Urban and Economic Transformation of Accra, Ghana*, Syracuse, NY: Syracuse University Press.

Grant, R. and P. Yankson (2003) 'City profile: Accra', *Cities*, 20(1): 65–74.

Gray, A. (2009) 'Emplacing displacement: cultural landscapes of refugee-hosting in Ukwimi, Zambia', Unpublished PhD thesis, University of Kansas.

Gupta, A. and J. Ferguson (1992) 'Beyond "culture": space, identity, and the politics of difference', *Cultural Anthropology*, 7: 6–23.

Gurnah, A. (1987) *Memory of Departure*, New York: Grove Press.

— (1988) *Pilgrims Way*, London: Jonathan Cape.

— (1990) *Dottie*, London: Jonathan Cape.

— (1994) *Paradise*, New York: New Press.

— (1996) *Admiring Silence*, New York: New Press.

— (2001a) *By the Sea*, New York: New Press.

— (2001b) 'The wood of the moon', *Transition*, 10(4): 88–112.

— (2004) 'Writing and place', *World Literature Today*, 78(2): 26–8.

— (2005) *Desertion*, London: Bloomsbury.

— (2006) 'Beside the seaside', *New Statesman*, 25 September, pp. 66–7.

Gutale, A. (2008) 'The Alliance Framework: a micro-level approach to diagnosing protracted conflict in south central Somalia', Unpublished Masters thesis, University of Kansas.

Guyer, J. (2004) *Marginal Gains: Monetary Transactions in Atlantic Africa*, Chicago, IL: University of Chicago Press.

Guyer, J., L. Denzer and A. Agbaje (eds) (2002) *Money Struggles and City Life: Devaluation in Ibadan and Other Urban Centers in Southern Nigeria, 1986–1996*, Portsmouth, NH: Heinemann.

Halla, F. (2005) 'Critical elements in sustaining participatory planning: Bagamoyo Strategic Urban Development Planning Framework in Tanzania', *Habitat International*, 29: 137–61.

Hamdan, G. (1964) 'Capitals of the New Africa', *Economic Geography*, 40: 239–53.

Hamilton, R. (2007) 'Rethinking the African diaspora: global dynamics', in R. Hamilton (ed.), *Routes of Passage: Rethinking the African Diaspora*, East Lansing: Michigan State University Press, pp. 1–40.

Hampwaye, G. (2008) 'Local economic development in the city of Lusaka, Zambia', *Urban Forum*, 19: 187–204.

Hampwaye, G., E. Nel and C. Rogerson (2007) 'Urban agriculture as local initiative in Lusaka, Zambia', *Environment and Planning C: Government and Policy*, 25: 553–72.

Hannerz, U. (1996) *Transnational Connections: Culture, People, Places*, New York: Routledge.

Hansen, K. (1997) *Keeping House in Lusaka*, New York: Columbia University Press.

— (2008) 'Getting stuck in the compound: some odds against social adulthood in Lusaka, Zambia', *Africa Today*, 15: 3–16.

Hansen, K. and M. Vaa (eds) (2004) *Reconsidering Informality: Perspectives from Urban Africa*, Uppsala: Nordic Africa Institute.

Hansen, S. (2007) 'Civil war economies, the hunt for profit and the incentives for peace (the case of Somalia)', Unpublished report on businesses in Mogadishu funded by Norwegian Agency for International Development.

Harrison, P. (2003) 'Fragmentation and globalization as the new meta-narrative', in P. Harrison, M. Huchzermeyer and M. Mayekiso (eds), *Confronting Fragmentation: Housing and Urban Development in a Democratizing Society*, Cape Town: UCT Press.

— (2006a) 'On the edge of reason: planning and urban futures in Africa', *Urban Studies*, 43(2): 319–35.

— (2006b) 'Integrated development plans and Third Way politics', in U. Pillay, R. Tomlinson and J. du Toit (eds), *Democracy and Delivery: Urban Policy in South Africa*, Pretoria: HSRC Press.

Harrison, P., A. Todes and V. Watson (2008) *Planning and Transformation: Learning from the Post-Apartheid Experience*, New York: Routledge.

Hart, K. (1973) 'Informal income opportunities and urban employment in Ghana', *Journal of Modern African Studies*, 11(1): 61–89.

Hartley, A. (2003) *The Zanzibar Chest*, New York: Atlantic Monthly Press.

Harvey, D. (1973) *Social Justice and the City*, Baltimore, MD: Johns Hopkins University Press.

— (1989) *The Condition of Postmodernity: An Enquiry into the Origins of Cultural Change*, Oxford: Blackwell.

— (1996) *Justice, Nature, and the Geography of Difference*, Oxford: Blackwell.

— (2000) *Spaces of Hope*, Edinburgh: Edinburgh University Press.

— (2005) *A Brief History of Neo-*liberalism, New York: Oxford University Press.

Hashi, A. (1996) *Weapons and Clan Politics in Somalia*, Self-published, Mogadishu.

Hayuma, A. M. (1981) 'Dodoma: the planning and building of the new capital city', *Habitat International*, 5: 653–80.

Healey, P. (2000) 'Planning in relational space and time: responding to new urban realities', in G. Bridge and S. Watson (eds), *A Companion to the City*, Oxford: Blackwell.

Helff, S. (2009) 'Illegal diasporas and African refugees in Abdulrazak Gurnah's *By the Sea*', *Journal of Commonwealth Literature*, 44: 67–80.

Hendriks, B. (2010) 'City-wide governance networks in Nairobi: towards contributions to political rights, influence and service delivery for poor and middle-class citizens?', *Habitat International*, 34(1): 59–77.

Hess, J. (2006) *Art and Architecture in Postcolonial Africa*, Jefferson, NC: McFarland & Co.

Hirsch, J. and R. Oakley (1995) *Somalia and Operation Restore Hope: Reflections on Peacemaking and Peacekeeping*, Washington, DC: United States Institute for Peace Press.

Hitchcock, P. (2007) 'Postcolonial failure and the politics of nation', *South Atlantic Quarterly*, 106(4): 727–52.

Holleman, H. (1997) *Graham's Town: The Untold Story*, Grahamstown: The Black Sash.

Holtzman, J. (2000) *Nuer Journeys, Nuer Lives: Sudanese Refugees in Minnesota*, Needham Heights, MA: Allyn & Bacon.

Home, R. (1997) *Of Planting and Planning: The Making of British Colonial Cities*, London: Spon.

Home, R. and H. Lim (2004) *Demystifying the Mystery of Capital: Land Tenure and Poverty in Africa and the Caribbean*, London: Glasshouse Press.

Howe, J. (1997) 'Relations between the United States and United Nations in dealing with Somalia', in W. Clarke and J. Herbst (eds), *Learning from Somalia: The Lessons of Armed Humanitarian Intervention*, Boulder, CO: Westview Press, pp. 173–90.

Hoyle, B. (1979) 'African socialism and urban development: the relocation of the Tanzanian capital', *Tijdschrift voor Economische en Sociale Geografie*, 70: 207–16.

Hughes, D. (1994) *Afrocentric Architecture: A Design Primer*, Dayton, OH: Greydon Press.

Human Rights Watch (2007) *Shell-Shocked: Civilians under Siege in Mogadishu*, New York: Human Rights Watch.

Hyden, G. (1999) 'Governance and the reconstitution of political order', in R. Joseph (ed.), *State, Conflict and Democracy in Africa*, Boulder, CO: Lynne Rienner, pp. 179–96.

Hyden, G., J. Court and K. Mease (2004) *Making Sense of Governance: Empirical Evidence from Sixteen Developing Countries*, Boulder, CO: Lynne Rienner.

Ikejiofor, U. (1997) 'Planning and the political process: sifting some underlying issues in the development of Abuja, Nigeria's new capital', *Third World Planning Review*, 19(3): 271–87.

— (1998) 'Access to land, development control and low-income housing in Abuja, Nigeria: policy, politics and bureaucracy', *Planning Practice and Research*, 13(3): 299–309.

— (2006) 'Equity in informal land delivery: insights from Enugu, Nigeria', *Land Use Policy*, 23: 448–59.

ILO (International Labour Organization) (1972) *Employment, Incomes and Equality: A Strategy for Increasing Productive Employment in Kenya*, Geneva: ILO.

Imam, A., B. Mohammed, D. Wilson and C. Cheeseman (2008) 'Country report: solid waste management in Abuja, Nigeria', *Waste Management*, 28: 468–72.

Jack, M. (2009) '2500 walk out as strike action hits bay', *The Herald* (Port Elizabeth), 21 July, p. 1.

Jackson, P., P. Crang and C. Dwyer. (2004) 'Introduction: the spaces of transnationality', in P. Jackson, P. Crang and C. Dwyer (eds), *Transnational Spaces*, London: Routledge, pp. 1–23.

Jama, A. (1996) *The Origins and Development of Mogadishu AD 1000 to 1850*, Uppsala: Uppsala University Studies in African Archeology.

James, D. (2007) *Gaining Ground? 'Rights' and 'Property' in South African Land Reform*, New York: Routledge.

Jordhus-Lier, D. (2010) 'The Struggle against informalization in the city of Cape Town', in I. Lindell (ed.), *Africa's Informal Workers: Collective Agency, Alliances, and Transnational Organizing*, Uppsala: Nordic Africa Institute, pp. 115–29.

Joseph, M. (1999) *Nomadic Identities: The Performance of Citizenship*, Minneapolis: University of Minnesota Press.

Kalipeni, E. (1999) 'The spatial context of Lilongwe's growth and development', in P. T. Zeleza and E. Kalipeni (eds), *Sacred Spaces and Public Quarrels: African Cultural and Economic Landscapes*, Trenton, NJ: Africa World Press, pp. 73–108.

Kaluwa, B. (1994) 'The delivery of urban services in Malawi: the case of housing', in K. Wekwete and C. Rambanapasi (eds), *Planning Urban Economies in Southern and Eastern Africa*, Brookfield, VT: Avebury, pp. 249–74.

Kapchan, D. (2008) 'Performing the festive sacred in Morocco: Sufi tourism and the promise of sonic translation', Paper presented to the Kansas African Studies Center Seminar Series, 21 April.

Kaplan, D., J. Wheeler and S. Holloway (2004) *Urban Geography*, Hoboken, NJ: John Wiley and Sons.

Karcher, T. (2004) *Understanding the 'Victory Disease,' from the Little Bighorn to Mogadishu and Beyond*, Global War on Terrorism Occasional Paper 3, Combat Studies Institute Press, Fort Leavenworth, KS.

Karta, Y. (2010) Author's personal communication with Yaganami Karta, University of Maiduguri, 1 May.

Kashi, E. (photography) and M. Watts (ed.) (2008) *Curse of the Black Gold: 50 Years of Oil in the Niger Delta*, Brooklyn, NY: powerHouse Books.

Kaspin, D. (1995) 'The politics of ethnicity in Malawi's democratic transition', *Journal of Modern African Studies*, 33(4): 595–620.

Kaus, M. (2002) 'What *Black Hawk Down* leaves out: that Somali raid really was more a debacle than a victory', *Slate*, 21 January, www.slate.com.

Kawka, R. (2002) 'The physiognomic structure of Maiduguri', in R. Kawka (ed.), *From Bulamari to Yerwa to Metropolitan Maiduguri: Interdisciplinary Studies on the Capital of Borno State, Nigeria*, Cologne: Rödiger Köppe Verlag, pp. 33–63.

Kazan, F. (2002) 'Recalling the other Third World: Nuruddin Farah's *Maps*', in D. Wright (ed.), *Emerging Perspectives on Nuruddin Farah*, Trenton, NJ: Africa World Press, pp. 369–494.

Kearney, J. (2006) 'Abdulrazak Gurnah and the "disabling complexities of parochial realities"', *English in Africa*, 33(1): 47–58.

Kehinde, A. (2007) 'Narrating the African city from the diaspora: Lagos as a trope in Ben Okri and Chika Unigwe's short stories', in F. Demissie (ed.), *Postcolonial African Cities: Imperial Legacies and Postcolonial Predicaments*, London: Routledge, pp. 73–88.

Kgositsile, K. (2009) 'In the naming' (poem), *Wordstock* (Grahamstown), 8 July, p. 2.

Khamis, S. (2009) 'Contemporary prose fiction from Zanzibar from the 1990s to the present', in E. Zubkova, M. Gromov, S. Khamis and K. Wamitila (eds), *Outline of Swahili Literature: Prose Fiction and Drama*, 2nd edn, Leiden: Brill, pp. 156–70.

Kinuthia, M. (1992) 'Slum clearance and the informal economy in

Nairobi', *Journal of Modern African Studies*, 30(2): 221–36.

Kipfer, S. (1996) 'Whose sustainability? Ecology, hegemonic politics and the future of the city', in R. Keil, G. Wekerle and D. Bell (eds), *Local Places in the Age of the Global City*, Montreal: Black Rose Books, pp. 117–24.

Kirkby, J., P. O'Keefe and C. Howorth (2001) 'Introduction: rethinking environment and development in Africa and Asia', *Land Degradation and Development*, 12: 195–203.

Kironde, J. (1993) 'Will Dodoma ever be the new capital of Tanzania?', *Geoforum*, 24(4): 435–53.

— (1994) 'The evolution of the land use structure of Dar es Salaam, 1890–1990: a study in the effects of land policy', Unpublished PhD thesis, University of Nairobi.

— (2000) 'Understanding land markets in African urban areas: the case of Dar es Salaam, Tanzania', *Habitat International*, 24: 151–65.

— (2004) 'Regulatory framework for affordable shelter: the case of Dar es Salaam', in G. Payne and M. Majale (eds), *The Urban Housing Manual: Making Regulatory Frameworks Work for the Poor*, London: Earthscan (on CD-ROM with the volume).

— (2006) 'The regulatory framework, unplanned development and urban poverty: findings from Dar es Salaam, Tanzania', *Land Use Policy*, 23: 460–72.

Kitilla, M. (2008) Personal communication between author and Martin Kitilla, director, Capital City Development Corporation, Dodoma, 28 June.

Kjellen, M. (2006) *From Public Pipes to Private Hands: Water Access and Distribution in Dar es Salaam, Tanzania*, Stockholm: Stockholm University Press.

Knight, J. (1992) *Institutions and Social Conflict*, Cambridge: Cambridge University Press.

Knox, P. and L. McCarthy (2005) *Urbanization: An Introduction to Urban Geography*, 2nd edn, Upper Saddle River, NJ: Pearson Prentice Hall.

Koegelenberg, I. (2009) 'Turning the lens on Grahamstown', *Cue* (Grahamstown), 10 July, p. 8.

Kombe, W. (2005) 'Land use dynamics in peri-urban areas and their implications on the urban growth and form: the case of Dar es Salaam, Tanzania', *Habitat International*, 29: 113–35.

Kombe, W. and V. Kreibich (2000) *Informal Land Management in Tanzania*, SPRING Research Series 29, University of Dortmund, Dortmund.

Konadu-Agyemang, K. (1991) 'Reflections on the absence of squatter settlements in West Africa', *Urban Studies*, 28: 139–51.

— (2001) 'Structural Adjustment Programs and housing affordability in Accra, Ghana', *Canadian Geographer*, 45(4): 528–44.

Kondoro, J. (1995) 'The impact of SAPs on urban and industrial pollution in Tanzania: the case study of Dar es Salaam city', in M. Bagachwa and F. Limbu (eds), *Policy Reform and the Environment in Tanzania*, Dar es Salaam: University of Dar es Salaam Press, pp. 227–49.

Konings, P. (2006) '"Bendskin" drivers in Douala's New Bell neighborhood: masters of the road and the city', in P. Konings and D. Foeken (eds), *Crisis and Creativity: Exploring the Wealth of the African Neighborhood*, Leiden: Brill, pp. 46–65.

Konings, P. and D. Foeken (eds) (2006) *Crisis and Creativity: Exploring the Wealth of the African Neighborhood*, Leiden: Brill.

Konings, P., R. van Dijk and D. Foeken (2006) 'The African neighborhood: an introduction', in P. Konings and D. Foeken (eds), *Crisis and Creativity: Exploring the Wealth of the African Neighborhood*, Leiden: Brill, pp. 1–21.

Koolhaas, R. (2002) 'Fragments for a lecture on Lagos', in O. Enwezor et al. (eds), *Documenta 11, Platform 4: Under Siege: Four African Cities: Freetown, Johannesburg, Kinshasa, Lagos*, Ostfildern-Ruit: Hatje Cantz, pp. 173–84.

— (2003) *Lagos/Koolhaas*, Video produced by Pieter van Huystee and VPRO Television, directed by B. van der Haak, Brooklyn, NY: First Run/Icarus Films.

Koolhaas, R. and the Harvard Design School Project on the City (2000) 'Lagos', *Mutations*, Bordeaux/Barcelona: arc en rêve centre d'architecture/ACTAR, pp. 650–720.

Koonings, K. and D. Kruijt (2009) 'Introduction', in K. Koonings and D. Kruijt (eds), *Megacities: The Politics of Urban Exclusion and Violence in the Global South*, London: Zed Books, pp. 1–7.

Korn, F. (2006) *Born in the Big Rains: A Memoir of Somalia and Survival*, New York: Feminist Press.

Koser, K. (2003) 'New African diasporas: an introduction', in K. Koser (ed.), *New African Diasporas*, London: Routledge, pp. 1–16.

Kruijt, D. (2008) 'Divided cities: urban informality, exclusion, and violence', in L. Boer (ed.), *A Rich Menu for the Poor: Food for Thought on Effective Aid Policies*, The Hague: Ministry of Foreign Affairs, pp. 323–32.

Kruijt, D. and K. Koonings (2009) 'The rise of megacities and the urbanization of informality, exclusion and violence', in K. Koonings and D. Kruijt (eds), *Megacities: The Politics of Urban Exclusion and Violence in the Global South*, London: Zed Books, pp. 8–26.

Kuper, L., H. Watts and R. Davies (1958) *Durban: A Study in Racial Ecology*, London: Jonathan Cape.

Kurth, M. (2004) 'Through my eyes', in M. Eversmann and D. Schilling (eds), *Battle of Mogadishu: Firsthand Accounts from the Men of Task Force Ranger*, New York: Ballantine, pp. 66–119.

La Sage, A. and N. Majid (2004) 'The livelihoods gap: responding to the economic dynamics of vulnerability in Somalia', in R. Ford, H. Adam and E. Ismail (eds), *War Destroys, Peace Nurtures: Reconciliation and Development in Somalia*, Asmara: Red Sea Press, pp. 367–90.

Larbi, W., A. Antwi and P. Olomo-laiye (2003) 'Land valorization processes and state intervention in land management in peri-urban Accra, Ghana', *International Development Planning Review*, 25(4): 355–71.

Larsen, K. (2009) 'Introduction', in K. Larsen (ed.), *Knowledge, Ritual and Religion: Repositioning and Changing Ideological and*

Material Circumstances among the Swahili on the East African Coast, Uppsala: Nordic Africa Institute, pp. 11–37.

Lefebvre, H. (1991) *The Production of Space*, Oxford: Blackwell.

Lemansky, C. and S. Oldfield (2009) 'The parallel claims of gated communities and land invasions in a southern city: polarized state responses', *Environment and Planning A*, 41: 634–48.

Lerise, F. (2000) 'Urban governance and urban planning in Tanzania', in S. Ngware and J. Kironde (eds), *Urbanising Tanzania: Issues, Initiatives, and Priorities*, Dar es Salaam: University of Dar es Salaam Press, pp. 88–116.

— (2005) *Politics in Land and Water Use Management*, Dar es Salaam: Mkuki na Nyota Publishers.

Lie, J. (1995) 'From international migration to transnational diaspora', *Contemporary Sociology*, 24: 303–6.

Lindell, I. (2002) *Walking the Tight Rope: Informal Livelihoods and Social Networks in a West African City*, Stockholm: Stockholm University Press.

— (2010) 'Changing landscapes of collective organizing in the informal economy', in I. Lindell (ed.), *Africa's Informal Workers: Collective Agency, Alliances, and Transnational Organizing*, Uppsala: Nordic Africa Institute, pp. 1–30.

Lipietz, B. (2008) 'Building a vision for the post-apartheid city: what role for participation in Johannesburg's City Development Strategy?', *International Journal of Urban and Regional Research*, 32(1): 135–63.

Little, P. (2003) *Somalia: Economy without State*, Bloomington: Indiana University Press.

Livermon, X. (2008) 'Sounds in the city', in S. Nuttall and A. Mbembe (eds), *Johannesburg: The Elusive Metropolis*, Durham, NC: Duke University Press, pp. 271–84.

Lloyd, R. (2003) 'Defining spatial concepts toward an African urban system', *Urban Design International*, 8: 105–17.

Locatelli, F. and P. Nugent (2009) 'Introduction', in F. Locatelli and P. Nugent (eds), *African Cities: Competing Claims on Urban Spaces*, Leiden: Brill, pp. 1–13.

Loomba, A. (1998) *Colonialism/ Postcolonialism*, London: Routledge.

Lugalla, J. and C. Kibassa (2003) *Urban Life and Street Children's Health: Children's Accounts of Urban Hardships and Violence in Tanzania*, Hamburg: Lit Verlag.

Lupala, A. and J. Lupala (2003) 'The conflict between attempts to green arid cities and urban livelihoods: the case of Dodoma, Tanzania', *Journal of Political Ecology*, 10: 25–35.

Lwanda, J. (2008) 'Poets, culture and orature: a reappraisal of the Malawi political public sphere, 1953–2006', *Journal of Contemporary African Studies*, 26(1): 71–101.

Lyons, T. and A. Samatar (1995) *Somalia: State Collapse, Multilateral Intervention, and Strategies for Political Reconstruction*, Washington, DC: Brookings Institution.

Mabogunje, A. (1990) 'Urban planning and the post-colonial state in Africa: a research overview', *African Studies Review*, 33(2): 121–203.

— (2001) 'Abuja: the promise, the performance and the prospects', in M. Kalgo and O. Ayileka (eds), *The Review of the Abuja Master Plan*, Ibadan: Fountain Publications.

MacGregor, D. (2009) 'Fun street performers give festival a boost', *Daily Dispatch* (East London), 9 July, p. 1.

Maira, J. (2001) 'Sustainable Dar es Salaam programme, Tanzania – evolvement, development, and experiences in implementing environmental strategies through investments and policy initiatives', in *Implementation and Replication of the Sustainable Cities Programme Process at City and National Level: Case Studies from Nine Cities*, Nairobi: UN Environment Programme, pp. 35–50.

Makinda, S. (1993) *Seeking Peace from Chaos: Humanitarian Intervention in Somalia*, Boulder, CO: Lynne Rienner.

Malaquais, D. (2006) 'Douala/Johannesburg/New York: cityscapes imagined', in M. Murray and G. Myers (eds), *Cities in Contemporary Africa*, New York: Palgrave Macmillan, pp. 31–52.

Malbert, R. (2005) 'Introduction', *Africa Remix: Contemporary Art of a Continent*, London: Hayward Gallery, p. 11.

Maliyamkono, T. (2000) *The Political Plight of Zanzibar*, Dar es Salaam: Tema Publishers.

Manger, L. and M. Assal (2006) 'Diasporas within and without Africa – dynamism, heterogeneity, variation', in L. Manger and M. Assal (eds), *Diasporas within and without Africa*, Uppsala: Nordic Africa Institute, pp. 7–31.

Manji, A. (2006) *The Politics of Land Reform in Africa: From Communal Tenure to Free Markets*, London: Zed Books.

Manona, C. (1988) 'Small town urbanization in South Africa: a case study', *African Studies Review*, 31(3): 95–110.

Marchal R. (2006) 'Resilience of a city at war: territoriality, civil order, and economic exchange in Mogadishu', in D. Bryceson and D. Potts (eds), *African Urban Economies: Viability, Vitality or Vitiation?*, Basingstoke: Palgrave Macmillan, pp. 207–29.

Marx, J. (2008) 'Failed state fiction', *Contemporary Literature*, 49(4): 597–633.

Massey, D. (1994) *Space, Place, and Gender*, Minneapolis: University of Minnesota Press.

Mbembe, A. (2001) *On the Postcolony*, Berkeley, CA: University of California Press.

— (2003) 'Necropolitics', *Public Culture*, 15(1): 11–40.

Mbembe, A. and S. Nuttall (2004) 'Writing the world from an African metropolis', *Public Culture*, 16(2).

— (2008) 'Introduction: Afropolis', in S. Nuttall and A. Mbembe (eds), *Johannesburg: The Elusive Metropolis*, Durham, NC: Duke University Press, pp. 1–33.

Mbewe, M. (2002) Interview with Samalila Ukhondo Waste Group secretary Mzamose Mbewe, conducted by author and Wilma Nchito, 23 December.

Mbwiliza, J. (2000) 'The birth of a political dilemma and the challenges of the quest for new politics in Zanzibar', in T. Maliyamkono (ed.), *The Political Plight of Zanzibar*, Dar es Salaam: Tema Publishers, pp. 1–34.

McAuslan, P. (2007) 'Law and the poor: the case of Dar es Salaam', in A. Philippopoulos-Mihalopoulos (ed.), *Law and the City*, London: Routledge-Cavendish, pp. 171–87.

McCarney, P. and R. Stren (eds) (2003) *Governance on the Ground: Innovations and Discontinuities in Cities of the Developing World*, Washington, DC: Woodrow Wilson Center Press.

McDonald, D. (2002) 'What is environmental justice?', in D. McDonald (ed.), *Environmental Justice in South Africa*, Cape Town: UCT Press, pp. 1–48.

— (2008) *World City Syndrome: Neoliberalism and Inequality in Cape Town*, London: Routledge.

— (2009) 'Electric capitalism: conceptualising electricity and capital accumulation in (South) Africa', in D. McDonald (ed.), *Electric Capitalism: Recolonising Africa on the Power Grid*, London: Earthscan, pp. 1–49.

McEwan, C. (2003) 'Material geographies and postcolonialism', *Singapore Journal of Tropical Geography*, 24(3): 340–55.

— (2009) *Postcolonialism and Development*, New York: Routledge.

Mennasemay, M. (2009) 'A Millennium Development Goal for Ethiopia: some conceptual issues', *Africa Today*, 55(1): 3–32.

Mercer, C., B. Page and M. Evans (2008) *Development and the African Diaspora: Place and the Politics of Home*, London: Zed Books.

Meyer, D. (1992) 'Racial residential desegregation in Grahamstown',

Unpublished BA Honors thesis, Rhodes University.

Middleton, N. and P. O'Keefe (2003) *Rio Plus Ten: Politics, Poverty, and the Environment*, London: Pluto.

Mitchell, J. C. (1969) *Social Networks in Urban Situations: Analyses of Personal Relationships in Central African Towns*, Manchester: Manchester University Press.

Mitchell, K. (2005) 'Hybridity', in D. Atkinson, P. Jackson, D. Sibley and N. Washbourne (eds), *Cultural Geography: A Critical Dictionary of Key Concepts*, London: I. B. Tauris, pp. 188–93.

Mitchell, T. (1988) *Colonizing Egypt*, Cambridge: Cambridge University Press.

Mitlin, D. and D. Satterthwaite (2004) 'Introduction', in D. Mitlin and D. Satterthwaite (eds), *Empowering Squatter Citizen: Local Government, Civil Society and Urban Poverty Reduction*, London: Earthscan, pp. 3–21.

Mitullah, W. (2008) 'Decentralized urban service delivery in Nairobi: institutional issues and challenges', *Regional Development Dialogue*, 29(2): 55–70.

— (2010) 'Informal workers in Kenya and transnational organizing: the challenge of sustainability', in I. Lindell (ed.), *Africa's Informal Workers: Collective Agency, Alliances, and Transnational Organizing*, Uppsala: Nordic Africa Institute, pp. 184–201.

Mjojo, B. (1989) 'Urban development: the case of Lilongwe 1920–1964', University of Malawi Chancellor College History Department Seminar Series, Paper no. 12, Zomba.

Mlia, J. (1975) 'Malawi's new capital city: a regional planning perspective', *Pan-African Journal*, 8: 387–401.

Mohammed, A. (1999) *Anatomy of a Failure: Causes and Consequences of the Somalia Tragedy*, Mogadishu: Community Concern Somalia.

— (2001) 'State–civil society relationship for democracy and sustainable development: a case study of municipal governance in Zanzibar town', Unpublished MA thesis, University of Dar es Salaam.

Mohammed, M. (1998) *Recolonization beyond Somalia*, Self-published, Mogadishu.

Møller, V. (2008) 'Living in Rhini: a 2007 update on the 1999 Social Indicators Report', Research Report no. 14, Institute of Social and Economic Research, Rhodes University, Grahamstown.

Montgomery, T. (2003) 'Foreword', in *The United States Forces, Somalia After Action Report and Historical Overview, The United States Army in Somalia, 1992–1994*, Washington, DC: United States Army Center of Military History.

Moon, K. (2009) 'Disappearing heritage of Dar es Salaam', *ArchiAfrika Newsletter*, May, pp. 6–11.

Moore, G. (2002) 'Maps and mirrors', in D. Wright (ed.), *Emerging Perspectives on Nuruddin Farah*, Trenton, NJ: Africa World Press, pp. 509–20.

Mooya, M. and C. Cloete (2007) 'Informal urban property markets and poverty alleviation: a conceptual framework', *Urban Studies*, 44: 147–65.

Mophophe, A. (2009) '(Not) heading for Nombulelo', *Cue* (Grahamstown), 10 July, p. 8.

Morah, E. (1992) 'Housing development in Nigeria's new capital at Abuja', *African Development Review*, 12(1): 64–86.

— (1993) 'Why Nigeria obtained the new capital that it did: an analysis of officials' disposition in housing development', *International Review of Administrative Sciences*, 59: 251–7.

Moreland, S. and E. Richards (2009) 'All's not fair at Fiddler's Fair', *Grocott's Mail* (Grahamstown), 7 July, p. 3.

Moyer, E. (2004) 'Popular cartographies: youthful imaginings of the global in the streets of Dar es Salaam, Tanzania', *City and Society*, 16(2): 117–43.

— (2006) 'Not quite the comforts of home: searching for locality among street youth in Dar es Salaam', in P. Konings and D. Foeken (eds), *Crisis and Creativity: Exploring the Wealth of the African Neighborhood*, Leiden: Brill, pp. 163–96.

Mudimbe, V. (1988) *The Invention of Africa*, Bloomington: Indiana University Press.

Muhajir, M. (1993) 'Settlement planning improvement in Zanzibar: towards a framework for implementation', Unpublished MA thesis, Curtin University of Technology, Perth.

— (2011) 'How planning works in an age of reform: land, sustainability, and housing development traditions in Zanzibar', Unpublished PhD thesis, University of Kansas.

Mukangara, D. (2000) 'Race, ethnicity, religion, and politics in

Zanzibar', in T. Maliyamkono (ed.), *The Political Plight of Zanzibar*, Dar es Salaam: Tema Publishers, pp. 35–54.

Murray, M. (2008a) *Taming the Disorderly City: The Spatial Landscape of Johannesburg after Apartheid*, Ithaca, NY: Cornell University Press.

— (2008b) 'The city in fragments: kaleidoscopic Johannesburg after apartheid', in G. Prakash and K. Kruse (eds), *The Spaces of the Modern City: Imaginaries, Politics, and Everyday Life*, Princeton, NJ: Princeton University Press, pp. 144–78.

Murunga, G. (1999) 'Urban violence in Kenya's transition to pluralist politics, 1982–1992', *Africa Development*, 24(1/2).

— (2007) 'Governance and the politics of structural adjustment in Kenya', in G. Murunga and S. Nasong'o (eds), *Kenya: The Struggle for Democracy*, Dakar: Codesria, pp. 263–300.

Murunga, G. and S. Nasong'o (eds) (2007), *Kenya: The Struggle for Democracy*, Dakar: Codesria.

Myers, G. (1994) 'Making the socialist city of Zanzibar', *Geographical Review*, 84(4): 451–64.

— (1996a) 'Democracy and development in Zanzibar? Contradictions in land and environment planning', *Journal of Contemporary African Studies*, 14(2): 221–45.

— (1996b) 'Isle of cloves, sea of discourses: writing about Zanzibar', *Ecumene*, 3(4): 408–26.

— (2003) *Verandahs of Power: Colonialism and Space in Urban Africa*, Syracuse, NY: Syracuse University Press.

— (2005) *Disposable Cities: Garbage, Governance, and Sus-tainable Development in Urban Africa*, Aldershot: Ashgate.

— (2006) 'The unauthorized city: late colonial Lusaka and post-colonial geography', *Singapore Journal of Tropical Geography*, 27(3): 289–308.

— (2008a) 'Sustainable development and environmental justice in African cities', *Geography Compass*, 2(3): 695–708.

— (2008b) 'Peri-urban land reform, political-economic reform, and urban political ecology in Zanzibar', *Urban Geography*, 29(3): 264–88.

— (2009) 'Africa', in R. Kitchin and N. Thrift (eds), *International Encyclopedia of Human Geography*, London: Elsevier, pp. 25–30.

— (2010a) 'Social construction of peri-urban places and alternative planning in Zanzibar', *African Affairs*, 109(437): 575–95.

— (2010b) 'Representing the other, negotiating the personal and the political', in M. Crang, L. McDowell, S. Herbert and D. DeLyser (eds), *Handbook of Qualitative Research in Human Geography*, London: Sage, pp. 373–87.

Myers, G. and M. Muhajir (1997) 'Localizing Agenda 21: environmental sustainability and Zanzibari urbanization', *Third World Planning Review*, 19: 367–84.

Myers, G. and M. Murray (2006) 'Introduction: situating contemporary cities in Africa', in M. Murray and G. Myers (eds), *Cities in Contemporary Africa*, New York: Palgrave Macmillan, pp. 1–25.

Myers, G. and F. Owusu (2008) 'Cities of sub-Saharan Africa', in S. Brunn, M. Hays-Mitchell and D. Zeigler (eds), *Cities of the World*, 4th edn, Lanham, MD: Rowman and Littlefield, pp. 341–83.

Nasong'o, S. (2007) 'Political transition without transformation: the dialectic of liberalization without democratization in Kenya and Zambia', *African Studies Review*, 50(1): 83–108.

Nast, H. (1994) 'The impact of British imperialism on the landscape of female slavery in the Kano Palace, northern Nigeria', *Africa*, 64: 34–73.

Nava, M. (2007) *Visceral Cosmopolitanism: Gender, Culture and the Normalisation of Difference*, Oxford: Berg.

NAZ (National Archives of Zambia) (1957–1961) 'African suburbs and hostels, private compounds and townships: unauthorized compounds 1957–1961', Lusaka Urban District Council (LUDC) file 1/4/24, National Archives of Zambia, Lusaka.

Ndi, A. (2007) 'Metropolitanism, capital and patrimony: theorizing the postcolonial West African city', in F. Demissie (ed.), *Postcolonial African Cities: Imperial Legacies and Postcolonial Predicaments*, New York: Routledge, pp. 11–24.

Ndjio, B. (2006a) 'Intimate strangers: neighbourhood, autochthony and the politics of belonging', in P. Konings and D. Foeken (eds), *Crisis and Creativity: Exploring the Wealth of the African Neighborhood*, Leiden: Brill, pp. 66–87.

— (2006b) 'Douala: inventing life in an African necropolis', in M. Murray and G. Myers (eds), *Cities in Contemporary Africa*,

New York: Palgrave Macmillan, pp. 103–18.

Ngaboh-Smart, F. (2000) 'Secrets and a new civic consciousness', *Research in African Literatures*, 31(1): 129–36.

— (2001) 'Nationalism and the aporia of national identity in Farah's *Maps*', *Research in African Literatures*, 32(3): 86–102.

— (2004) *Beyond Empire and Nation: Postnational Arguments in the Fiction of Nuruddin Farah*, Amsterdam: Rodopi.

Ngcukana, L. (2009) 'Water at last – but from tanks', *Daily Dispatch* (East London), 21 July, p.1.

Ngugi wa Thiong'o (1986) *Decolonising the Mind: The Politics of Language in African Literature*, London: James Currey.

Njami, S. (2005) *Africa Remix: Contemporary Art of a Continent*, London: Hayward Gallery.

Njeru, J. (2006) 'The urban political ecology of plastic bag waste problems in Nairobi, Kenya', *Geoforum*, 37: 1046–58.

Njoh, A. (2003) *Planning in Contemporary Africa: The State, Town Planning and Society in Cameroon*, Aldershot: Ashgate.

Njoroge, M. (2009) 'Interview with Kenyan architect Maranga Njoroge by Berend van der Lans', *ArchiAfrica Newsletter*, September, pp. 2–3.

Njwabane, M. (2009) 'Municipal workers threaten national strike', *Daily Dispatch*, 16 July, p. 4.

Nnkya, T. (2007) *Why Planning Does Not Work? Land Use Planning and Residents Rights in Tanzania*, Dar es Salaam: Mkuki na Nyota Press.

Nolan, K. (2002) *Black Hawk*

Down: The Shooting Script, New York: Newmarket Press.

Nossiter, A. (2009) 'Nigeria confirms death of Islamic sect's leader', *New York Times*, 31 July, p. 8.

Nunan, F. and N. Devas (2004) 'Accessing land and services: exclusion or entitlement?', in N. Devas (ed.), *Urban Governance, Voice, and Poverty in the Developing World*, London: Earthscan, pp. 164–85.

Nussbaum, M. and A. Sen (1993) 'Introduction', in M. Nussbaum and A. Sen (eds), *The Quality of Life*, Oxford: Clarendon Press, pp. 1–6.

Nuttall, S. (2008) 'Literary city', in S. Nuttall and A. Mbembe (eds), *Johannesburg: The Elusive Metropolis*, Durham, NC: Duke University Press, pp. 195–218.

Nuttall, S. and A. Mbembe (eds) (2008) *Johannesburg: The Elusive Metropolis*, Durham, NC: Duke University Press.

Nyairo, J. (2006) '(Re)configuring the city: the mapping of places and people in contemporary Kenyan popular song texts', in M. Murray and G. Myers (eds), *Cities in Contemporary Africa*, New York: Palgrave Macmillan, pp. 71–94.

Nyerere, J. (1967) *Ujamaa Vijijini* [Ujamaa in the villages], Dar es Salaam: Government of Tanzania.

— (1968) *Uhuru na Ujamaa* [Freedom and socialism], Dar es Salaam: Government of Tanzania.

— (1970) *Uhuru na Maendeleo* [Freedom and development], Dar es Salaam: Government of Tanzania.

— (1972) *Decentralization*, Dar es Salaam: Government of Tanzania.

Nyquist, T. (1983) 'African middle class elite', Occasional Paper no. 28, Institute for Social and Economic Research, Rhodes University, Grahamstown.

Obrist van Eeuwijk, B. (2009) 'The daily governance of environmental health: gender perspectives from Dar es Salaam, Tanzania', in G. Blundo and P.-Y. Le Meur (eds), *The Governance of Daily Life in Africa: Ethnographic Explorations of Public and Collective Services*, Leiden: Brill, pp. 301–15.

O'Connor, A. (1983) *The African City*, London: Hutchinson University Library.

Oguine, I. (2007) 'Lagos v. Abuja', *New Internationalist*, April, p. 29.

Oldfield, S. (2002) 'Partial formalization and its implications for community governance in an informal settlement', *Urban Forum*, 13(2): 102–15.

Omari, C. and E. Lukwaro (1978) 'Settlement patterns and Ujamaa', *Tanzania Notes and Records*, 83: 1–8.

Omasombo, J. (2005) 'Kisangani: a city at its lowest ebb', in A. Simone and A. Abouhani (eds), *Urban Africa: Changing Contours of Survival in the City*, Dakar: Codesria, pp. 96–119.

Ong, A. (2006) *Neoliberalism as Exception: Mutations in Citizenship and Sovereignty*, Durham, NC: Duke University Press.

Otiso, K. (2002) 'Forced evictions in Kenyan cities', *Singapore Journal of Tropical Geography*, 23: 252–67.

Pacione, M. (2004) *Urban Geography: A Global Perspective*, 2nd edn, New York: Routledge.

Parnell, S. (2007) 'Urban governance in the South: the politics of rights

and development', in K. Cox,
M. Low and J. Robinson (eds), *A Handbook of Political Geography*, London: Sage, pp. 595–608.

Parnell, S. and J. Robinson (2006) 'Development and urban policy: Johannesburg's City Development Strategy', *Urban Studies*, 43(2): 337–55.

Patel, Z. (2006) 'Of questionable value: the role of practitioners in building sustainable cities', *Geoforum*, 37: 682–94.

Payne, G. (2002) *Land, Rights, and Innovation: Improving Tenure Security for the Urban Poor*, London: ITDG Publishing.

Peck, J. and A. Tickell (2002) 'Neoliberalizing space', *Antipode*, 34(3): 380–404.

Peffer, J. (2009) *Art and the End of Apartheid*, Minneapolis: University of Minnesota Press.

Petterson, D. (2002) *Revolution in Zanzibar: An American's Cold War Tale*, Boulder, CO: Westview Press.

Pieterse, E. (2005) 'At the limits of possibility: working notes on a relational model of urban politics', in A. Simone and A. Abouhani (eds), *Urban Africa: Changing Contours of Survival in the City*, Dakar: Codesria, pp. 138–73.

— (2008a) *City Futures: Confronting the Crisis of Urban Development*, London: Zed Books.

— (2008b) 'Towards an agenda for action on African urbanization: an argument arising from the African Urban Innovations Workshop', Cape Town: African Centre for Cities.

— (2010) 'Cityness and African urban development', *Urban Forum*, 21: 205–19.

Pile, S. and N. Thrift (1995) 'Introduction', in S. Pile and N. Thrift (eds), *Mapping the Subject: Geographies of Cultural Transformation*, New York: Routledge.

Pillay, U., R. Tomlinson and J. du Toit (2006) 'Introduction', in U. Pillay, R. Tomlinson and J. du Toit (eds), *Democracy and Delivery: Urban Policy in South Africa*, Cape Town: HSRC Press, pp. 1–21.

Portes, A. (1997) 'Globalization from below: the rise of transnational communities', Paper from the ESRC Transnational Communities Program, www.transcomm. ox.ac.uk.

Portes, A., M. Castells and L. Benton (1989) *The Informal Economy: Studies in Advanced and Less Developed Countries*, Baltimore, MD: Johns Hopkins University Press.

Potts, D. (1985) 'The development of Malawi's new capital at Lilongwe: a comparison with other new African capitals', *Comparative Urban Research*, 10(2): 42–56.

— (1986) 'Urbanization in Malawi with special reference to the new capital city of Lilongwe', Unpublished PhD thesis, University College London.

— (1994) 'Urban environmental controls and low income housing in southern Africa', in H. Main and S. Williams (eds), *Environment and Housing in Third World Cities*, New York: John Wiley, pp. 207–23.

— (2006) 'City life in Zimbabwe at a time of fear and loathing: urban planning, urban poverty, and Operation Murambatsvina', in

M. Murray and G. Myers (eds), *Cities in Contemporary Africa*, New York: Palgrave Macmillan, pp. 265–88.

— (2009) 'The slowing of sub-Saharan Africa's urbanization: evidence and implications for urban livelihoods', *Environment and Urbanization*, 21(1): 253–9.

— (2011) *Circular Migration in Sub-Saharan Africa: Re-inventing the Wheel?*, Woodbridge: James Curre.

Powell, C. (2002) Speech of US Secretary of State Colin Powell to the National Academy of Sciences meeting, 30 April.

Power, M. (2003) *Rethinking Development Geographies*, London: Routledge.

Prestholdt, J. (2008) *Domesticating the World: African Consumerism and the Geneologies of Globalization*, Berkeley: University of California Press.

Rakodi, C. (1986) 'Colonial urban planning in Northern Rhodesia and its legacy', *Third World Planning Review*, 8: 193–218.

Rawls, J. (1971) *A Theory of Justice*, Cambridge, MA: Harvard University Press.

Rawson, D. (1994) 'Dealing with disintegration: US assistance and the Somali state', in A. Samatar (ed.), *The Somali Challenge: From Catastrophe to Renewal?*, Boulder, CO: Lynne Rienner, pp. 147–87.

Razack, S. (2004) *Dark Threats and White Knights: The Somalia Affair, Peacekeeping, and the New Imperialism*, Toronto: University of Toronto Press.

Rizzo, M. (2002) 'Being taken for a ride: privatization of the Dar es Salaam transport system,

1983–1998', *Journal of Modern African Studies*, 40(1): 133–57.

Roberts, J. (2007) 'Globalizing environmental justice', in R. Sandler and P. Pezzullo (eds), *Environmental Justice and Environmentalism: The Social Justice Challenge to the Environmental Movement*, Cambridge, MA: MIT Press, pp. 285–307.

Robins, S. (2006) 'When shacks ain't chic! Planning for "difference" in post-apartheid Cape Town', in S. Bekker and A. Leilde (eds), *Reflections on Identity in Four African Cities*, Johannesburg: African Minds, pp. 97–117.

— (2008) *From Revolution to Rights in South Africa: Social Movements, NGOs and Popular Politics after Apartheid*, Rochester, NY: Boydell & Brewer.

Robinson, J. (1990) '"A perfect system of control"? State power and "native locations" in South Africa', *Environment and Planning D: Society and Space*, 8(2): 135–62.

— (1996) *The Power of Apartheid: State, Power, and Space in South African Cities*, Oxford: Butterworth Heinemann.

— (1998) '(Im)mobilizing space – dreaming of change', in H. Judin and I. Vladislavic (eds), *Blank_: Architecture, Apartheid and After*, Rotterdam: NAi Publishers, pp. 163–71.

— (2002a) 'Global and world cities: a view from off the map', *International Journal of Urban and Regional Research*, 26(3): 531–54.

— (2002b) '(Post)colonial geographies at Johannesburg's Empire Exhibition, 1936', in A. Blunt and C. McEwan (eds), *Post-*

colonial Geographies, London: Continuum, pp. 115–31.

— (2003) 'Postcolonialising geography: tactics and pitfalls', *Singapore Journal of Tropical Geography*, 24(3): 273–89.

— (2004) 'A world of cities', *British Journal of Sociology*, 55(4): 569–78.

— (2006) *Ordinary Cities: Between Modernity and Development*, Abingdon: Routledge.

— (2008) 'Developing ordinary cities: city visioning processes in Durban and Johannesburg', *Environment and Planning A*, 40: 74–87.

Robinson, J. and S. Parnell (2011) 'Travelling theory: embracing post-neoliberalism through Southern cities', *Urban Geography* (forthcoming).

Roble, A. (photographs) and D. Rutledge (essays) (2008) *The Somali Diaspora: A Journey Away*, Minneapolis: University of Minnesota Press.

Rodrigues, C. (2009) 'Angolan cities: urban (re)segregation?', in F. Locatelli and P. Nugent (eds), *African Cities: Competing Claims on Urban Spaces*, Leiden: Brill, pp. 37–53.

Roe, G. (1992) 'Beyond the city limits: anatomy of an unplanned housing settlement in Lilongwe, Malawi', Unpublished paper, Centre for Social Research, University of Malawi.

Rohregger, B. (2006) 'Shifting boundaries of support: re-negotiating distance and proximity in trans-local support relations in an urban fringe area in Lilongwe city Malawi', *Ethnic and Racial Studies*, 29(6): 1153–68.

Roy, A. (2005) 'Urban informality: toward an epistemology of planning', *Journal of the American Planning Association*, 71(2): 147–58.

— (2007) 'The location of practice: a response to John Forester's "Exploring urban practice in a democratizing society: opportunities, techniques and challenges"', *Development Southern Africa*, 24(4): 623–8.

Ruiters, G. (2002) 'Race, place and environmental rights: a radical critique of environmental justice discourse', in D. McDonald (ed.), *Environmental Justice in South Africa*, Cape Town: UCT Press, pp. 112–26.

— (2006) 'Social control and social welfare under neoliberalism in South African cities: contradictions in free basic water services', in M. Murray and G. Myers (eds), *Cities in Contemporary Africa*, New York: Palgrave Macmillan, pp. 289–308.

Ruokoranta, K. and M. Kiiselli (2007) Author interview with Keijo Ruokoranta and Matti Kiiselli at the Finland Ministry for Foreign Affairs, Helsinki, 8 May.

Sachs, W. (2002) 'Ecology, justice, and the end of development', in J. Byrne, C. Martinez and L. Glover (eds), *Environmental Justice: Discourses in International Political Economy*, Brunswick, NJ: Transaction Publishers, pp. 19–36.

Sack, R. (1997) *Homo Geographicus: a Framework for Action, Awareness, and Moral Concern*, Baltimore, MD: Johns Hopkins University Press.

— (2002) 'Geographical progress

toward the real and the good', in R. Sack (ed.), *Progress: Geographical Essays*, Baltimore, MD: Johns Hopkins University Press, pp. 113–30.

SACN (South African Cities Network) (2006) *State of the Cities Report 2006*, Braamfontein: SACN.

Saff, G. (1996) 'Claiming a space in a changing South Africa: the "squatters" of Marconi Beam, Cape Town', *Annals of the Association of American Geographers*, 86(2): 235–55.

Sahnoun, M. (1994) *Somalia: The Missed Opportunities*, Washington, DC: United States Institute for Peace Press.

Saleh, M. (2009) 'The impact of religious knowledge and the concept of *Dini Wal Duniya* in urban Zanzibari life-style', in K. Larsen (ed.), *Knowledge, Renewal and Religion*, Uppsala: Nordic Africa Institute Press.

Salm, S. and T. Falola (eds) (2005) *African Urban Spaces in Historical Perspective*, Rochester, NY: University of Rochester Press.

Saltmarsh, M. (2009) 'Somalis' money is lifeline for homeland', *New York Times*, 12 November, p. A13.

Sam, P. (2002) 'Indoor air pollution assessment within selected residential areas in the Greater Accra-Tema Metropolitan Region, Ghana, West Africa', Unpublished PhD thesis, University of Kansas.

Samatar, A. (1994) 'Introduction and overview', in A. Samatar (ed.), *The Somali Challenge: From Catastrophe to Renewal?*, Boulder, CO: Lynne Rienner, pp. 3–20.

— (2002) 'Somalia: Statelessness as Homelessness', in A. Samatar and A. Samatar (eds), *The African State: Reconsiderations*, Portsmouth, NH: Heinemann, pp. 217–51.

Samatar, S. (2000) 'Are there secrets in *Secrets?*', *Research in African Literatures*, 31(1): 137–43.

Samuelson, M. (2007) 'The city beyond the border: the urban worlds of Duiker, Mpe and Vera', in F. Demissie (ed.), *Postcolonial African Cities: Imperial Legacies and Postcolonial Predicaments*, New York: Routledge, pp. 89–102.

Santos, M. (1979) *The Shared Space: The Two Circuits of the Urban Economy in Underdeveloped Countries*, London: Methuen.

Sassen, S. (1991) *The Global City: New York, London, Tokyo*, Princeton, NJ: Princeton University Press.

Schler, L. (2007) 'The unwritten history of ethnic co-existence in colonial Africa: an example from Douala, Cameroon', in P. Ahluwalia, L. Bethlehem and R. Ginio (eds), *Violence and Non-Violence in Africa*, London: Routledge, pp. 27–43.

Schlyter, A. (1999) *Recycled Inequalities: Youth and Gender in George Compound, Zambia*, Uppsala: Nordic Africa Institute Press.

— (2002) *Empowered with Ownership: The Privatisation of Housing in Lusaka, Zambia*, Roma: National University of Lesotho.

— (2006) 'Esther's House: one woman's "home economics" in Chitungwiza, Zimbabwe', in D. Bryceson and D. Potts (eds), *African Urban Economies: Viability, Vitality, or Vitiation?*,

New York: Palgrave Macmillan, pp. 254–77.

Schneider, J. and I. Susser (eds) (2003) *Wounded Cities: Destruction and Reconstruction in a Globalized World*, New York: Oxford University Press.

Scholz, W. (2008) *Challenges of Informal Urbanisation: The Case of Zanzibar/Tanzania*, Dortmund: SPRING Centre, University of Dortmund.

Schweitzer, L. and M. Stephenson (2007) 'Right answers, wrong questions: environmental justice as urban research', *Urban Studies*, 44: 319–37.

Scott, D. and C. Oelofse (2005) 'Social and environmental justice in South African cities: including "invisible stakeholders" in environmental assessment procedures', *Journal of Environmental Planning and Management*, 48: 445–67.

Semuso (1997–2006) 'Semuso Mradi wa Maji na Maendeleo Zanzibar' [Sebleni-Muungano-Sogea Project for Water and Development], Unpublished records of the Semuso Umoja wa Mradi wa Maji na Maendeleo community-based organization, Zanzibar.

Sen, A. (1993) 'Capability and well-being', in M. Nussbaum and A. Sen (eds), *The Quality of Life*, Oxford: Clarendon Press, pp. 30–53.

— (1999) *Development as Freedom*, New York: Knopf.

Sheffer, G. (1986) 'A new field of study: modern diasporas in international politics', in G. Sheffer (ed.), *Modern Diasporas in International Politics*, London: Croom Helm, pp. 1–15.

Shepherd, N. and N. Murray (2007)

'Introduction: space, memory and identity in the post-apartheid city', in N. Murray, N. Shepherd and M. Hall (eds), *Desire Lines: Space, Memory and Identity in the Post-Apartheid City*, London: Routledge, pp. 1–18.

Sheriff, A. (1987) *Slaves, Spices and Ivory: Integration of an East African Commercial Empire into the World Economy, 1770–1873*, London: James Currey.

Sheriff, B. (2002) 'Urbanization and social cohesion: the role of voluntary associations in Maiduguri', in R. Kawka (ed.), *From Bulamari to Yerwa to Metropolitan Maiduguri: Interdisciplinary Studies on the Capital of Borno State, Nigeria*, Cologne: Rüdiger Köppe Verlag, pp. 147–58.

Short, J. (2004) 'Black holes and loose connection in the global urban network', *Professional Geographer*, 56: 295–302.

Shrader-Frechette, K. (2002) *Environmental Justice: Creating Equality, Reclaiming Democracy*, Oxford: Oxford University Press.

Sibley, D. (1995) *Geographies of Exclusion: Society and Difference in the West*, London: Routledge.

Sidaway, J. (2000) 'Postcolonial geographies: an exploratory essay', *Progress in Human Geography*, 24(4): 591–612.

Simatele, D. and T. Binns (2008) 'Motivation and marginalization in African urban agriculture: the case of Lusaka, Zambia', *Urban Forum*, 19: 1–21.

Simon, D. (1992) *Cities, Capital and Development: African Cities in the World Economy*, London: Belhaven Press.

Simone, A. (2001a) 'Straddling the divides: remaking associational

life in the informal African city',
*International Journal of Urban
and Regional Research*, 25(1):
102–17.

— (2001b) 'On the worlding of
African cities', *African Studies
Review*, 44(2): 15–42.

— (2001c) 'Between ghetto and
globe: remaking urban life
in Africa', in A. Tostensen,
I. Tvedten and M. Vaa (eds),
*Associational Life in African
Cities: Popular Responses to the
Urban Crisis*, Uppsala: Nordic
Africa Institute, pp. 46–63.

— (2004) *For the City Yet to Come:
Changing African Life in Four
Cities*, Durham, NC: Duke
University Press.

— (2006) 'Pirate towns: reworking
social and symbolic infrastructures in Johannesburg and
Douala', *Urban Studies*, 43(2):
357–70.

— (2007a) 'Assembling Douala: imagining forms of urban sociality',
in A. Cinar and T. Bender (eds),
*Urban Imaginaries: Locating
the Modern City*, Minneapolis:
University of Minnesota Press,
pp. 79–99.

— (2007b) 'Sacral spaces in two
West African cities', in P. Ahluwalia, L. Bethlehem and R. Ginio
(eds), *Violence and Non-Violence
in Africa*, London: Routledge,
pp. 63–83.

— (2008) 'People as infrastructure:
intersecting fragments in
Johannesburg', in S. Nuttall and
A. Mbembe (eds), *Johannesburg:
The Elusive Metropolis*, Durham,
NC: Duke University Press,
pp. 68–90.

— (2010) *City Life from Jakarta
to Dakar: Movements at the
Crossroads*, London: Routledge.

Simone, A. and A. Abouhani
(2005) *Urban Africa: Changing
Contours of Survival in the City*,
Dakar: Codesria.

Sinyangwe, B. (2000) *A Cowrie
of Hope*, Portsmouth, NH:
Heinemann.

Sirve, H. (2003) 'Program preparation phase, suggested outline for
the Inception Report', Presented
to the Planning Workshop for
Sustainable Management of
Land and Environment (SMOLE)
program, 29/30 October,
Bwawani Hotel, Zanzibar.

Sivaramakrishnan, K. (1997) 'Urban
governance: changing realities', in
M. Cohen et al. (eds), *Preparing
for the Urban Future: Global
Pressures and Local Forces*,
Washington, DC: World Bank.

Smiley, S. (2007) 'Patterns of urban
life and urban segregation in Dar
es Salaam, Tanzania', Unpublished PhD thesis, University of
Kansas.

— (2009) 'The city of three colors:
segregation in colonial Dar es
Salaam, 1891–1961', *Historical
Geography*, 37: 193–213.

Smith, D. (2004) 'Social justice
and the (South African) city:
retrospect and prospect', *South
African Geographical Journal*,
86: 1–6.

Smith, N. (1997) 'The satanic geographies of globalization: uneven
development in the 1990s', *Public
Culture*, 10(1): 169–89.

SMOLE (Sustainable Management
of Land and Environment)
(2004) *Strategic Plan 2005–2015*,
Zanzibar: SMOLE.

Söderstrom, O. (2005) 'Representation', in D. Atkinson, P. Jackson,
D. Sibley and N. Washbourne
(eds), *Cultural Geography:*

A Critical Dictionary of Key Concepts, London: I. B. Tauris, pp. 11–15.

Soja, E. (1968) *The Geography of Modernization in Kenya*, Syracuse, NY: Syracuse University Press.

— (1979) 'The geography of modernization: a radical reappraisal', in D. Taylor and R. Obudho (eds), *The Spatial Structure of Development*, Boulder, CO: Westview Press, pp. 28–45.

— (1989) *Postmodern Geographies: The Reassertion of Space in Critical Social Theory*, London: Verso.

— (1996) *Thirdspace: Journeys to Los Angeles and Other Real-and-Imagined Places*, Cambridge, MA: Blackwell.

— (2000) *Postmetropolis: Critical Studies of Cities and Regions*, Oxford: Blackwell.

— (2001) 'Exploring the postmetropolis', in C. Minca (ed.), *Postmodern Geography*, Oxford: Blackwell, pp. 37–56.

— (2010) *Seeking Spatial Justice*, Minneapolis: University of Minnesota Press.

Soja, E. and C. Weaver (1976) 'Urbanization and underdevelopment in East Africa', in B. Berry (ed.), *Urbanization and Counter-Urbanization*, Beverly Hills: Sage, pp. 233–65.

Stevenson, J. (1995) *Losing Mogadishu: Testing US Policy in Somalia*, Annapolis, MD: Naval Institute Press.

Stoller, P. (1999) *Jaguar: A Story of Africans in America*, Chicago, IL: University of Chicago Press.

— (2002) *Money Has No Smell: The Africanization of New York City*, Chicago, IL: University of Chicago Press.

— (2003) 'Marketing Afrocentricity: West African trade networks in North America', in K. Koser (ed.), *New African Diasporas*, London: Routledge, pp. 71–94.

— (2005) *Gallery Bundu: A Story about an African Past*, Chicago, IL: University of Chicago Press.

Stren, R. (1985) 'Urban studies in Africa', *Canadian Journal of African Studies*, 19(1): 211–16.

— (1994) 'Urban research in Africa, 1960–92', *Urban Studies*, 31(4/5): 729–43.

— (2003) 'Introduction: toward the comparative study of urban governance', in P. McCarney and R. Stren (eds), *Governance on the Ground: Innovations and Discontinuities in Cities in the Developing World*, Washington, DC: Woodrow Wilson Center Press, pp. 1–30.

Sugnet, C. (1998) 'Nuruddin Farah's *Maps*: deterritorialization and "the postmodern"', *World Literature Today*, 72(4): 739–46.

Swanson, M. (1977) 'The sanitation syndrome: bubonic plague and urban native policy in the Cape Colony, 1900–1909', *Journal of African History*, 18: 387–410.

Swilling, M. and E. Annecke (2006) 'Building sustainable neighbourhoods in South Africa: learning from the Lynedoch case', *Environment and Urbanization*, 18: 315–32.

Swilling, M., A. Simone and F. Khan (2003) '"My soul I can see": the limits of governing African cities in a context of globalization and complexity', in P. McCarney and R. Stren (eds), *Governance on the Ground: Innovations and Discontinuities in Cities in the Developing World*, Washington,

DC: Woodrow Wilson Center Press, pp. 220–50.

Tait, J. (1997) *From Self-Help Housing to Sustainable Settlement: Capitalist Development and Urban Planning in Lusaka, Zambia*, Brookfield, VT: Avebury.

Trefon, T. (2009) 'Hinges and fringes: conceptualizing the peri-urban in Central Africa', in F. Locatelli and P. Nugent (eds), *African Cities: Competing Claims on Urban Spaces*, Leiden: Brill.

Tripp, A. (1997) *Changing the Rules: The Politics of Liberalization and the Urban Informal Economy in Tanzania*, Berkeley: University of California Press.

Turok, I. (2001) 'Persistent polarisation post-apartheid? Progress towards urban integration in Cape Town', *Urban Studies*, 38(13): 2349–77.

Ukoha, O. and J. Beamish (1997) 'Assessment of residents' satisfaction with public housing in Abuja, Nigeria', *Habitat International*, 21(4): 445–60.

UN-Habitat (2008) *The State of African Cities 2008: A Framework for Addressing Urban Challenges in Africa*, Nairobi: UN Habitat.

— (2009) *The Sustainable Cities Program in Zambia 1994–2007: Addressing Challenges of Rapid Urbanization*, Nairobi: UN Habitat.

— (2010) *The State of African Cities 2010: Governance, Inequality and Urban Land Markets*, Nairobi: UN Habitat.

Vale, L. (2008) *Architecture, Power, and National Identity*, 2nd edn, London: Routledge.

Van der Merwe, I. and A. Davids (2006) 'Demographic profiles of Cape Town and Johannesburg', in S. Bekker and A. Leilde (eds), *Reflections on Identity in Four African Cities*, Johannesburg: African Minds, pp. 25–44.

Varley, A. (2002) 'Private or public: debating the meaning of tenure legalization', *International Journal of Urban and Regional Research*, 26: 449–61.

Visser, G. (2001) 'Social justice, integrated development planning and post-apartheid urban reconstruction', *Urban Studies*, 38(10): 1673–99.

— (2004) 'Social justice, integrated development planning and post-apartheid urban reconstruction', *Urban Studies*, 38: 1673–99.

Vivan, I. (1998) 'Nuruddin Farah's Beautiful Mat and its Italian plot', *World Literature Today*, 72(4): 786–90.

Waste Management Unit, Lusaka City Council (2006) 'Waste collection services in peri-urban areas', Unpublished report, Lusaka City Council Waste Management Unit, Lusaka.

Watson, V. (2002) *Change and Continuity in Spatial Planning: Metropolitan Cape Town under Political Transition*, London: Routledge.

— (2003) 'Conflicting rationalities: implications for planning theory and ethics', *Planning Theory and Practice*, 4(4): 395–408.

— (2007) 'Engaging with difference: understanding the limits of multiculturalism in planning in the South African context', in N. Murray, N. Shepherd and M. Hall (eds), *Desire Lines: Space, Memory and Identity in the Post-Apartheid City*, London: Routledge, pp. 67–79.

Watts, H. (1957) 'Grahamstown: a socio-ecological study of a small South African town', Unpublished PhD thesis, Rhodes University.

Weiss, B. (2005) 'The barber in pain: consciousness, affliction and alterity in urban Africa', in A. Honwana and F. de Boeck (eds), *Makers and Breakers: Children and Youth in Postcolonial Africa*, Trenton, NJ: Africa World Press, pp. 102–20.

— (2009) *Street Dreams and Hip Hop Barbershops: Global Fantasy in Urban Tanzania*, Bloomington: Indiana University Press.

Western, J. (1985) 'Undoing the colonial city?', *Geographical Review*, 75: 335–57.

— (1996 [1981]) *Outcast Cape Town*, 2nd edn, Berkeley: University of California Press.

— (2001) 'Africa is coming to the Cape', *Geographical Review*, 91(4): 617–40.

Williams, R. (2006) '"Doing history": Nuruddin Farah's *Sweet and Sour Milk*, subaltern studies, and the postcolonial trajectory of silence', *Research in African Literatures*, 37(4): 161–76.

Willis, K., B. Yeoh and S. Fakhri (2004) 'Introduction: transnationalism as a challenge to the nation', in B. Yeoh and K. Willis (eds), *State/Nation/Transnation: Perspectives on Transnationalism in the Asia-Pacific*, London: Routledge, pp. 1–15.

Winters, C. (1982) 'Urban morphogenesis in francophone black Africa', *Geographical Review*, 72(2): 139–54.

Wisner, B. (1994) '*Jilaal, Gu, Hagaa*, and *Der*: living with the Somali land, and living well', in A. Samatar (ed.), *The Somali Challenge: From Catastrophe to Renewal?*, Boulder, CO: Lynne Rienner, pp. 27–64.

Wright, D. (1998) 'History's illuminated prints: negative power in Nuruddin Farah's *Close Sesame*', *World Literature Today*, 72(4): 733–8.

— (2004) *The Novels of Nuruddin Farah*, Bayreuth: Bayreuth University Press.

Wright, G. (1991) *The Politics of Design in French Colonial Urbanism*, Chicago, IL: University of Chicago Press.

Yeboah, I. (2003) 'Demographic and housing aspects of structural adjustment and emerging urban form in Accra, Ghana', *Africa Today*, 10: 107–19.

— (2006) 'Subaltern strategies and development practice: urban water privatization in Ghana', *Geographical Journal*, 172(1): 50–65.

— (2008a) 'Globalization and the sub-Saharan African city', Paper presented to the Annual Meeting of the Association of American Geographers, Boston, MA, 17 April.

— (2008b) 'Ethnic emancipation and urban land claims: disenfranchisement of the Ga of Accra, Ghana', *Geographical Research*, 46(4): 435–45.

— (2008c) *Black African Neo-Diaspora: Ghanaian Immigrant Experiences in the Greater Cincinnati, Ohio, Area*, Lanham, MD: Rowman & Littlefield.

Yeoh, B. (2001) 'Postcolonial cities', *Progress in Human Geography*, 25(3): 456–68.

Yewah, E. (2001) 'The nation as a contested construct', *Research in African Literatures*, 32(3): 45–56.

Young, R. (2001) *Postcolonialism: An Historical Introduction*, Malden, MA: Blackwell.

Zeleza, P. T. (2005) 'The politics and poetics of exile: Edward Said in Africa', *Research in African Literatures*, 36(3): 1–22.

Index

informal sector, 71, 77
informal settlements, 69, 71–8,
  87–101, 192; definition of, 87,
  88–93; everyday life in, 93–5;
  planning responses to, 95–10
informality, 11, 14, 15, 28, 33,
  41, 46, 58, 64, 81, 93, 194;
  creativity of, 83; planning for,
  78–87; rationality of, 86 see also
  reinformalization
informalization, trend towards, 73
infrastructure, people as, 12
insecurity, 197
institutions, functionality of, 124
Integrated Development Plan (South
  Africa), 58
International Labor Organization,
  33; report on Nairobi, 72
invisibility, 11, 14, 23, 192
involution, 53
Isandla Institute (Cape Town), 47
Isegawa, Moses, 174
Islam, political, 157
Islamic Courts Union (ICU)
  (Somalia), 148

Jack Marapodi (Lusaka), 31
Jenkins, Rachel, 48
Joe Slovo Park (JSP) (Cape Town),
  97–8
Johannesburg (South Africa), 26,
  79, 197
John Howard (Lusaka), 31
John Laing (Lusaka), 31
justice: environmental, 121; issues
  of, 121–6

Kabulonga suburb (Lusaka), 37
Kaffir farming, 29
Kalikiliki neighborhood (Lusaka),
  36, 40
Kansas African Studies Center, 163
Kapwepwe, Mulenga, Like Choosing
  between Eating and Breathing, 41
Karume, Amani, 128
Kaunda, Kenneth, 37, 38
Kenya, 116–18

Kgositsile, Keorapetse, 142–3, 184
Kibaki, Mwai, 104
Kibera settlement (Kenya), 105
Kikwete, Jakaya, 67
Kingelez, Bodys Isek, 188; Projet
  pour le Kinshasa du troisième
  millénaire, 188
Kinshasa, 10, 17, 19, 53, 114–15,
  134, 157; gang territorialization
  in, 115; piracy in, 144
Kisangani (Congo), 145
Kombe, Wilbard, 66–7, 100
Konings, P., 114
Koolhas, Rem, 9–10
Koonings, K., 144
Korle Lagoon (Ghana), 99
Kreibich, Volker, 66–7, 100
Kruijt, D., 144
KwaFord (South Africa), 26
Kwazekele township (South Africa),
  57–8

Lagos, 9–10; piracy in, 144
land: allocation of, 67; indigenous
  markets of, 85; informal holdings
  of, 84; subdivision of, 80; urban
  markets, 78
land laws: in Tanzania, 85; in
  Zanzibar, 130–1
land reform, in Accra, 84–5
land struggles, 18
Land Tenure Act (1992) (Zanzibar),
  130–1
Langa, Moshekwa, 188; Collapsing
  Guides, 188
Lefebvre, Henri, 24–5, 26, 45, 160
Lerise, Fred, 47
Liberia, 22, 50
Libya, 96
Lilongwe (Malawi), 17, 18, 45,
  59–61, 69
Local Authorities Transfer Fund
  (LATF) (Kenya), 117
Local Authority Service Delivery
  Action Plan (Kenya), 117
Los Angeles, 24, 25, 26, 37; as
  African city, 26

About Zed Books

Zed Books is a critical and dynamic publisher, committed to increasing awareness of important international issues and to promoting diversity, alternative voices and progressive social change. We publish on politics, development, gender, the environment and economics for a global audience of students, academics, activists and general readers. Run as a co-operative, Zed Books aims to operate in an ethical and environmentally sustainable way.

Find out more at:

www.zedbooks.co.uk

For up-to-date news, articles, reviews and events information visit:

http://zed-books.blogspot.com

To subscribe to the monthly Zed Books e-newsletter, send an email headed 'subscribe' to:

marketing@zedbooks.net

We can also be found on **Facebook**, **ZNet**, **Twitter** and **Library Thing**.

www.ingramcontent.com/pod-product-compliance
Lightning Source LLC
Chambersburg PA
CBHW030359270326
41926CB00009B/1175